Praise for *Hol*

"Gianni Russo walks the walk an ci-
nating. A worthy read."

—Robert De Niro

"Russo tells a fascinating story about how a kid from New York's Little Italy grew up to be a genuine mobster (and actor, singer, and restaurateur). . . . It's a hell of a story, and Russo comes across as a hell of an interesting guy."

—*Booklist*

"Russo's writing style reads like narration from *Goodfellas*. . . . Fans of mob movies and unlikely success stories will find Russo's account compelling."

—*Library Journal*

"Recounting a life that reads like a narrative for a mob-movie script, a mobster, actor, and Las Vegas presence delivers numerous eye-opening revelations about national and world events. . . . Russo is an engaging raconteur."

—*Kirkus Reviews*

"In this robust, fast-paced memoir, Russo describes his life, going from being a real-life mobster to landing a role playing one in *The Godfather*. . . . [his] exhilarating memoir packs a punch."

—*Publishers Weekly*

"Gianni Russo is a true character who has led a most colorful life."

—Gay Talese

"Gianni Russo has seen a lot, done a lot, and tells it all. Amazing."

—Nick Pileggi

HOLLYWOOD GODFATHER

MY LIFE IN THE MOVIES AND THE MOB

GIANNI RUSSO

with Patrick Picciarelli

ST. MARTIN'S GRIFFIN
NEW YORK

This is a work of nonfiction. However, the names of certain individuals have been changed to protect their privacy, and dialogue has been reconstructed to the best of the authors' abilities.

Published in the United States by St. Martin's Griffin, an imprint of St. Martin's Publishing Group

www.stmartins.com

Designed by Steven Seighman

The Library of Congress Cataloging-in-Publication Data is available upon request.

ISBN 978-1-250-18139-8 (hardcover)
ISBN 978-1-250-18140-4 (trade paperback)
ISBN 978-1-250-18141-1 (ebook)

Our books may be purchased in bulk for promotional, educational, or business use. Please contact your local bookseller or the Macmillan Corporate and Premium Sales Department at 1-800-221-7945, extension 5442, or by email at MacmillanSpecialMarkets@macmillan.com.

First St. Martin's Griffin Edition: 2020

D 10 9 8 7 6 5 4

Were it not for my faith in God and the help of St. Anthony would I have reached my seventy-fifth year and be able to thank our men and women in the service of our country for their sacrifice to keep this nation strong and a wonderful place to live in freedom.

CONTENTS

CONTENTS

HOLLYWOOD GODFATHER

PROLOGUE

I don't visit the old neighborhood as often as I used to. While it occasionally brought back some unpleasant memories, I had my share of enjoyable recollections, too. It's those nostalgic remembrances that draw me back, but these days not too frequently.

Manhattan's Little Italy was different back then; I'm talking sixty-five years ago, when Little Italy was composed of—surprise—Italians! Today the neighborhood has diversified, predominantly because of an influx of Asians. Chinatown and Little Italy always shared a common border, with the ethnic Chinese encroaching into the Italian neighborhood as years went on.

Eventually Chinese nationals from the People's Republic began fleeing their homeland in record numbers with the help of professional human smugglers, called "snakeheads." These illegals, unable to speak English—much like the Italian immigrants from the previous century—mixed in among the Italians and were later joined by Vietnamese refugees after the war. By the 1970s, Little Italy was getting squeezed, with young Italians leaving the hundred-year-old Italian sanctuary for the greener pastures of the outer boroughs. The neighborhood shrank from a ten-block-square area to less than three square blocks. The Little Italy of my youth is now Minuscule Italy.

My name is Gianni Russo. You'll be reading about my family, how I was separated from them at a tender age, and how I came to lead a life that I could never have imagined.

In the 1950s, I was like every other kid in Little Italy, anonymous and oblivious of what lay north of Houston Street. Mine was an insular world of old-school Italians, most of who arrived in America with grandiose dreams of striking it rich in the country where the streets were paved with gold and riches waited for all those willing to work hard. It turned out that the streets were paved with cobblestones, and most immigrants never left the neighborhood, instead scratching out a living for pennies, or making names for themselves in the emerging American Mafia.

I'm not anonymous anymore. I'm most recognized as an actor, having had a feature role in *The Godfather* and numerous other films and television shows, but I've also been behind the scenes as a writer and producer of countless others. My other life, as a Mafia associate, spans over sixty years, but I've also done well in legitimate business.

I'm recognized, and for an actor that's a good thing. But when I go down to the old neighborhood, I'd rather walk the streets and blend into the crowd.

The Little Italy of my youth eventually became a tourist mecca, with suburbanites going downtown for a genuine Italian experience. While they are nothing new—tourists have been going to this part of town for as long as anyone can remember—most of the old restaurants they visited are generally gone, taken over by non-Italians preparing Italian cuisine without the warmth of the mom-and-pop joints I remember so well.

It's a sunny autumn day and I find myself on Mulberry Street, which runs through the heart of Little Italy. I stop momentarily at number 247, the Ravenite Social Club, as notorious a hangout as ever existed anywhere in the country. It was here that gangster John Gotti was welcomed like a conquering Caesar shortly after Gambino crime family boss "Big Paul" Castellano was gunned down in midtown Manhattan. It was Gotti who had given the execution order, and then assumed command of the largest Mafia family in the United States. It was also Gotti who ran the family into the ground a few short years later, and weakened the mob beyond repair by his inability to recognize that the Mafia was a *secret* organization. Gotti never met a reporter he didn't like, and the mob paid the price for his love of the spotlight. I knew Gotti very well, although I'd rather that I hadn't, but that's a story I'll share later.

Tourists flock past me, bumping my shoulder, excusing themselves, while I stare at the facade of the old Ravenite, whose doorway I walked through many times, always under the watchful eye of a platoon of federal agents filming everyone for posterity—and possible criminal prosecution.

That epicenter of the American Mafia is now a shoe store. A floor once trod upon by handmade Italian footwear now sells sneakers. Gotti, surely burning in whatever kind of hell exists, must be wondering what became of La Cosa Nostra—"this thing of ours." He ought to know—his incompetent leadership was instrumental in getting the mob where it is today.

The street fragrances are what I miss most about the neighborhood—a mélange of aromas emanating from a wide variety of ethnic Italian and Asian restaurants. The iconic Italian eateries that remain have moved to more spacious locales. La Luna, where a sequence from *The Godfather* was filmed, is now located across the street from the original site, and Umberto's Clam House, where notorious mobster Joey Gallo was murdered in front of his wife, made the move a few doors down the same street. While the food may still be top-notch, the historic ambience of the original locations was left behind. Tourists can no longer sit at the same table where *Godfather* mobster Clemenza stuffed his face while his driver waited patiently for him in the car, never realizing that he'd never make it home that night because he had set up Don Corleone for assassination. What *Godfather* aficionado can forget Clemenza uttering the unforgettable words to the assassin in the backseat after the driver was dispatched, "Leave the gun. Take the cannoli."

Mafia "made men" no longer hang out on the street looking tough and world-weary, absorbing the admiring glances of neighborhood women and teenage boys who, if things work their way, will join their ranks when they get older, instead of playing tough-guy roles by sporting ninety-mile-an-hour slicked-back hair and enough jewelry to sink a boat.

It's a calmer Little Italy these days; the electricity is gone, as are the old mafiosi, who are either dead or serving lengthy prison sentences. The row tenement where I lived is still there, a building that was old when McKinley was president, now subdivided into studio apartments renting for two thousand dollars a month.

The old dons, killers, and corrupt politicians are still very much alive in my memories, as are the iconic movie stars, celebrities, Popes, and presidents. You'll meet them.

This is my story.

1

A DEATH IN SIN CITY

Las Vegas, Nevada: October 28, 1988

Las Vegas is like no other place in the world. The city has a worldwide reputation for nonstop partying, gambling, and the availability of any kind of sex you can think of, and some that can't be conjured up even on the mind-bending drugs that were as plentiful as popcorn in a movie theater.

And when you owned the hottest club in town, every night was a party. My name is Gianni Russo and I owned that club, cleverly called Gianni Russo's State Street. My name and reputation brought the beautiful people into my club; celebrities mingled with gangsters, politicians, megarich titans of industry from around the world, and the occasional U.S. president.

I was reaping the benefits of my acting career, connections to the mob, international political and religious affiliations, and just plain brass balls. In the world in which I traveled, you needed all that, plus glibness and a take-no-bullshit personality, coupled with a willingness to take chances. And I took chances, many of which I think back on today and wonder how I have survived to tell my story.

I played Carlo Rizzi in the movie *The Godfather*, Don Corleone's

Judas son-in-law, whose betrayal cost the heir apparent to the crime family and oldest boy, Sonny, his life. While that role launched my show-business career, I didn't get to where I was at the tender age of thirty-nine without having been associated with some of the most powerful people in the world, many legitimate, but most not so much.

But on this cool autumn night, I was thinking in the moment, my mind racing, greeting every one of my three hundred–plus patrons, and trying to focus on everything around me. This was a ten-thousand-square foot high-end club with prices to match, and with a very cohesive and jovial crowd, but you never knew what could happen in the blink of an eye with booze flowing like water spilling over the Hoover Dam, and people flying on enough coke and other drugs to keep Charlie Sheen happy for a month.

I'd opened the club in 1981 in a vacant building off a strip mall, located between the Sahara Hotel and the Hilton International Hotel. My intention was to attract my celebrity friends, who would, in turn, draw high-rolling tourists and politicians looking for photo ops.

The club was a success from the jump. Frank Sinatra, Dean Martin, Paul Anka, Engelbert Humperdinck, Louis Prima, Wayne Newton, the two Dons (King and Rickles), and numerous other A-listers made the club their second home. Stephen Shirripa, who would later become an actor and star on *The Sopranos,* was one of my doormen. But you don't attract and keep big names as customers, friends of mine or not, unless you provided great food, flash, and class. I also went all out on the décor, both inside and outside.

The club was located at the end of the dimly lit State Street. I had freshly painted Dumpsters on the street, which overflowed with what appeared to be mountains of garbage (in reality, bags stuffed with newspapers), to give the impression of a depressed, tough neighborhood, so that people would get the feeling they were slumming. At the end of the street, where a patron had to turn a corner to get to the club, that all changed; what assaulted the senses was opulence on steroids.

A fifty-foot red carpet ended at the club's red-and-white awning entrance. The door was flanked by two mirror-polished brass plaques with my name in flaring cursive writing, announcing their arrival at Gianni Russo's State Street. Patrons were greeted by doormen in formal wear when they were admitted after knocking on the door, and perused by a blinking eye through a peephole. Customers loved the decadence of it all.

Once inside, a small army of the best-looking men and women in Vegas greeted them. I hired only beautiful people, all required to wear tuxedos, although the women accessorized with black stockings under tight-fitting shorts, and revealing crisp white shirts, topped off with bow ties. Eighty-six women worked in shifts, serving food and drinks, while the men tended bar and did any required heavy lifting. Every woman who entered my club got a long-stemmed rose from me personally, which set the mood for what was to come: an evening of fine dining, great live music, and enough people-watching to cause a bad case of whiplash.

Nothing much impressed me anymore, having been around the block more than once, but every day I marveled at the sheer energy of the club—the electricity in the air, the customers trying to outdress one another, as if to say, Look at me; I'm sharp, rich, young, and ready to party!

I'd come a long way from being a crippled, tough New York kid with little formal education and no prospects for the future. I was successful and loving every minute of it.

I heard the commotion before I knew what was causing it. Gales of laughter, shouts across the room in greeting, boisterous applause for my piano player, these were the norm, but this was the sound of a collective sucking in of air, coupled with gasps and a high-pitched scream.

I pushed through the crowd to a booth at the back end of the main dining room. A group of customers was standing there frozen, staring at a small woman, well dressed, who sat in a booth with her hands to her face, crying hysterically as she tried to staunch a current of blood flowing through her fingers, a male figure hovering over her.

I grabbed the guy by the shoulder and spun him around. He appeared to be Hispanic, about thirty, maybe five foot six, and was thin and well dressed in a suit and tie. I recognized him and the woman as a couple who had arrived at the club less than a half hour ago. The red rose I had presented to the lady now lay on the table and was drenched with a different shade of crimson.

She had been slashed on the face and had suffered severe, deep wounds around her left eye. There was no uniformity to the cuts as would have been evident if made with a knife. She appeared to have gotten jabbed a few times with cut glass.

"Hey, motherfucker, get your fucking hands off me!" the man hollered, his eyes wild with fury as I shoved him away from the woman.

"What happened to you?" I asked as I gently pried her hand away from her face and replaced it with a linen napkin. I got wailing sobs in response.

The crowd began to retreat backward as the sound of sirens emerged in the distance. Someone had called the cops, and, I assumed, an ambulance.

I grabbed the woman's date by a lapel. "Get the fuck out of here. Now!" I gave him a shove and he banged into the table. I could handle the police; I knew every cop on the force, but a bloody brawl in a licensed premise was a quick way to lose that license.

The guy bounced off the table and went for the woman. "She's coming with me, man."

"She's not going any-fucking-where, shithead. She needs medical attention," I told him.

I had one eye on him and the other on his date. I didn't see a weapon, which turned out to be a broken champagne bottle that this dickhead still had in his hand, held down alongside his leg and hidden from my view.

He yelled something unintelligible, and in a nanosecond, he brought the jagged bottle up and slashed at my face. I was quick enough to tilt my head backward, but he caught me on the chin in a sweeping motion that would later take eighty-four stitches to close. Customers began to take off for the exits.

I felt no immediate pain but realized I was cut when an ocean of blood erupted from the wound. Edged-weapon wounds on thin skin over bone bleed profusely, and he had gotten me square on a bone. Blood was everywhere.

My custom-made Nat Weiss Sea Island cotton shirt was covered in blood, with enough left over to splatter my new Brioni suit. I was enraged; I'd waited six months for that shirt. I'd been hurt badly in the past by professionals, and I could handle that, but fuck with my wardrobe and you've got a problem.

I swerved back to get fighting room as Bottleman made another lunge at me, yelling, "Fuck you!"

I was armed with two gold-plated, five-shot custom-made .25-caliber revolvers in the pockets of my vest, and I was duly licensed by the state of Nevada to carry them.

He slashed at me and missed. I drew one of the guns and fired a shot into his forehead. He stood there in amazement as he brushed at his face as if swatting a mosquito. This guy was shot between the eyes and he wasn't reacting. In fact, it pissed him off; I figured he had to be coked up and not feeling any pain. I made a quick mental note to get a bigger-caliber gun. He came for me again, and I parried to the right to avoid the bottle while putting another round in his head and three more in his chest. He went down like a dumped load of wet laundry and lay still, very dead.

My heart was pumping like an air hammer as a platoon of cops came charging into the club. I was covered with blood and had a dead guy at my feet. This was not the way I had planned my evening.

The cops were great, professional and accommodating. I'd had a great working relationship with the LVPD over the years and took good care of them. They ate and drank well in my club and never got a check, which was probably the reason I was being interviewed in my office instead of cuffed to a bed in some emergency room while they sorted out the particulars of the shooting.

I was being questioned by a captain named Koontz while the morgue attendants dealt with the dead guy and detectives interviewed witnesses. Koontz and I went back many years.

"So, Gianni, I'm assuming you shot this asshole *after* he cut you, right?" Koontz was a big guy with over twenty years on the job and knew what questions to ask so I wouldn't incriminate myself.

I was holding a towel to my wound to stop the bleeding. I didn't want to go to the hospital until I got the preliminaries out of the way. "Shooting? What shooting?" I deadpanned.

Koontz mumbled something about my being a wiseass and read me my rights, which was standard operating procedure just to cover his ass should I turn out to be the aggressor rather than a victim.

"Yeah, of course," I said. "Fucking jerkoff cut up his girlfriend like she was a watermelon. How's she doing, by the way?"

"Missed her eye by a millimeter. Lucky. What started the fight?"

"Who the fuck knows. I wasn't invited until later."

"Well, you killed a guy and we gotta go through the motions. No one's disputing it was a good shooting, but the law's the law."

We went back and forth while he took notes, and in an hour I was in Sunrise Hospital, being stitched up by Dr. Elias Ghanem, who was also known as "Dr. Feelgood," the late Elvis Presley's personal physician and the man to see for anything that ailed you.

The next day, several friends suggested that I get good legal representation, should some zealot DA decide to make an example of me and charge me with a crime. Attorney Robert Shapiro's name came up several times, and I decided to see him, just to have him handy should I require his services.

I made an appointment for the following morning, and after closing the club at 6:00 A.M., I flew to Los Angeles to meet the lawyer who would one day represent O. J. Simpson in his infamous double-murder case.

I was beyond exhausted when I arrived at Shapiro's law firm. Shapiro was on the phone when I was ushered into his office. He motioned me to have a seat and raised a finger, which I assumed to mean he would be with me in a minute, not the half hour I spent listening to him gab with someone who apparently meant more to him than I did.

Finally, I couldn't take this asshole's rudeness anymore. I got up, leaned across his desk, grabbed the phone from his hand, and hung it up for him. He looked like the jury had just told him O.J. was not guilty—eyes wide, mouth agape, registering an expression of utter disbelief.

"Listen, jerkoff," I said, "no one treats me like you just did. I had an appointment, and I'm watching you talk on the phone. Go fuck yourself. Have a nice day."

I left L.A. determined to take care of my own problems.

I took it easy at home for the next few days, feeling absolutely no remorse about the shooting. This hadn't been my first shooting incident and it wouldn't be my last. It was a righteous homicide, in that I had been defending not only myself but anyone else in the club who might have become the victim of further slashings.

Captain Koontz called me and said that while I had nothing to worry about legally, I still might have a problem.

"What kind of problem?"

"The guy you iced, Lorenzo Morales, was in town to conduct business."

I didn't like where this was going. "What kind of business?"

"Cocaine business. Flew in from Colombia last week to set up a supply chain for his good friend Pablo Escobar."

Fuck me.

"My advice to you, Gianni, is to get this shit straightened out before you get a visit," said Rex Bell, the district attorney of Las Vegas. He was my neighbor and a good friend. We were sitting in my living room, sipping drinks, a week after the shooting. "My office will go through the motions with the grand jury, but you've got to address your own safety."

Pablo Escobar, for those of you who live in a cloistered convent, was the mass-murdering cocaine overlord of Colombia's Medellín cartel, the biggest importer of cocaine to the United States in the world. I had just killed a highly placed emissary of his business, and common sense would dictate that he might be pissed off.

When Colombian drug dealers seek revenge, they do it in a big way to make a point. Before they kill the intended target, they kill the target's family, his friends, his neighbors, and his friggin' pets. Then, when it's the target's turn, he goes out in the most violent manner, usually tortured and left to be discovered in a public place.

"Straightened out how?"

Rex shrugged. "You know any Colombians in the trade?"

I thought about it. While I didn't know anyone personally in the cartels, I knew people who knew connected people in Colombia, but I didn't think I had a problem that I couldn't handle. I had very close friends in organized crime, Italians, not Colombians, and I figured I was safe. After all, I was defending myself when I shot the asshole. The mob I knew had a sense of honor, and had I shot one of their own, I'd have gotten a pass because I wasn't the aggressor and the dead guy was in the wrong; he had cut up a defenseless woman. I figured that all gangsters had a secret handshake and the incident would die on the vine.

I shared this notion with Rex.

"Hey, I bow to your superior knowledge in this area," he said. After draining his glass, he got up to leave. "If they send you some kind of message, let me know."

I got a message all right, and it wasn't very subtle.

I lived in a very beautiful home on La Paloma Avenue, in an upscale section of Vegas. Cops and private security patrols cruised the area nonstop. So it was to my great surprise when I arrived home a few days later and found a "message" in the middle of the living room floor.

A four-foot circle of blood, surrounded by three bowls filled with dead chickens and salamanders with needles through their heads, greeted me. In the center of the circle were two pictures: one of me and another of my daughter, Carmen. These weren't family snapshots taken off the mantel; they were surveillance pictures taken with a telephoto lens.

Shocked as I was at what I was looking at, my first thought was, Whoever did this had to be Houdini to get past my security system and locks. The house was locked up tighter than a crab's ass, which is waterproof. To this day, it's a mystery to me how anyone penetrated my high-tech security setup without leaving a trace. I was upset, not so much for me, but for the safety of my daughter.

I called Captain Koontz, who was at my house within minutes. He stared at the artwork on my floor and scratched his head. "What the fuck is it?"

"You're supposed to tell me. It's why you're here," I said.

"Let me make a call."

He summoned an anthropology professor at the University of North Las Vegas, who knew exactly what it was as soon as she arrived.

"What you've got here," she said, "is a Colombian death warning. You have enemies in Colombia?"

"Yeah, you might say that," I said. Koontz rolled his eyes.

Now my family was involved. I wouldn't trust my daughter's safety to a deal between the Italians and Colombians. Even if I could arrange it, it might not work. I needed to handle this problem personally. While I had no contacts in the Medellín cartel, I knew people who probably did.

John Gotti had assumed command of the Gambino crime family with the demise of the family's boss, Paul ("Big Paul") Castellano, whose life came to an abrupt halt after he and his driver, Tommy Bilotti, were gunned down in front of Sparks Steak House in midtown Manhattan on December 16, 1985. Not many in the family liked Big Paul, because he was an elitist, greedy boss. Among his most ardent detractors was John Gotti, a Gambino captain of a Queens crew, who had Big Paul killed despite the murder not being sanctioned by the Commission—the governing body of the Mafia—which had to give the go-ahead when a boss was going to be whacked. John had declared himself the new boss of the Gambinos before Big Paul hit the ground.

Gotti, now three years into his reign, wasn't that popular among the rank and file, either. I wasn't a big fan, because he was too full of himself and enjoyed getting dogged by the media whenever he was out and about hitting the nightspots in Manhattan, which was often.

Gotti loved the spotlight and never truly got the message that the Mafia was a secret organization. His big mouth would eventually find him a permanent guest of the feds in the Unites States Penitentiary, in Marion, Illinois. The FBI had a big-time hard-on for the guy and made it its mission to see him behind bars.

He was no great fan of mine, either. While I wasn't a made guy, I did command the respect of wiseguys, mainly because I was a man of my word, had included them in many of my moneymaking enterprises, and knew when to keep my mouth shut, which was always. I'd always liked my independence and didn't want to be owned by a "family," and being "made" was my idea of being a slave in a nice suit.

John was, however, the boss of the largest Mafia family in the country and as such had connections with other criminal entities all over the world. It was with this knowledge that I grudgingly sought him out to help me get the Colombian target off my family's back. I'd do anything to protect my daughter, even if it meant seeking an audience with John Gotti.

To see a man of Gotti's stature, you went to him; he didn't come to you. His seat of power was the Ravenite Social Club, located at 247 Mulberry Street, in the heart of Manhattan's Little Italy. John held court there and enjoyed basking in the admiration—real or imagined—of his minions a few nights a week. I had arranged a sit-down with

Gotti over the phone through "Joe (the German) Watts," a Gambino enforcer and rabid loyalist.

I took a flight to LaGuardia Airport, planning to arrive early at the Ravenite so as to show respect to Gotti, which he demanded. Gotti once famously had a guy murdered because he chose not to comply with a summons from Gotti to meet him at the Ravenite. I figured if I got stuck in traffic, I might as well shoot myself. First and foremost was my daughter's safety. If it took talking to Gotti with the respect I didn't think he deserved, I'd do it.

I took a taxi to within two blocks of the Ravenite and hoofed it the rest of the way, seeking to be as low-profile as I could, a difficult task given Gotti's notoriety. Before I entered the club, I waved to the unseen FBI agents in the tenement across the street, whose job it was to record the comings and goings of everything Gotti. I didn't give a damn if they saw me; the only thing they could accuse me of was having lousy taste in friends. I knocked, and some goon let me in. The Ravenite Social Club was nothing like Gianni Russo's State Street, that's for damn sure.

Gotti was in the back room of the club, which looked like it had been decorated by Stevie Wonder. Nothing matched. He was seated in a red plastic chair at a Formica table, a glass of red wine close by. Joe Watts, forever the devotee, was standing behind the boss with his arms crossed over his chest. Watts would eventually serve heavy prison time for not flipping on Gotti when the Gambino boss was being betrayed to the feds by his underboss and others. Look up the word *gangster* in the dictionary and you should see a picture of Joe Watts. He believed in the Mafia, its history and blood oath. Always elegantly attired, Watts would be the one who would teach Gotti how to dress when he became a media darling. Prior to that, Gotti wore sweatsuits most of the time and didn't know Brioni from baloney. Since then, Gotti had always dressed elegantly. His suits were top-shelf, as were his shirts and shoes. Always immaculately coiffed, his silver hair neat and in place, he looked like an executive, which I suppose he was, in a manner of speaking.

Gotti gave a condescending smile and we did the usual cheek kisses. Gotti nodded toward a chair. I sat.

"So," he said with a mirthless smile, "you're a fucking killer, now, huh?" He might have looked elegant on the outside, but as soon as he opened his mouth you knew whom you were dealing with—basically, a degenerate gambler whose command of the language was no better or worse than the soldiers who worked for him. A running joke was that whatever Gotti bet on, you did the opposite.

I had just walked in the door and he was busting my balls already. Because of my role in *The Godfather*, the shooting at my club had made the TV show *Entertainment Tonight*. Getting publicity was not something Gotti liked for anyone other than himself.

Gotti could be a loudmouthed drunk. I recall once when Frank Sinatra was performing at Carnegie Hall, his son, Frank Junior, was appearing at the same time at Tavern on the Green, in Central Park. Junior was no senior, but he had a decent voice and put on a good show.

On the night in question, Frank had given me a pile of tickets to see his son's act. For a reason I'm still not able to figure out, I invited a few of the Gambinos, and so as not to incur the wrath of Gotti, I invited him, too. If Gotti felt slighted, he would take out his anger the best way he knew how, which was to kill the offender, so rather than deal with that, he became part of our entourage.

In between songs, Frank Junior would recount stories about his dad, which lent a homey, nostalgic slant to his act. Truth be told, most people came to see Junior's act because of the stories he told about his dad.

Frank Junior would refer to his father as "Frank." He had always done this in his act, and no one gave a damn—except for John Gotti. The more he drank, the meaner Gotti would get; he was a nasty, loudmouth drunk. On this particular night, Gotti took exception to Frank Junior's calling his father by his first name, and he let everyone know it.

"Hey," Gotti yelled from the audience, "he's your father; have some respect!"

There were at least two hundred people in the audience, and when Gotti bellowed his disapproval, everything stopped, including Junior's act. Junior laughed it off, dropped the patter, and went into a song. When he was finished, he started in again with "Frank this" and "Frank that." I don't know where he thought Gotti had gone, but now the Queens capo was pissed and felt disrespected.

"What're you, some kinda fuckin' jerk?" Gotti shouted. "I'm sittin' right here, you fuckin' mook. Call your father 'Dad,' or I'll come up there and break your fucking legs."

This time, Junior got the message. He went right to a song, which he dedicated to "my father."

All was peaceful for the rest of the set, but this is the type of person Gotti was. He had a big mouth, and when oiled up, he wasn't shy about using it.

Now in the Ravenite, I got down to my dilemma, laying it all out while Gotti listened. In the end, he said he'd set up a connection in Colombia but that the rest was up to me. While there had always been tension between us, and maybe one of the reasons he helped me was because I was highly thought of by people he respected, he came through for me. Or perhaps he was setting me up to get murdered and be out of his way for once and for all.

I was going to have a contact in Bogotá. What reception I was going to get was another matter. I can't say I wasn't concerned, but I had to face Escobar; there was no other way to go.

We'll continue with my journey to Colombia to get the cartel off my back a little later in my story. As for the present, it's better you know who I am and how factors I had no control over led me down a path that was littered with gangsters.

2

A CHILDHOOD LOST

New York's Little Italy in the 1940s and 1950s was a tight-knit neighborhood consisting of crowded tenements and enough Italian restaurants and *salumerias* to feed the standing army of a good-size country. The captivating aromas emanating from these specialty-food establishments hung over the neighborhood in downtown Manhattan like fog blanketing London.

The neighborhood never expanded past its original ten-square-block boundaries and was crammed to the breaking point with families looking to survive and retain their connection to the old country. Italian Americans stuck together, and rather than push to the outer boroughs, these hardworking souls chose to be around families they either knew from Italy and with whom they had shared the trip over to America, where the streets were supposedly paved with gold, or Italian families they had met upon their arrival. Their common language, loyalty to all things Italian, and family values had created a very cohesive community.

I lived with my parents and two sisters, Theresa and Joanne, in a crowded, two-bedroom tenement on Mulberry Street, the epicenter of Little Italy. My parents had one bedroom, my sisters the other. I was relegated to a closet, where I slept with a can of heating kerosene near my head. To this day, I wonder if constantly breathing in those fumes at such a tender age might have damaged me in some way.

Coincidentally, both sides of my family are named Russo. My grandfather on my father's side, Vito Russo, and his brother John Russo had a burning desire to emigrate to America at the turn of the last century, but coming from Sicily was going to be a problem. The Black Hand, a gang of thugs with ties to the Sicilian Mafia, had wreaked havoc in lower Manhattan upon their arrival from the old country. They preyed on their own people, extorting money from small businesses, murdering those who wouldn't pay, and bombing their stores, which created collateral damage to non-Italians. Indicating you were Sicilian wasn't the politically correct thing to do if you had a desire to go to America.

The brothers journeyed to Naples, Italy, to figure a way to say they were Napolitano, in order to grease the wheels of immigration. Whom should they meet in Naples but sisters Theresa and Lilly Russo (no relation), who were born and raised in Naples and who also wanted to go to America. The brothers' brother (my great-uncle Angelo) was a mafioso with great influence, and he arranged with the immigration authorities to have the four Russos go to America together as married couples from Naples. Vito and Theresa would marry before the journey, John and Lilly upon arrival in America.

While Italian families are historically patriarchal, with a strong father figure at the helm, my father, Louis, broke that mold by disregarding the traditional role as family breadwinner and doing whatever he wanted to do, which wasn't much. He was more concerned with impressing people (particularly women) than being around to raise his family. He had a no-show job on the docks, provided by Albert Anastasia (who would later run Murder, Inc.) and his brother, Anthony, who ran the docks and were both well-respected members of the Mafia, and who were very tight with my great-uncle Angelo. My father would show up every week on the docks for his no-show job to get his paycheck. My great-uncle Angelo would also be instrumental in getting many members of the Mafia into the United States from the old country over the years, and had garnered a lot of respect, and in the Mob, respect is everything. Oddly, Angelo never had an interest in emigrating to America, and he spent his time being a highly respected Mafia boss in Palermo, Sicily.

Having respect was better than being canonized, and my great-uncle enjoyed a solid reputation until the day he was hanged in 1948, executed by the Sicilian government for a laundry list of crimes going back generations.

The Mafia permeated every fabric of life in Little Italy. If you didn't have a family member in the Mafia, you knew someone who was "connected." Italian immigrants didn't rely on local government to solve problems; they relied on the mob. In that part of New York, you were either Italian or you were an outsider. New York's politicians, at least in our little world, were mostly Irish. While you might find a stray politico who was other than an Irishman, the police department was top-heavy with Irish cops who had no love for "ginzos," as some cops so diplomatically called us. So you were either "us" or "them." The Mafia was "us."

If you had a problem—an unreasonable landlord, a disagreement with a local merchant, a child being abused by a bully, or any other issue you couldn't handle yourself—you went to the local crew captain, who would "fix" the problem. Needed money? A job? You knew a guy, or that guy knew a guy who could help you out. This is how the neighborhood was run and flourished.

My mother, Inez, a name my father disliked (he called her "Dotty"), was a mixed-Italian and Western European beauty who had family blood in numerous cities throughout Italy. She married my father when she was sixteen, had two daughters in under two years, and me at eighteen. She was often compared to Rita Hayworth in the looks department, and was a stay-at-home mom, as were the other Italian women in the neighborhood. Any man worth the description would never allow his wife to work, and he supported his family financially and morally.

My father, however, was more interested in having a good time on the street than in being a good family man. There was many a time I'd wave to him as I passed him on the block, and he'd ignore me, like I didn't exist. The last thing he wanted to be associated with was a wife and three kids. I even saw him on the street one day sporting a yarmulke, the traditional headgear of Jewish men. I didn't want to know what that was about.

My mother did the best she could raising us while my father was out somewhere doing his thing. I was instilled with strong religious beliefs from as early as I can remember. My paternal grandmother and I would go to Mass literally every day. I carried around a little plastic Saint Anthony statuette, which I still have today. I was only five, maybe six years old, but that solid religious foundation would give me solace during stressful times. Unbeknownst to me, shortly I'd come to rely on the comfort of my faith sooner than expected, and it helped me survive a horrific period in my young life.

My father was a very jealous person, and for no apparent reason, other than that he was a serial cheater, he assumed everyone else was, too, including my mother. My father heard that my mother had had a male visitor in our apartment several times while he wasn't home, so he got a few of his friends to ambush the poor bastard upon leaving the apartment. They beat the guy severely and stopped the assault only when they realized that the "other man" was one of my mother's brothers.

My father was careless and out of control when it came to his lifestyle, and there came a point where he couldn't afford to keep his various women in the manner to which they had become accustomed without a new plan.

My mother had developed frequent headaches—nothing more serious, undoubtedly, than the trauma of being married to my father. Seeing an opening, my father utilized his Mafia connections to get my mother institutionalized in an asylum for the mentally ill. Back then, all it took was a word from a mob-connected guy and things got done. One day she was home; the next day she was gone, locked up against her will.

Mom was absent, only to be replaced by one of my father's girlfriends, who moved into our apartment, bag and baggage. Shortly thereafter, my sisters and I were parceled out to relatives while my mother was literally held persona non grata in a nuthouse. She would be locked up there for two years, until her brothers worked against all odds and got her out. Her freedom brought us all together, once again, in our apartment on Mulberry Street. Why she returned home to more misery can only be blamed on the accepted Italian social mores at the time: A wife belonged at home with her husband and her kids. Divorce? There was no such thing in religious Italian families. You made do with what you had. This was the 1940s and Gloria Steinem was still in elementary school.

My existence might not have been idyllic, but I was about to enter a phase where my home life would be like living in heaven, compared to what I was about to go through.

I woke up one morning in the summer of 1949, when I was seven years old, and had no feeling in my left arm and leg. Initially, I thought little about it; sleeping in a confined closet had cut off my circulation many times in the past. Only this time, the numbness didn't go away. I remember my mother taking me to a clinic, where I was poked and prodded and returned home. I don't recall being privy to information as to what was wrong with me; I was too young to be in the adult loop. The numbness remained through the following night.

Bright and early the next morning, an ambulance made its way down Mulberry Street and stopped in front of my building. It had come for me.

I was asleep when two male attendants in white uniforms entered my apartment. My first recollection of knowing something was going on was hearing my mother's sobs from the kitchen. Her wails had awakened me. Oddly, I didn't find this to be upsetting, because I'd heard her crying many times, due to my father's antics, and thought the current tears were because of an argument between my parents. It was only when the door to my closet/bedroom opened and I saw the white-uniformed men and my mother like I had never seen her before, with a look of shock, hurt, dismay, and fear spread across her striking face, that I realized something else was going on. A feeling of dread spread over me like volcanic ash.

"What's wrong, Mama?" I managed to squeak out. The left side of my body was still numb and the radiating fear that was making its way through me made it all that more difficult for me to stand up.

"These men, honey," she said, "are going to take you for some tests. About your leg, your arm. You'll be home soon." Even at my tender age, I doubted her words because of the pained expression on her face.

I grabbed her around the waist while the two hulking attendants mumbled something to each other. I began crying, the tears flowing uncontrollably. "You coming with me, Mama?" I wailed through tears that clouded my vision.

My mother cradled my head. "Yes, Gianni, I'm coming with you. Everything will be okay."

The ambulance guys had a collapsible stretcher, which was easy enough to get up the building's stairs, but it would be useless with me as a passenger. The narrow stairway couldn't accommodate the stretcher fully deployed.

With no fanfare, one attendant grabbed me under my arms while the other took hold of my ankles and proceeded to carry me down the stairs to the ambulance. I was a skinny, lightweight kid, but I fought like hell, crying and screaming as my mother tried to calm me. I had no idea where I was going or why. The fear and terror were palpable.

My mother held my hand for the fifteen-minute ride to Bellevue Hospital, telling me everything would be okay, but I heard little of what she said. I was hyperventilating and felt like I was sucking for air. I had my little plastic Saint Anthony statue with me and held it in a white-knuckled grip, and my faith in God gave me the courage to keep breathing. That statue never left my side, ever. As I write this description of one of the most horrific days of my life, I still have with me the same Saint Anthony statue I had with me that terrible day. It gave me, and still gives me, sustenance.

I was placed on a gurney upon our arrival at Bellevue. My mother continued to hold my hand as I was wheeled into the building. Most of what transpired that first day is lost to time, but I do remember calming down a little while my mother and a nurse prepared paperwork. I kept on asking when we were going home. The nurse, whom I remember as kind but officious, kept smiling and saying, "In a few days, we need to do some tests."

I was wheeled into an elevator and taken to a large room with a white sign above the entrance that read QUARANTINED AREA POLIO WARD.

I might've been seven, but I wasn't stupid. I knew what polio was and now I knew I had it. The disease was spreading across the nation at an alarming rate, some 58,000 new cases reported yearly, with about a 9 percent mortality rate. Among those who survived, many were left paralyzed or partially paralyzed for life. The disease mostly attacked children, cause unknown. I can't describe the horror I experienced as I was separated from my mother and was led, screaming and wailing, into that ward as my mother was restrained from following me inside. My Saint Anthony statue was taken away from me for a short period of time and sterilized.

I would be in that ward and one like it a few floors higher for five years. This would be my home. I wouldn't be permitted to leave the hospital for the entire time. I would never play, never have a friend my own age, and never feel rain or sunshine on my face. I would not see my family or get a visitor for my entire stay there. Five long years—to a kid, it was like an eternity. I would endure things that no adult should ever experience, let alone a child. There was no school to attend, because the prevailing thought of hospital administrators was that most of the patients wouldn't survive to become productive members of society, so why waste resources educating us?

If it hadn't been for the caring and love of one particular nurse, I would've gone insane.

I was just a kid.

The cavernous ward housed twenty boys around my age. Each of us had a bed with a thin mattress and a metal cabinet where we kept our meager possessions. The bed was on wheels. On the ceiling was a metal runner with a drape attached. When we were examined by hospital staff, which was almost daily, the drape would be drawn for privacy, as it was at night, after the mandatory lights-out. If the family of a patient had money, their kid was placed in a private or semiprivate room across the hall. We were kept segregated from those kids, and I can't recall ever seeing them once they were removed from the ward.

The kids who couldn't breathe on their own were locked into an iron lung, a huge torpedolike contraption that did the breathing for the patient. Those poor kids had only their heads protruding from the contraption and were in that damn thing 24/7. At least I had some mobility. I would be helped out of bed occasionally for physical therapy to keep my limbs from atrophying further. If I wanted to move around on my own, I'd roll out of bed onto the floor and drag myself around the ward with my good arm. My usual destination was a window where I could view the outside world.

I remember I cried for a long time, maybe months. No one on the staff could console me, but none of them tried very hard. Some mornings I would wake up and one or more of the beds in the ward would be empty. Kids would die during the night and be carted away on squeaky-wheeled gurneys. After a while, I dreaded the sound of that squeak, because I knew one of the kids had passed away during the night, and the body was taken away before the rest of us could see it the next morning.

I made no friends out of necessity, for fear that anyone I became attached to might die in the middle of the night and would be gone from my life. Over sixty-five years later, I'm still difficult to get close to. I can count my acquaintances in the hundreds, but close friends? Maybe four. I have a primordial fear of losing people I love. Some guys I know who were in combat in Vietnam experienced similar feelings of dreading abandonment when their buddies died in combat, and spent the rest of their lives avoiding connecting with people who tried to get close to them. The beginnings of PTSD were planted in me when I was seven.

I needed my mother. What I got was Delores Barone, a saint who became my surrogate mom, and who protected and counseled me when she arrived about six months into my stay.

Delores was sixteen or seventeen and a real beauty. She had olive skin, long chestnut hair, and a huge chest. I might've been only seven years old and very sick, but I knew tits when I saw them. My juices were beginning to flow even at that tender age.

When I arrived in the ward, Delores was a candy striper, a member of a relatively new organization of hospital volunteers formed in 1944. She wore a red-and-white pinafore-style dress and worked under the direct supervision of nurses. In a few years, Delores would become a nurse and be in charge of my ward.

We hit it off immediately. I became instantly enamored and developed my first crush, and I fantasized about us running off together. The mind of a seven-year-old boy is imaginative, and mine was even more so. I was constantly thinking about being healthy and free, and how Delores and I would live happily ever after. It kept me sane.

For her part, Delores was the ultimate professional. In the beginning, she read to me and we would talk for hours by my bed. Later, when she had an office, we'd spend hours in there conversing about everything. When I was with her, she had the magical power to distract me from my pain, boredom, and fear. I looked forward to her coming to work. On her days off, I'd think about her until she returned to work.

The first two years or so, I was pretty much confined to my bed unless I chose to drag myself around the ward floor. While some of the physical therapy protocol had me attempting to walk with the aid of the therapists, most of my strength building was done with the aid of English bicycle tire tubes while I lay in bed. The tubes were attached to my disabled left leg and arm, and I'd do arm and leg curls, sometimes for hours. By year three, I was beginning to see some results. I was regaining strength and range of motion, but after years of inactivity, the muscles on that side of my body were noticeably smaller. But even a slight improvement in muscle tone spurred me on to try even harder with the bike tubes.

One day, when I was about ten years old, Delores called me into her office, shut the door, and sat me down.

"Gianni," she said conspiratorially, "do you know Harold, the nurses' aide?"

"Yeah, sure. Everybody knows him. He's one of the physical therapy guys, right?" Harold was a young black man in his early twenties.

She leaned in closer. My heart started doing flip-flops. "Well, Harold has a problem, and you're getting to be that age where I should tell you about him."

She had my attention, not so much for what she was about to tell me, but I was now closer to those mammoth breasts than I'd ever been before. And she smelled great, too.

"Harold likes boys, Gianni, boys about your age, maybe a little older. You know what I'm saying?"

I'd heard rumors about Harold from the other kids—how he'd rub their bodies a little too long during therapy and talk about sex. I'd never had a problem with him, because he wasn't assigned to me, and I told Delores as much.

"He's got free run of the place and can go anywhere he wants on the floor. I'm just telling you to be careful. Watch out for him." She cleared her throat. "You're a very good-looking boy, Gianni"—She's noticed! I thought—"and you're the exact type he likes."

Later, before she left for the day, Delores came to my bed to say good night, which she did every day. This time she added, "Remember what I said, Gianni, when we talked before about Harold." Delores was always upbeat, and she laughed and smiled a lot. Now she looked as serious as the priests who would occasionally wander through the ward offering religious guidance.

I got the message. Delores scared me enough to get me thinking about defending myself should I run into trouble, be it with Harold the Pervert or any other problem that might come my way. In a ward packed with twenty kids with varying degrees of mobility, anything could happen and usually did. These incidents usually involved petty fistfights, but every now and then someone would pull an improvised weapon, if only to threaten someone.

The Harold thing seemed a bit more hazardous, so I decided to make my own makeshift weapon. To that end, I found the porter's broom on my way to the bathroom, jammed a portion of it under a radiator, and broke off a section a little over two feet long. I fashioned one end to spearlike sharpness by rubbing it against the grout between the tiles on the bathroom floor. It took me about a week, but I wound up with a formidable tool with which to defend myself should the need ever arise.

My senses on high alert, I watched my back constantly, especially when Harold wandered through the ward. Whenever he even approached the vicinity of my bed, Delores would materialize like the angel she was and give Harold the stink eye until he left the area. He never bothered me, and after a while my thoughts went from self-preservation back to Delores's breasts. I decided to hide my newly honed spear in the place I would be most vulnerable to an attack: the bathroom.

Everyone in the wards used the toilet bowls, even to pee, because most couldn't stand for even short periods of time to use the urinals. The bowls were side by side against a wall, and there was a drape suspended from the ceiling that you could pull around the bowl for privacy. Behind the bowls was a radiator mounted on the wall; it was around eighteen inches off the floor and went all around the room. I hid the spear on my right (strong) side between the radiator and the wall behind the third toilet bowl. I practiced drawing it to a defensive position while I sat on the bowl. Sometimes I'd spend over an hour on the toilet, honing the point to a deadly, sharper point. I would recite the rosary over and over again to keep my mind occupied while I scraped the broom handle through the grout.

There were six toilets in the bathroom, and sometimes when I needed to go, the third toilet would be taken. I would wait until it was unoccupied rather than use any of the others. These days, this discipline would be called "situational awareness." I thought of it as just being smart. Eventually, my discipline would save me from an attack or even death. But for now, it was comforting to have a weapon at the ready should I require it.

About a year passed and I hadn't had any problems with Harold, and with hormones beginning to rage like the Colorado River, all thoughts turned to Delores and her Magic Tits.

By this time, I had pretty good upper-body strength, mostly from dragging myself on the floor for years, but my left leg was still a little weak, and my left arm still a bit atrophied. I relied on the numerous rails affixed to every wall in the facility to help the patients get around. Most of my time was spent with Delores, and she caught me stealing glances at her chest on numerous occasions. I tried to be subtle, but I wasn't very good at it, and I felt my face reddening constantly.

One night, she was working an evening shift, and I made my way to her office as I usually did and sat down. She was behind her desk, doing some paperwork, when she suddenly looked up and caught me once again with my eyes riveted on those humongous mammaries. Being red-faced was becoming my natural color.

She had never mentioned my actions before; a simple glance was enough for me to avert my eyes and begin jabbering about something unrelated to breasts. This time, I didn't have the chance to say anything before she said, "You do that a lot, Gianni."

I played dumb. "Do what?"

She ignored my ridiculous attempt at a comeback. "Would you like to see them?" Delores said very matter-of-factly.

I just stared at her. I was both scared and excited at the same time.

"Go close the door, Gianni," she said as she stood up and began unbuttoning her blouse.

She didn't have to ask me twice. I struggled to my feet, reached for the door, and shut it. I looked at her, my eyes wide as manhole covers.

"Now come here." She had all her buttons undone and was pulling the blouse from her skirt.

I grabbed the rail on the wall and took one shuffling step in her direction.

"No," she said, holding up a manicured hand. "Don't use the rail. Walk on your own. You can do it."

I'd never walked without the aid of the rails before, but I would've done a slow stroll over hot coals to get closer to her. I forgot I even had a problem walking, and made my way to her without the support of the wall rail.

I stood in front of her, my knees weak as she held open her blouse. I was transfixed and stood there, using her desk for support.

"Would you like to touch them?" she asked with a smile.

"Uh-huh," I said dumbly, and inched closer, using the desk to guide me.

"Only if you let go of the desk." She backed up as far as she could go without colliding with the wall, maybe seven or eight feet. "Now walk to me." She held out her hands.

I crossed the room without any problem and gently placed my hands on those lovely breasts that I'd been fantasizing about for years. I didn't linger for long, withdrawing my hands after a few seconds.

Delores grinned. She was, and remains, one of the few truly sultry women I've known in my life. I was so happy, I thought I was going to cry.

She stood there in front of me, making no move to button her blouse.

"Do you know what you've done here today, Gianni?"

I didn't know what to say. I held those luscious tits, I thought, but how do I put that into acceptable words?

"I, uh, I mean, we, uh . . ." I managed to get out.

"You walked without the rails, without support," she said. Did she have tears in her eyes?

I did, didn't I? I thought. I felt really proud of myself, and for that one brief instant, her tits became secondary; my independence was primary. I knew I was going to be okay. I wasn't going to be a cripple.

We met in her office for what I called "Tit Therapy" until I left the wards. Toward the end, she lifted her bra, if only for the brief caress I gave her breasts with my shaking hands. If I had been permitted to do this from day one, I could've joined the Flying Wallendas within a few months. No amount of elastic-band extensions could get the results I'd gotten in a relatively short period of time using Tit Therapy. I was motivated, that's for sure.

The Salk vaccine became national news. Dr. Jonas Salk, while working at the University of Pittsburgh School of Medicine, developed a polio vaccine. Clinical trials were ordered and patients at Bellevue suffering from this devastating illness were chosen to be part of the trials. Half of the kids in my ward were given the vaccine—roughly ten kids—while the rest got nothing, not even a placebo. I was among those not receiving the vaccine, and I was devastated. I cried myself to sleep upon being told I wasn't part of the experimental group. While I was making strides toward normalcy, the disease had too many unknowns associated with it for me to think that I was on my way to being cured. Was my remission temporary? Was it truly a remission, or had my exercising combated the atrophying consequences of the disease? And did the psychological effects of Delores's "therapy" have anything to do with my improvement, or were her tits a placebo? Too many questions, too many doubts about my future.

I desperately wanted to be a part of the group receiving the experimental vaccine, but I could do nothing about being left out. All the kids with pull (read: the rich kids across the hall) were in the group getting the vaccine. We peons in the wards had to rely on the luck of the draw, and I was unlucky.

It turned out that not being chosen for the vaccine injections may have worked to my benefit. Shortly after the inoculations began, an inordinate number of the kids receiving it began dying in higher numbers than was the norm. The problem was never addressed, or at least not shared with the patients.

Life, for what it was worth, went on. My routine was comprised of physical therapy, waiting for Delores to begin her shift, and praying. Delores had me moved to a bed by a window. This was a big deal—tantamount to a bean counter in a company getting the corner office. There were no other distractions—no movies, books, or TV—just the dull, predictable, repetitive daily grind, so the window view was a respite. All I could see was First Avenue and sooty office buildings, but it might as well have been Shangri-la.

Without Delores, I would have descended into a pit of depression, like most of the other kids in the ward. She surprised me one day with a new transistor radio. I latched onto it like a life preserver; it was my free pass to the outside world. I would spend hours listening to radio shows like *Inner Sanctum*, *The Goldbergs*, and *Amos 'n' Andy*. The fictional characters became my family and friends. I was always into music, and during the day, when my shows weren't on, I'd tune in to WNEW for the current popular music of the day.

I was a rabid Frank Sinatra fan, made more so when I discovered that he and I shared the same birthday, December 12. I marveled at the man's talent and his "fuck you" persona. He was king of the world in the 1950s and never relinquished much of that power in the coming decades. If someone had told me at that time that Sinatra and I would become great friends and that he'd be the godfather to my son, I'd have recommended having them committed to one of the loony wards upstairs.

The day that changed my life forever began with the usual morning visit by the physical therapy staff and counting the minutes until Delores arrived. She showed up for her day shift and waved to me as she went into her office to clear up some overnight paperwork. I had her timed to the second; I had to wait about twenty minutes before I could stop in and see her, at which point in time my day would officially begin. But before that happened, I needed to make a trip to the john.

The bathroom was empty. I positioned myself on the third bowl and drew the curtain around me. Almost immediately, I felt the presence of someone else in the room. I didn't hear or see anyone; it was just a feeling creeping though my soul that someone was standing outside my drawn curtain.

Suddenly, the curtain was swept aside and Harold the Pervert loomed in front of me. He was not that tall, but to a kid sitting on a toilet, he looked huge.

"Hey, kid," he said with a leer. "I've got something for you." He undid his belt, unfastened his pants, and unzipped and dropped his drawers in what seemed like less than a second. He held his dick in his hand like some kind of weapon.

Fear ran through me like an icicle. I looked to his immediate left and right, considering a dash for freedom, but I was in no position to make a stealthy move while sitting on a toilet bowl. I didn't know how fast I could move under the best of circumstances anyway.

Harold said, "It's a Tootsie Roll, kid. Put it in your mouth." He took a step toward me and grabbed the back of my head, applying pressure to bring it down.

I must have rehearsed reaching for my spear a hundred times, and now my muscle memory kicked in. I reached behind me with my right hand and grabbed the spear, swinging it into position and guiding it with my left hand toward Harold's chest. He had no time to react, and he either didn't notice that I now held a deadly weapon in my hands or just didn't care, because he kept on applying pressure to the back of my head.

With all the strength I could muster, I rammed the spear at an upward angle into the pedophile's left chest area. I recall feeling a nanosecond of resistance, probably the weapon ricocheting off a rib. The son of a bitch jumped backward and began emitting high-pitched screams.

The spear dislodged in my white-knuckle grip, and he began running around the bathroom with blood spurting from the wound.

I sat in wide-eyed horror at what I'd just done. My first reaction was that I hadn't stabbed him hard enough, and as soon as he recovered from the shock of the blow, he'd come back at me, grab my spear, and use it on me.

Within seconds, however, he ran out of steam and dropped to his knees as his blood continued to spurt and gather around him on the tile floor.

Delores burst into the bathroom as Harold keeled over on his face and lay still. Her expression of horror twisted her beautiful face into something unrecognizable. She was carrying a blanket wherever she was going when she heard the screams, and she immediately threw it over my head to shield me from the bloody gore that lay in front of me.

She tried to coax me off the bowl, but I was almost too numb to move.

"Gianni, you've gotta get up, sweetie. C'mon now," she said gently.

I could hear other adults entering the bathroom, shouting, screaming, cursing. I tried to get the blanket off my head, but Delores held it firmly over me. She embraced me and pulled me into a standing position.

"I'm gonna lead you, sweetie. Don't worry, everything will be okay."

All the sexual fantasies I had about this woman over the years suddenly vanished. If her current embrace had occurred under different circumstances, it would've fulfilled yet another desire that I could have envisioned as something sexual in my adolescent-boy brain. Now she became a mother figure; helping, nourishing, protecting, and I reverted from the budding stud I thought I was to being a helpless child.

The next few hours were a blur. Delores removed the blanket once we were clear of the bathroom and took me to another ward a few floors above where I'd been staying. She stayed with me the rest of the day, never asking me what had happened. Thinking back on the incident as an adult, I figure she pretty much knew what had occurred and didn't want me to relive it.

I was never questioned by another adult—no hospital bosses, and, oddly, no cops. It was as if the attack and my response to it had never occurred. Delores did tell me that Harold had died, and only because I asked her if he was okay. The knowledge that I'd killed a man confused me more than frightened me. Sure, I was scared, but not because of what I'd done, but because of the consequences of my actions. I had absolutely no remorse, because I had defended myself. Would anyone believe that I'd stabbed Harold in an act of self-defense, or was I going to wind up in some kind of jail for juvenile delinquents, a term that was used to describe kids who did anything from reading comic books to, well, killing someone?

To this day, I don't know how the incident was handled. Many years later, I'd get a call from an NYPD detective who had inherited what he called "the cold case" regarding Harold's death, but I'm getting ahead of the story.

I remained in the ward where Delores had taken me until the day I was discharged from Bellevue. Out of nowhere, I was told I was being released. No one told me why. I felt strong, although my left leg and arm were still a bit atrophied, but they would return to normal in time.

I was going home; thanks for stopping by.

I had mixed emotions about leaving. Bellevue had been my home for five crucial years of my life, and the experience hadn't been all that bad as soon as Delores came into my orbit. Killing that pedophile, which had given me bad dreams for a while, was all but gone from my thoughts. I had effectively blocked out the episode. That ward was all I knew, and it was with great trepidation that I looked forward to the day when I'd go out into the real world.

I equate my feelings with those of convicts who spend years in prison, all of a sudden to be thrust out into a world with which they are unfamiliar when their sentences are complete. Their comfort zone was the prison; mine was the ward—both prisons of sorts.

I'd missed a good portion of my childhood and I was bitter. I was certainly hostile toward my parents. They hadn't visited me or contacted me once. It was as if I no longer existed once my mother had dropped me off the day I was admitted to the polio ward. I was old beyond my years and certainly not in a forgiving mood.

I was waiting with Delores when my mother arrived to pick me up. My mother acted like nothing had happened, like the five years I was gone was a blip in time. I fully expected to have her ask me how my day was going, but I got a hug and small talk instead. She looked the same—still beautiful, but beaten by life. She had come alone—no father, no sisters.

My parting with Delores was tearful. We kept in touch for a few years but gradually drifted apart. I never forgot her. I did track her down about twenty years ago and we spoke by phone. She was living out west with her family. We reminisced. It was a very emotional reunion.

I tried my best to resume my life at home, but my heart wasn't in it. Relations with my family were strained, my resentment palpable. My sisters were like strangers. I can't imagine what problems they had in the five years that I was gone. Living with my father was always difficult at best, horrendous at worst, and the psychological damage they endured must've been traumatizing. No one asked me about those five years I had been exiled; I was expected to pick up where I had left off, but that wasn't going to happen.

My family was the same: my father still out and about doing his thing, my mother the dutiful wife, my sisters involved with their friends and school, me the odd kid out.

My mother talked to me about getting back to school. I was almost twelve and would've had to resume where I'd left off. She registered me for school, but I didn't go. I wasn't about to be the world's oldest second grader, so no thanks.

I began spending less and less time at home, returning at night because I had nowhere else to go. I didn't even want to do that, but I needed a way to support myself before I could make a clean break.

This was no easy task for a kid who had just reentered society. Panhandling was out of the question. I was too proud and looked down scornfully on people who did that; still do to this day. If you're physically able, there's always a legitimate way to make money if you set your mind to it.

Magnatti's Bakery was located on Mott Street, close to where I lived. It was a fixture in the neighborhood, and my family had been going there ever since I could remember. One of my earliest memories was going there with my mother a few times a week and getting fresh hot bread right out of the oven.

Funzi Magnatti, the owner, was a nice man, about fifty years old. A hard worker, he opened his business before sunrise and didn't leave until it was dark, which was typical of the Italian work ethic in the neighborhood. It was a trait I admired, although when it came to my father, that way of life was foreign to him.

I approached Mr. Magnatti with a request: Give me a job and a place to stay and he could pay me whatever he deemed fair. An honorable man, he paid me the going hourly rate and said I could bunk down in the room where he stored his bags of flour. The room was spacious enough, and I shared it with a chute that extended to street level and was used to dump the bags of flour in the basement, where my room was located. The bags of flour would serve as my bed. The basement was dry, with virtually no humidity, and it was a welcome change from the damp tenement where my parents and sisters lived.

I was on the night shift, because that was when the bread was baked. My job was to prepare the bread mixture by combining a fifty-pound bag of flour with two pounds of lard, along with salt and water. Mr. Magnetti had a machine that did the mixing, but I elected to do it by hand in order to build muscle. My left arm was still a bit smaller than my right arm, but after a few months of making bread, I was making progress.

I went home occasionally to say hello, and was gone in a flash. I didn't want to be there, but the Italian ethic that dictated that family was paramount to everything else in life had been ingrained in me from birth. I did the bare minimum: *Hello. How're you doing? Goodbye.*

I didn't require much sleep. I was up and around by midmorning, my brain churning with ways to make more money.

One day I wandered into a little stationery store a few doors down from Magnatti's Bakery with an idea.

More and more people were using ballpoint pens, which had come way down in price since the end of World War II. While they had sold for around $12.50 a pen back then (about $166 in 2017 money), the price had plummeted in the 1950s to about $2, when they became a popular option over the high-maintenance fountain pen.

I introduced myself to the owner, a wizened old Jewish man, replete with yarmulke, who was behind the counter.

"Mr. Rabinowitz, my name is Gianni Russo and I've got a business proposition for you." I extended my hand.

The old man shook my hand and stared down at me over his reading glasses for what seemed like a lifetime. Without altering his gaze, he called to an unseen person in the back room of the store.

"Hey, Moishe!" he said in a high-pitched tone. "You hear that? I've got a young man here wants to make me a business proposition." There was no response from the back. "So, why should I listen to anything you have to say, young man?"

I was ready for doubt, given my age. "Because, Mr. Rabinowitz," I said, "I'm gonna make you an offer you can't refuse," a prophetic pronouncement I would hear again, uttered from the mouth of Marlon Brando years later on the set of *The Godfather.*

We struck a deal. Mr. Rabinowitz would sell me ballpoint pens at twenty cents a pen and I would be on my own to resell them. He fronted me the first fifty pens after I used Mr. Magnatti as a reference.

My plan was to go to the Wall Street area and sell them to office workers at a minimum of a dollar a pen. This was the beginning of my entrepreneurial career, something that has remained with me until this day.

I had a preemptive plan in place: I surveyed various businesses in the Financial District to ascertain when they paid their employees; then I'd go back on paydays to hawk my pens. I charged what I thought I could get away with, usually a dollar, sometimes a little bit more. These were cheap plastic pens, but at half the price brick-and-mortar stores were selling them for. I was doing pretty well, making a profit of about thirty dollars a day.

A few months later, Mr. Rabinowitz began to stock miniature ballpoint pens encrusted with faux jewels, and I envisioned a different demographic: women.

I abandoned the world of Wall Street high finance and headed to the Theater District in midtown, where I figured my target audience wouldn't disappear after the lunch hour. There were tourists by the thousands in Times Square, and how could you send a postcard home to East Cupcake, Arkansas, without a pen?

Armed with a cigar box full of pens, I hawked them, saying, "I've got beautiful pens! Could you help me out, please?" I was either the world's best pen salesman or my customers took pity on me. Either way, I cared little, just as long as I was making money.

I began averaging between thirty and sixty dollars a day in profits, not a bad payday for the 1950s. After a while I had hundreds of dollars stuffed in coffee cans at Magnatti's Bakery. I needed a bank account to stash the dough (pardon the pun) but couldn't open one because I was too young. I wasn't about to ask my parents to open an account for me, thinking that my father would probably loot the account when his nightclub tabs came due.

Mr. Magnatti stepped up to the plate and opened the account in his name, in trust for me. Within a few months, I had fifteen hundred dollars saved. Always thinking of ways to make more money, I decided to move my business to midtown and the Upper East Side, where the well-heeled New Yorkers lived, and where the priciest hotels were located.

I set up shop outside the Sherry-Netherland Hotel on Fifth Avenue, across from Central Park, every morning. Business was great, and I'd often run out of pens by early afternoon. The hotel traffic would've been enough to sustain me, but the pedestrian flow on the avenue was nonstop, too.

3

THE AMBASSADOR, MARILYN MONROE, AND MY MAFIA EDUCATION BEGINS

Every morning at ten o'clock, a well-dressed man around fifty years old and wearing a suit and tie, topped off with a fedora, would come out of the Sherry-Netherland with at least one other man, sometimes two. Whoever the older man was, he seemed to be in charge, and they would disappear around the corner on foot. After a few days, the older man came up to me.

"What've you got, kid?" he asked. He had a rough, throaty voice but appeared pleasant enough.

"Pens," I said, "lots of 'em. Want one?"

"Not today, but take this." He already had a bill in his hand, and he stuffed it into my jacket pocket. "Have a good day." And he was gone.

I retrieved the bill. Five dollars! The only time I'd gotten a fiver was when I was making change. This was indeed my lucky day, only I didn't realize how lucky I truly was.

The man stopped by and spoke briefly to me every day. I figured he lived in the hotel, but I would find out later that he didn't. You could set your watch by the guy—out in the morning at 10:00 A.M. sharp. I'd get a five-dollar bill every day.

This went on for a few more weeks and nothing changed. Still got my fiver every day, and he never bought a pen. What did change, however, was that after he gave me the bill, he'd touch my shoulder before he went wherever he and his friends were going. It was a subtle touch and wasn't bothersome, until one day when I found out what it meant.

I still went to Mass at the Church of the Most Precious Blood on Mulberry Street early every day. One day after Mass, I went into the religious objects store located next door to the church (it's still there today, in the same location). In the window was a small statue of a deformed man, and I was curious as to what it meant. The owner told me that the statue represented an old Sicilian belief that by touching a crippled person's deformity, it would bring you luck.

It took a few seconds to sink in. That man who gave me the fiver every day was touching my atrophied arm for luck! I was fucking incensed. I wanted to get back at him, but I also considered the five bucks I was getting every day. After a few minutes of contemplative soul-searching, I thought, Screw it. My self-respect was worth more than five dollars.

I had two things going for me in my life up until this time: my faith in God and my friendship with Delores Barone at Bellevue. Of course, God was always omnipresent, and I could lean on Him whenever I felt abandoned, but Delores had been out of my life since I'd left the hospital. When I found out that the five-dollar guy was, in effect, using me, I had that feeling of helplessness all over again. Who was there in this world that could be trusted? Certainly not my family, definitely not the "system," which had kept me locked up for five years. Now I felt as if this total stranger who I'd thought was befriending me and treating me kindly had an ulterior motive.

While the unearned five dollars a day was nice, I wasn't going to stand for being someone's four-leaf clover. I went to a novelty store down the street and bought a pink rabbit's foot, with a specific plan in mind.

Later on, same thing: I got a smile, a five-dollar bill, and a shoulder touch.

"Hey," I said, brushing his hand away, "this is for you," and I handed him the rabbit's foot.

He stared at it for a moment. "What's this?"

"You want luck?" I said, seething. "Now you have a rabbit's foot. Keep your hands off me."

The pleasant demeanor I'd gotten used to seeing vanished. He stared at me and his eyes narrowed.

"Hey, Blackie," he said to his buddy, "the kid's got balls." Now he was smiling. Blackie thought this was funny, too, or maybe because his boss was smiling, he thought he should, too.

Almost as an afterthought, he asked, "What's your name, kid?"

"Gianni Russo," I said, still sullen.

"Where you from?"

I didn't want to go into my family situation, and that I was currently residing in a bakery, so I just said, "I live with my parents on Mulberry Street."

He grunted. "I know a Russo . . . Angelo Russo."

"That's my uncle," I said proudly.

"Angelo Russo is your uncle?"

"Great-uncle, my grandfather's brother," I said.

I had his interest. "He's from the neighborhood where you live, right?" I got the feeling I was being tested.

"No, Palermo, in Sicily." Next question.

"What's he do in Palermo?"

"Capo regime," I said. Uncle Angelo was the captain of his own Mafia crew, and now I was sure this guy knew exactly what the Italian term for that was.

The man smiled. He turned to Blackie. "You believe this? Small world."

He appraised me for a few moments, then reached into his pocket and came out with a wad of money thicker than my thigh. He peeled off two bills, both hundreds, and extended them to me. I was hesitant to take it. He gestured with the money. "Take it, kid."

I took it.

Then he turned to his buddy. "Blackie, take the box."

Blackie snatched the box full of pens from my hand. I stood there dumbfounded.

"I like you, kid. You work for me now. Your pen days are over. I need someone to run errands for me . . . see people, drop stuff off, pick stuff up." He looked at Blackie, a swarthy character, also dressed in an expensive suit, but he seemed out of place in it, as if it were a uniform, not something he would choose to wear.

"Tomorrow morning at eleven-thirty," he said to me, "meet Blackie here under the clock in the lobby of the Waldorf. You know where that is?"

Who didn't know where the Waldorf-Astoria, the swankiest hotel in New York, was? "Yeah, sure," I said.

"Don't be late," he said. "Never be late . . . for anything." He stared at me for a few seconds, then left, with Blackie in tow.

The doorman at the hotel had watched the entire episode. I saw him chuckling to himself and shaking his head. I walked over to him.

"Who was that guy?" I asked, jerking my thumb over my shoulder.

"*That guy*," the doorman said, mimicking me, "is the Ambassador."

"Huh," I said, bewildered.

The doorman rolled his eyes. "Frank Costello."

Nothing more needed to be said by way of explanation. I had just disrespected the most powerful gangster in the United States.

I was under the clock in the Waldorf's lobby ten minutes early the next day. Blackie, who turned out to be Mr. Costello's bodyguard and enforcer, was right on time. He handed me a pile of envelopes with names and addresses on them, all in midtown.

"Drop these off, then go to these addresses." He handed me a paper with addresses and names on them. "Ask for these people; they'll have something for you. By the way, Mr. Costello knows your uncle Angelo."

Costello's reaction to my uncle's name seemed logical now. I nodded. "And could you tell Mr. Costello to call me by my name . . . Gianni? I'm not a kid."

"Listen, kid," Blackie said without rancor, "Mr. Costello can call you whatever he wants, understand?"

From the day I met him until the day he died, in 1973, Frank Costello called me "the Kid." The name stuck and spread. To everyone in the mob, I'd be known as the Kid for many years to come, long after I entered adulthood. As for Mr. Costello, I would come to find out later during conversations with him that he, Carlo Gambino, the boss of the crime family that still bears his name, and Charles "Lucky" Luciano, who organized crime in 1933, came to this country with the help of my great-uncle Angelo and his magic connections. A small world indeed.

Most of the addresses I was being directed to were bars, restaurants, hotels, and nightclubs. I'd pick up envelopes with the letter *C* on them, and then drop them off with the maître d' at the Copacabana on East Sixtieth Street, the hottest club in New York. Jules Podell was the owner of record, but it was really Mr. Costello who owned the place. He would hold court there several times a week after dinner. He always went home to The Majestic for dinner with his family—always. He was an old-school gangster, and very well respected, not only by his peers—if, in fact, he had any—but by politicians and some cops (those he had in his pocket), as well. He would become the model for Don Corleone in the book *The Godfather*, by Mario Puzo.

I wasn't certain what was in the envelopes, and I wasn't about to ask, but I wasn't stupid, either. The places I stopped by were obviously policy banks and bookie joints. After a while, I surmised I was picking up money and betting slips. Back then, the mob's main source of income was gambling; drug dealing was strictly forbidden. I kept my mouth shut and did what I was told. For my trouble, I was given money, lots of it. A hundred dollars a day was the norm, sometimes more, particularly if I had to go to the Copa later at night.

As time went on, and I became more trusted, I was permitted more entrée into Mr. Costello's world. I'd go to the barbershop in the Plaza Hotel, one of the mob's biggest policy operations, and pick up slips and cash, which I'd deliver to the Copa. I never gave Mr. Costello anything personally; at the Copa, I'd drop off whatever I had with Carmine, the maître d', even if Mr. Costello was standing right in front of me.

The first time I went to the Wyndam, another midtown hotel, I was in for a bit of a shock. An entire floor was devoted to Mr. Costello's gambling operation. There had to have been five big rooms filled with men talking on at least forty phones, a loudspeaker spewing the results of horse races from racetracks across the country, and another group of men wearing eyeshades, entering figures in ledgers.

I'd go to the Wyndam several times a week, and there was the same cop on horseback in front of the hotel on every trip. I assumed this cop had to know what was going on in the hotel, and I mentioned it to Mr. Costello one night, figuring I was tipping off the boss to something of which he was unaware.

Mr. Costello laughed. "He's our cop, kid. Don't worry about it."

So here I was, a kid, and stopping by famous places I'd only heard about: '21,' Toots Shor's, Patsy's, the Latin Quarter, and the Barbizon Hotel. The list was endless.

My life was being mapped out, although I might not have realized it at the time. All I knew was that I was independent and free of my family. I was on my own with a pocketful of cash and I was loving it.

Whenever I had to deliver or pick up envelopes at the Copa, I'd use the kitchen entrance and would stay there until I was told to go upstairs to the lounge and see Carmine. I would only deal with Carmine, the maître d'; Mr. Costello never dealt with me directly if there were "civilians" around and we were conducting business, and the Copa was always crowded with customers.

One night, I dropped off a pile of envelopes stuffed with cash to Carmine, and I was about to leave when he said, "Hold up, kid."

Carmine, like all maître d's in New York, was smooth, impeccably dressed, and didn't say much, at least not to me. Well into his fifties, he had been at the Copa since day one (a waiter told me they'd built the club around him) and had Mr. Costello's complete trust.

"Take this envelope to the Barbizon," Carmine told me, "and ask for Mr. Florio; he's the night manager. He'll give you something to bring back." Then he winked at me, like I was supposed to know what he was talking about. So I winked back at him and took the envelope. Just two guys in the know, with shared secrets. Only I was barely a teenager and I didn't know much about anything. One of the reasons Mr. Costello kept me around was because I was always on time, didn't ask questions, was polite to everyone, and kept my mouth shut. By this time, I knew what an envelope containing cash felt like, and while this one wasn't stuffed, I knew it contained significant money, just from the feel of it.

I was sure Mr. Costello had checked out my family connections; made sure my uncle Angelo was really my uncle, and spoke to the bookies and policy guys I was meeting with on a daily basis to make sure I was a stand-up guy and didn't conduct myself like a typical teenage street mope.

The Barbizon Hotel was on Sixty-third Street, off Lexington Avenue, and was for females only. It had a sterling reputation, wasn't expensive, and attracted professional women from out of town, actresses, and students from the Katharine Gibbs secretarial school.

I got a good reception when I handed the envelope to Mr. Florio, who looked like a typical bean counter who walked like he had a stick up his ass, and practically tripped over himself getting to me from across the lobby. Obviously, he'd gotten a heads-up to expect an emissary from Frank Costello. While he may have expected a Cagney-type gangster, he got me instead. My only ID was the envelope, and that was all that was needed.

He stuffed the envelope in his jacket pocket and said, "Wait here."

He went to the reception desk and said something to the guy behind it, who promptly picked up a phone. Within ten minutes, three knockout young women, dressed smartly, sauntered out of the elevator and conferred with Mr. Florio. He pointed me out and the women walked over.

Two of them I recognized immediately: actresses Grace Kelly and Audrey Hepburn. The third woman was, and remains, a mystery.

I was awed. These women were the ones I was taking back to the Copa. Two months earlier, I'd been selling two-dollar pens on the street, and now I was escorting two famous actresses (maybe three) back to the Copa.

Grace Kelly looked at me quizzically and said, "You're our escort?"

I stood a little taller and said, "Yes, ma'am."

The women looked at one another and smiled.

"Lead the way," the woman unknown to me said.

I had walked to the hotel, but, needless to say, we were cabbing it back. We were in the backseat of a Checker cab, roomy enough to accommodate the four of us in the back. I sat on the jump seat and ogled the women, who were talking animatedly. They were dressed like they were going to a party, which they probably were.

I dropped them off at the main entrance to the Copa, and I went in through the kitchen, as usual. Curiosity get the better of me and I went upstairs. Mr. Costello was at his usual table with two male friends. They had been joined by the three women I'd just picked up. They all looked like they were having a good time.

I'd make a Barbizon run a few times a month, each time exchanging an envelope with cash for women, some well known, others not, and escort them back to the Copa. After I made sure they were inside, I'd leave. I wondered if these women were getting a cut of the money I'd brought to the hotel manager, and what were they doing for it. Mr. Costello and his buddies never dealt with small denominations, fifties and hundreds being the norm, and the envelopes I delivered to the hotel were well padded. I couldn't imagine that the hotel manager was getting all of it.

One rainy, miserable night I had dropped off envelopes to Carmine and was about to leave when he stopped me.

"Go upstairs. Mr. C. wants to see you."

I went up to the lounge. Mr. Costello was at his table alone. He indicated a chair. "Sit."

I sat, and said nothing.

"You still living downtown?" he asked.

I picked up on his not mentioning Mulberry Street, where I had told him I lived with my parents. I was sure he knew I was crashing in the bakery on bags of flour.

"Yes, sir," I said.

"You've been working later, and I can't see you going all the way downtown every night, particularly tonight, in this weather." He reached into his pocket and came out with a key on a metal ring. "I've got apartments all over town, kid. Might as well use them. They're vacant at night." He tossed me the key and gave me the address. "Stay there as long as you like. If you want to move or we close up an apartment, I'll steer you to another."

And so it came to pass that I'd be staying in Mr. Costello's wire rooms for the foreseeable future. These apartments were where Mr. Costello's men took bets, on anything from horses to sports. At any given time during the day, over twenty men were on telephones, taking bets from all over the city. These were very upscale Upper East Side and midtown apartments, which were vacated periodically to stay one step ahead of the cops. Sure, the police were being paid off, but Costello didn't want to draw the attention of neighbors. If the police were called to report a "gambling den," the cops would have to take action, bribes or not. I'd be out in the morning to start my day's work, just when the daily workers were arriving. Once the racetracks closed, they would leave.

I was pulling in five hundred dollars a week in cash, not including the not so rare bonuses, which usually meant an extra hundred or so periodically. I never did anything out of the ordinary to earn the bonuses, just did my job, but Mr. Costello was a generous man who appreciated trustworthiness, and I thought that he may have reasoned that I was giving money to my parents. I was not.

I learned a lot from him, not the least being loyalty, and keeping my word. I've done this all my life, and attribute my longevity and success in the legitimate business world, and my dealings with the mob, to being a man of my word, and showing respect to people who reciprocate in kind.

My father figure was Frank Costello, and I couldn't have done any better. I never felt fear around him, never felt used or disrespected. I learned from him that if you kept your word and worked hard, there was nothing you couldn't accomplish.

"Hey, kid," Mr. Costello said to me one night after I had just dropped off some envelopes to Carmine. We were at the Copa and he'd just arrived from dinner with his family.

"Yes, sir," I said, waiting for instructions.

He looked me up and down. "Listen, you need to tone up the wardrobe some . . . make that a lot." He was dressed in a sharply cut gray silk suit and red print tie.

I felt a little self-conscious, but I was neat and clean in well-pressed street clothes. Granted, I wasn't wearing a fine silk suit, but I wasn't in his league, either. I'm sure his tie cost more than my entire wardrobe.

"This isn't good, Mr. C.?" I asked, looking down at my duds.

"Not if you work for me, it isn't. You know Leighton's?"

I'd passed the renowned men's store on Broadway and Forty-sixth Street, and I knew Mr. C. bought a lot of his clothes there. Leighton's sold mostly imported Italian menswear and fine Italian shoes. I'd ogle the clothes and shoes in the window as I passed the store while running my errands, and remember that their alligator shoes ran $110 and up, a hefty price for the 1950s. Leighton's was where all the well-dressed wiseguys, as well as entertainers, bought their clothes.

"Yes, sir, I know the place. Pass it all the time."

"Here's what I want you to do." He removed a wad of bills from his pocket, popped the rubber band that kept his brick of cash from exploding, and peeled off several bills—gangsters never carried their money in wallets. "Go to Leighton's and get yourself some suits and shirts and shoes. Ask for Bobby; he'll take care of you."

I knew enough not to refuse the money. "Thank you, sir," I said, anxious to be able just to walk into Leighton's, let alone buy anything.

"Stick with me, kid" he said, smiling. "You'll have movie actresses falling all over you."

He didn't know how profound those words were to become.

I bought one suit, two shirts, a pair of shoes, and one tie. I gave Mr. C. back significant change. I couldn't see spending his money like a drunken sailor on shore leave. He'd been good to me and would continue to be good to me; I didn't want him to think I was a pig.

I was bitten by the clotheshorse bug. Since that day at Leighton's, fine clothes would become one of my many weaknesses—a virtual addiction. Being well dressed had residual effects, not the least of which was attracting women. And, of course, what's the use of wearing designer clothes if you look like a bag of shit? Keeping in shape became a way of life for me, which had as much to do with ego as it had to do with feeling well. Money is nice, but if you don't take care of your body, you'll die young and all the money in the world won't be any good to you. The very least is that you won't have the drive to work hard every day. And I was driven.

I had made my usual visit to the Copa one night to hand over a bunch of cash-stuffed envelopes when Carmine told me that there were several New York Yankees downstairs in the showroom with their wives and asked if I would like to take a peek. That was like asking any fourteen-year-old kid in the country if Superman believed in truth, justice, and the American way.

"You don't have to ask me twice," I said, and made for the basement showroom, one flight down.

The Yankees were in the lounge to see Sammy Davis, Jr., perform.

Sammy was a big draw, and the place was packed. I stood inconspicuously in the back of the small room (it seated about eighty people, so no matter where I was, I would be close to the ballplayers).

In attendance at a large round table were Micky Mantle, Yogi Berra, Whitey Ford, Hank Bauer, and Billy Martin, and their wives. They were there celebrating Billy Martin's twenty-ninth birthday, I would find out later. A few champagne bottles littered the table, and the conversation was animated, although given the din from the rest of the room, I couldn't hear what they were saying. Contributing to the clamor were the people at the table next to the ballplayers'; I would later find out these were eight men from a bowling league out on the town. They were louder than anyone else, and I assumed already oiled to the gills and showing it.

All conversation abruptly ended when the lights dimmed and the star of the show, Sammy Davis, Jr., emerged onstage to loud applause. The show hadn't been under way five minutes when the bowlers began shouting drunken racial epithets at Sammy, some pretty vile. Someone from the Yankees table told the bowlers to be quiet and got a slew of curses in return.

Billy Martin was the first off his chair, and I thought, Uh-oh, here it comes. In less than five seconds, the rest of the Yankees followed Martin, and a full-out brawl commenced. Tables, chairs, bottles, and booze flew everywhere. Patrons leaped to their feet and made for the exits. The ballplayers' wives wisely retreated to the nearest wall. In less than a minute the fight was over, with the bowlers sprawled out on the floor, all moving and moaning except for one guy, who lay motionless.

Cops were there in minutes, and that was my cue to depart. If anyone asked, I hadn't seen anything.

The press played it up big. The one unconscious man wound up with a concussion and a broken jaw. It was thought that Hank Bauer put that guy down, but none of the witnesses the cops managed to corral before they fled the scene had seen anything. *"Fight, what fight?"* Who in their right mind was going to testify against the New York Yankees? Doing that would be like kicking the Pope in the balls.

The media reported that a grand jury was going to be convened to bring possible assault indictments against the Yankees because, the bowlers insisted, one of the ballplayers had thrown the first punch, and the rest of the players had piled on them for no apparent reason. The bowlers swore they were just minding their own business when they were forced to defend themselves against a tableful of drunken criminals. This upset me, and I said as much to Mr. C.

"Those assholes were cursing at Sammy. They deserved what they got," I said. "Are the Yankees going to jail?"

"Don't worry about it, kid." Mr. Costello smiled knowingly.

The lines I was reading between were as wide as a five-lane highway. I comforted myself by rationalizing that the "fix" was in.

The grand jury met and called Mickey Mantle as one of its first witnesses. When asked if he had seen who attacked the bigoted asshole who got his jaw broken, Mantle deadpanned, "I think Roy Rogers rode through the Copa, and Trigger kicked the man in the head."

The grand jury chose not to indict anyone. I later found out that Mr. Costello made sure of that.

I was living large, with more money than I knew what to do with. My family was a distant (unpleasant) memory, and the only person I had to answer to was Frank Costello. Because I had his confidence, all of Mr. C.'s colleagues treated me with deference and respect. I didn't take advantage of Mr. C.'s faith in me. I was very respectful to literally everyone, from the mobsters to hotel shoe-shine guys. I never lost sight of the fact that I was just a kid, and no matter what leeway I had among the wiseguys, I knew I could be replaced if I developed an attitude.

Life was good. What could possibly go wrong?

I was walking down the street in midtown one day, pockets jammed with cash-stuffed envelopes, when a car pulled to the curb and a man in his thirties jumped out and headed right for me. I was sure I was about to get ripped off for the more than twenty grand I had on me. After a second of reflection, I asked myself, Who's stupid enough to rip off Frank Costello? If someone even contemplated the thought, they should've immediately shot themselves in the head, because if they'd gone through with it, their demise would've been much more unpleasant than a quick bullet to the brain.

The guy was wearing a brown uniform and had a patch on his shirt, and as he came closer, I was able to read it: TRUANT OFFICER.

My first pinch.

"Hey, kid," he said as he blocked my path, "how old are you?"

"Fifteen," I said. Why lie? He had me cold.

"Why aren't you in school?"

I shrugged. "I dunno."

The truant officer looked me up and down. If he searched me, I was screwed. The money would be confiscated and vouchered at the nearest police precinct, or maybe stolen, and Mr. C. would be highly pissed. But the officer didn't put a hand on me.

"What's your name? Now don't lie to me. You lie, and I see you on the street again, you're going to juvie."

Going to juvenile hall was the last thing I needed. Who knows how long I'd be there. I told him my real name and gave him my parents' address. He wrote a summons and handed it to me.

"Give that to your parents and get your ass in school. I'm filing the original with the city," he said. As he turned to go back to his car, he said, "And don't forget what I told you . . . juvie."

It was with great anxiety that I reported what happened to Mr. Costello later that night at the Copa. I was literally shaking in my new brogues. To my surprise, he put the summons in his pocket and looked at me for a long moment.

"You know, you need to go to school. I don't need any scrutiny from the law over a truant kid."

That was it, I figured. My career, for what it was worth, was over. I was going back to school and maybe back to the bakery. Mr. C. saw the concern on my face.

"Listen," he said. "When you're sixteen, you can quit school. That's the law in New York. Until then, I'm enrolling you in the Wilford Academy."

"Huh? What's that, Mr. Costello?"

"It's a beauty school. I know the owner, and it'll cover you legally. The day you turn sixteen, you leave. You can still work for me while you're going."

I was both relieved and pissed off. While I'd keep my job with him, I was going to be a hairdresser? From what little I knew about the trade, I assumed that men who went in for that sort of thing were queer (the word *gay* hadn't as yet entered the American lexicon).

Frank Costello sighed and put his arm around me. "I know what you're thinking, kid, but trust me, that school is going to be the best thing that ever happened to you. You're gonna get more pussy than Rudolph Valentino." He smiled.

"Who?"

Mr. Costello rolled his eyes. "Look him up."

The only person on the planet whom I trusted implicitly was Frank Costello. That said, I wanted to believe what he was telling me, but it seemed too weird to go along with. But it turned out he was right.

The Wilford Academy was located next to Lindy's restaurant, a Broadway hot spot on Seventh Avenue between Fifty-third and Fifty-fourth streets, right in the heart of the Theater District.

My first day of classes began the last week of September 1959. Mr. Costello paid for the tuition, or maybe called in a favor. I never really knew which. I needed to attend the school until December 12, when I'd turn sixteen. I didn't know what was expected of me, how many days a week or hours I'd have to put in, and this was a concern. The more time I spent in school, the less time I'd be on the street making my rounds and putting cash in my pocket.

My first day, I showed up on time, 8:00 A.M. That would be the last day I arrived at eight. After getting the lay of the land, and finding out what was expected of me, I scheduled my own hours.

A middle-aged woman with hair as high as Abe Lincoln's hat told me I had to sign in to comply with the law.

"Same time every day? Eight o'clock?" I asked.

She gave me a motherly smile. "Anytime you want, dear."

Apparently, she was in Mr. C.'s pocket.

I got in the groove immediately. I'd meet Blackie at the Waldorf as usual at 11:00 A.M., go to the school, sign in, and stay for an hour, maybe two, before I hit the street to run my errands. I'd show up at the school two or three days a week.

So, what did I learn? Shampooing. That's it. Not much of a skill set, but there were some protocols, mainly how to greet customers, rinsing, drying, and getting knots out of hair. After ten minutes, my education was complete. I kept returning to try to hook up with some really hot girls who were students. There were a few guys in the classes, but all were gay. I was like a kid in a candy store. Two girls in particular caught my eye, and I took both of them to the Copa (not at the same time) to impress them. It worked. I got the best tables, no checks, and greetings and handshakes from well-known people. The girls weren't even old enough to drink, but they didn't care. They were awestruck, and I scored more than Mickey Mantle.

By November, I was eligible to begin an internship in an established beauty salon, which would count toward my education hours. Maybe I was hanging out with too many criminals, but I called it a work-release program.

One day, emissaries from the Lilly Dache Beauty Salon—the preeminent beauty salon in New York, located on East Fifty-sixth Street—Mr. Kenneth (aka Kenneth Battelle) and Marc Sinclair, showed up at the school, looking for shampoo boys for the salon. Mr. Kenneth was the hairdresser to the stars. His clients included the entire female side of the Kennedy clan, plus Marilyn Monroe, Judy Garland, and many other Hollywood notables. Marc Sinclair was a renowned hair colorist. He and Mr. Kenneth were also lovers.

They both took one look at me, a good-looking olive-skinned Italian boy, and they immediately fell in love. It didn't make a difference that I'd put in less time at Wilford than the mailman; I was in. I didn't care for whom I worked, just as long as the time counted toward my New York State required education hours. It did. I'd have to put in a minimum of one hundred hours, or until December 12, whichever came first. All I knew was that the day I turned sixteen, I'd be gone. My graduate school would be the street. My plan was to put in the least number of hours I could at the salon, and devote as much time as I could to working for Mr. Costello.

The salon consisted of three floors and was elegant. The first floor housed the hat boutique and a reception desk; Lilly Dache was famous for her hat designs. An elaborate circular staircase led to the second-floor salon; the third floor housed the offices.

Since Mr. Costello had no involvement in my getting the job, I had no juice like I'd had at Wilford. I had to show up for work five days a week, but I could play with the hours. I always had time to do my real job, which was to collect gambling money and slips for Mr. Costello.

My first day at the salon, I was issued a uniform and given my duties. Shampooing hair involved more than just standing at the ready in front of a sink, waiting for customers. I had to escort the customers up the stairs to the salon, hang up their coats, make small talk without getting personal, help them on with their coats when they left, and smile a lot. The more personable I was, the more I made in tips. I was paid minimum wage, so tips were the name of the game. The cream of New York society, the wealthy, celebrities, and people who thought they were celebrities were my customers.

My first three customers came and went. My fourth customer was already seated, head back and hair in the sink, by the time I got back from helping my last wet head to the colorist. I was bored already, and it was only my first day on the job, and I didn't give much thought to whose head I was washing.

Private cubicles housed the wash stations. We were required to wash, rinse, and repeat. When I began the second round, my customer began moaning softly. This was new. Maybe I had magic hands. I continued washing, and the customer continued to moan softly.

"You're very good at this," she said in a breathy voice. "What's your name?"

Her voice sounded familiar. "Gianni," I said. And then it hit me. I was shampooing Marilyn Monroe!

"Keep going, Gianni. It feels wonderful."

My instantaneous erection also felt wonderful, and it didn't go away when I was finished with the shampooing. I was a teenage boy, and we could get hard-ons putting on our pants.

I had to walk her to the colorist, and I prayed my stiffy would vanish. I willed it away. Didn't work. All I could hope for was that everyone would have their eyes on Marilyn and not on my crotch. I didn't make eye contact with anyone and hoped for the best.

She came back to the salon often, and always asked for me as her shampoo boy.

Marilyn was very friendly. After a few visits and my talks with her, I got over the movie-star hype and saw her as an average person, albeit one with a dynamite body. We had similar backgrounds, and I thought she viewed me as someone she could confide in and felt that I'd understand what she was saying. Both of us had been abandoned as kids—me to the polio ward, her to an orphanage. She told me she could see the Warner Bros. and RKO studios in the distance from her ward and vowed that she'd wind up working there one day.

I was called into work one Saturday morning and was told that Marilyn wanted me to shampoo her hair. What else is new? I thought. This wasn't a surprise.

"No, not here, at the Waldorf," my supervisor told me. This wasn't a day I'd soon forget. She requested my presence at 5:00 P.M. I watched the clock like a condemned prisoner and arrived at the hotel promptly at five. I figured she was going out and needed me to help her with her hair.

Marilyn was alone in a lavish suite replete with an outdoor terrace, but the entire place looked like the set of a disaster movie. Clothes were thrown everywhere, dirty dishes were on a sofa, the bed was unmade, and she looked like a homeless waif without makeup. She was wrapped in a white terry-cloth towel and had a flute of champagne in her hand. "Want some?" she offered.

"Uh, no thanks." Actually, I could've used a few glasses to calm myself, but I felt obligated to turn it down.

"I'm gonna take a bath." She turned her back to me and began walking to the bathroom.

I thought this was my cue to leave for a while, and I said as much.

She turned in the doorway and smiled. "Don't be silly. Come in here with me."

Huh? I figured I couldn't have heard that right. I froze in place.

Marilyn glanced behind her. "Well? C'mon."

My mouth was sand-dry and my heart was pounding. As soon as I broke the threshold of the bathroom, she dropped the robe.

Like an idiot, I covered my eyes, which made her laugh.

Embarrassed, I dropped my hands and stared at her. I had no words. Turned out, I didn't need any. She smiled and got into the tub. "Come join me."

Trying to act cool, I squeaked out, "Sure." How's that for glib?

She giggled.

I began removing my clothes, praying I wouldn't trip on my pants and fall on my ass, and then entered the tub. I immediately moved to the opposite end, facing her. I'll be honest, I had no idea what to do, or what she expected.

We wound up in bed for the entire weekend, climbing out only when needed. It was my first experience with room service (I didn't even know what it was), and it was great. I didn't leave the suite for two days.

Monday morning, I was back on the street and on my way to work. I was exhausted, giddy, sore, and confused. I was passing thousands of people on the street, and I had a secret that could never be guessed: I'd just had sex with America's hottest movie star and sex symbol. I knew I couldn't tell anyone, and not necessarily because I was a gentleman. Who would believe me? I certainly wouldn't tell Mr. Costello, and I wasn't really close to anyone else. After a while, keeping our relationship, for what it was worth, secret became second nature.

I never mentioned it to a soul until thirteen years later, when *The Godfather* was in preproduction and Marlon Brando was talking about Marilyn. Marlon was one of her many lovers, and he was lamenting her early death.

He shook his head as he thought back wistfully. "She oozed sex. Man, she was great."

Unconsciously, I nodded in agreement.

Brando stared at me. "You bedded her?"

"Yeah," I said, and shrugged.

Brando did a double take. "Get the fuck outta here." He didn't know whether to believe me or not. "Tell me something on her body no one would know."

I jabbed at my upper right thigh. "Scar, right about here."

He let out a hearty laugh. "Well, fuck me. How old were you?

"Almost sixteen, but it went on for a while."

Brando didn't say anything. I could see he was doing the math in his head.

"Thirty-three," I said. "She was thirty-three in the beginning." It shouldn't have been a big deal that I told someone, but afterward I didn't feel right about it. Marilyn had been dead since 1962, but I still thought about her often.

We would meet often when she came to New York, and the relationship wasn't always about sex. She looked to me as a respite from the craziness that was Hollywood. We talked about everything except her career and the pressure that went with being a star. The commonality of our respective experiences growing up was often discussed. It may be hard to comprehend, but she reminded me of a naïve teenage girl; she didn't act her age. She had low self-esteem, and that always amazed me. Marilyn had more power in the movie business than she realized, just based on her box-office draw, but she chose to use sex for leverage. Practically all her costars were lovers, as were many others, both in and out of the business.

Marilyn usually wore the same disguise when we were out: dark wig and sunglasses.

Her tastes were simple. She liked walking over the Brooklyn Bridge; loved the view of Manhattan at night from the Brooklyn side. There was a dive bar called the Subway Inn on the East Side that she wanted to go to all the time, and an Italian restaurant, Gino's, on Lexington Avenue that she loved. The woman could eat. Her weight fluctuated, but she didn't really give a damn. By today's skinnier-is-better standards, she could be fleshy at times. But no mistake about it, she was all woman.

Marilyn liked the freedom of being with a regular person like me, and the anonymity of being able to go anywhere she wanted without being mobbed by fans.

One of her favorite things was for us to go to Central Park and just walk and talk. It was then that I saw her at her most relaxed. No one ever recognized her. She marveled at the freedom of being anonymous.

Marilyn and I would see each other until she died, but not very often.

In the beginning, I was still shampooing rich ladies' hair, and getting propositioned frequently. A day didn't go by without some horny cougar approaching me. Some were subtler than others.

Carol was the twentysomething wife of a very wealthy businessman, who would later do some federal prison time for financial crimes. He was quite a few years older than the missus. They lived in the South, but came to New York often. When they did, Carol had her hair done at Lilly Dache, and yours truly was her shampoo boy.

Carol wasn't one of the subtle ones, and we began having sex after her first visit. She'd give me the name of a hotel and I'd meet her there after work. This went on for a while; then one day her husband showed up at the salon and confronted me in private.

He looked to be in his late forties, maybe early fifties, average-looking, but I'm sure his money was quite handsome. I guess he wasn't much for small talk, because he got right to the point.

"You banging my wife?"

There didn't seem to be any anger; it was like he was asking me for the time. I was sure he already knew the answer to the question, so I was honest. "I am." Bye-bye job. I was this close to my sixteenth birthday, when I could legally walk away from my "schooling" at the salon and get back to mob business. I was going to get fired for sure, and Mr. Costello would be pissed. I'd never seen him angry and didn't want to.

Hubby stared at me momentarily, then reached into his pocket and came out with his wallet. He gave me a hundred-dollar bill.

I stood there dumbstruck and speechless. All I managed to say was, "Huh?"

He clapped me on the shoulder. "I've been looking to dump this broad for a while, just needed an excuse. So thanks. I just needed to know. If you want to keep fucking her, be my guest." And with that, he turned and walked out.

I opted out of that relationship.

There were others, most notably a wealthy socialite who came in every Friday, married and a looker, maybe early forties. I've forgotten her name, but I could set my watch by her. Appointment at two o'clock, in bed with her by five.

On December 12, 1959, I turned sixteen and walked away from the Lilly Dache Beauty Salon. No two weeks' notice, no goodbyes to the staff. No one at the salon contacted me to ask why I never showed up for work. My lawful education requirement met, I moved on.

I had been conducting my usual rounds for Mr. Costello while I'd been at the salon, but now that I had more time, he had plans for me. He met me in Peacock Alley, the bar in the Waldorf, right near the clock where I'd meet Blackie. He never talked business in the Copa, too many people around to suit him. Peacock Alley was his "office" and that's where he was most comfortable.

"You've been doing a good job, kid," he said. "I never have to worry about you on the street, and you're honest with the money. You like doing what you're doing? Could get a little boring, I imagine, no?"

Five hundred a week, plus bonuses? I'd sit on top of a flagpole all day for that kind of money. "Not really, Mr. Costello. I like the work, the people."

"Money don't hurt, either, I'd think, right?" he said.

"No, sir, not at all."

"Well, I'm gonna give you some extra responsibility," he said. "You're gonna do some traveling."

He laid it out simply enough. I was going to fly to Vegas and pick up a bag at the Sands Hotel.

"You'll do this once a month, maybe twice. In the cashier's cage. They'll be expecting you. Always on a Monday. You fly back, with a stop in Chicago to see a guy. He'll lighten the load a bit from the bag; you give the rest to Blackie when you get back. *Capiche?*"

"Got it."

"Any questions?"

Unless the directions were unclear, no way was I going to ask what was in the bag I'd be carrying. I shook my head. "No, sir." I'd been working in this business only a short time, but I knew I was going to be picking up the "skim," which was Mr. Costello's cut of the casino profits from the Sands casinos, which would include the weekend cash drops (hence the Monday pickups), which were always substantial.

Las Vegas was in its infancy back then, just beginning a tremendous boom, and the mob ran everything. Different families ran different hotels. The mob skimmed undeclared profits off the top, all in cash, to the tune of hundreds of millions of dollars a year.

I was the perfect courier. At sixteen I wouldn't be targeted by the feds, who were always on the lookout to bag a bagman who clearly fit the gangster stereotype, or scoop up someone whose picture already adorned their walls.

Despite my age, I didn't look like a pushover, either, should someone try to rip me off. Victims of street robberies are chosen because they look like victims: female, or if male, small, skinny, exhibiting an aura of fear, or not paying attention to their surroundings.

I was five foot ten, 170 pounds, and had developed good situational awareness skills after carrying around reams of cash from New York bookies. If I got taken off on the streets of Manhattan, I'd lose maybe thirty or forty grand, which was walking-around money to the mob. Now I'd be carrying over one million around. Mr. Costello had told me if I got held up, I should just hand over the bag. "It's only money. Just be sure and get the guy's name," he said with a grin.

Street stickup men wouldn't know what I was carrying; they'd look for targets of opportunity. I'd often imagine some junkie with a rusty steak knife who would get lucky if he was able to rob me. He'd have a stroke when he opened up the bag and saw what was in it. If that ever happened, my parting advice to the thief would be to spend the money quickly, because his days were numbered. You don't steal from the Mafia. I'm reminded of a well-known story of an incident that took place years later.

Two burglars ripped off the safe from Rao's Restaurant on Pleasant Avenue in Harlem, right in the heart of mob boss Anthony "Fat Tony" Salerno's turf. Rao's attracted an eclectic crowd—gangsters, celebrities, and politicians—and was off-limits to trouble. In fact, the entire street was safer than the Vatican Bank; you could double-park your Caddy on the block with the keys in it, and enjoy a meal in Rao's without fear of anyone ripping it off. Occasionally you'd come out and find your car had been hand-washed by a neighborhood kid looking for a tip.

The two mopes who took off Rao's must've been out-of-towners, because no New York burglar in his right mind would even consider hitting it unless they had a death wish. The jerkoffs in question were found in bad shape (and also dead) within twenty-four hours. The safe's contents were recovered. It wouldn't surprise me if the two master criminals didn't pony up all their own money before they met their expected demise.

I flew under a "John Smith" ticket via TWA to Las Vegas, arranged by Nick Nitti—grandson of the infamous Al Capone henchman Frank Nitti—who owned a travel agency in Chicago. This was obviously way before the Patriot Act and terrorists using airplanes as guided missiles. Airline ticketing personnel took your word for it when they asked your name, and you could take a flamethrower with you on a flight if it would fit it in the overhead storage compartment.

Upon my arrival in Las Vegas, it was with some trepidation that I presented myself to Sands casino pit boss Milton Frank, who would later be immortalized in the movie *Casino,* and played by Don Rickles. He escorted me inside the cashier's cage, where a leather tote bag crammed with thick sealed envelopes was waiting for me. Cashier's cages are very secure, for obvious reasons, and there're a limited number of personnel who can be admitted. I was one of the select few, apart from vetted casino employees, who were permitted into the cage.

The Sands was *the* hotel for wiseguys. Prime real estate were the rooms near the pool, which were laid out like one-story motels, but noticeably more opulent. Each room was named for a U.S. racetrack, and the wiseguys were put in rooms according to their family's geographic location; the Chicago Outfit guests stayed in rooms named after Illinois racetracks, New York guys stayed in rooms named for New York tracks, et cetera. This system made it easier for mob guys to know who was who and which family was represented by their presence. The closer you were to the pool, the higher your status in the mob.

No one really knew me, which was one of the reasons, I'm sure, that Mr. Costello chose me for the courier job. He had also told me to try to pick up on careless mob talk around the hotel and report back to him upon my return. At the time, I didn't realize the value of intelligence, and that anything I saw and heard might be beneficial to Mr. Costello's interests, but gangsters are a paranoid lot, and are always on the alert for betrayal. Anything I saw or heard might be valuable, whether I realized it or not, so I was attentive to my surroundings at all times. I was like a fly on the wall; no one paid much attention to me, other than being polite because of my status with Frank Costello.

I was comped for everything at the Sands; paid for nothing. I looked and carried myself like someone older than my age, had complete access to the bars, and would stop in for drinks. Even if I had been nine years old, I would've been served, because I was Frank Costello's emissary. I didn't make a pig of myself; had a few drinks, ate well, and watched the lounge acts. The lounge had a working model railroad that would roll past the tables laden with food. I fit in easily in a suit and tie, which was normal Vegas attire for a night on the town. These days, you can show up in shorts and flip-flops and be seated practically anywhere on the Strip.

Back then, singer Wayne Newton was an unknown (*he* looked like he was nine years old). He appeared in a Sands lounge act called Amato and Newton, which also included Wayne's brother, who later faded into obscurity after ripping Wayne off for big money. Louis Prima and Keely Smith did several shows a night in the lounge. Prima had more energy than a meth-addled outlaw biker and, along with Sam Butera and the Witnesses, put on a helluva show.

I also saw Howard Hughes around the hotel (before his waist-length hair and foot-long fingernail days). He was always accompanied by an entourage of former FBI and CIA agents, most notably Bob Maheu, a secretive former CIA spook who would later control Hughes's empire when the boss decided to become a hermit.

Jack Entrata, who was on paper as the sole owner of the Sands, had a private pool on the hotel grounds. Surrounded by an eight-foot opaque fence, it was a magnet for wiseguys and scantily clad and naked women. I had access to that pool, used it, but kept to myself. It was there that I saw a young Senator John F. Kennedy, our future president, do lines of cocaine off actress Juliet Prowse's less than fully clothed body.

I saw JFK at that pool quite a few times. He was being groomed to run for president, and his father, Joe, was using the mob to exert influence to make sure his son got elected. At the time, I wasn't privy to all the information regarding the mob's involvement in Kennedy's ascension, but as time passed, I was given more access to the Mafia's participation in the election process. For now, Kennedy was just another mob hanger-on with a penchant for cocaine and women. I would later overhear him go on and on about Prowse's shaved pussy. He was like a kid with a new toy. The more decadence he wanted, the more he got, all courtesy of the Mafia. The wiseguys were pretty soon going to have their own man in the White House, or so they thought.

Ava Gardner was also at poolside often, mostly in the company of women, whom, it was rumored, she favored. Actor Peter Lawford, was there, too, almost always accompanied by the randy John F. Kennedy.

Mr. Costello never went to Vegas to party with the Kennedys. He wanted nothing to do with them, or as he would so eloquently put it, "You can keep those Irish cocksuckers. I don't trust them." Turned out, Mr. Costello was a good judge of character, but more on that shortly.

Bag of cash in tow, I'd make a stop in Chicago on the way home to leave some tribute for the Outfit before continuing on to New York. The meeting places were varied, either social clubs that were mob-run or the Palmer House, a luxury downtown hotel.

Sam Giancana ran the Outfit, but I never gave him any envelopes personally. Bosses who had any longevity avoided meeting with underlings on my level, which at the time was lower than a street curb. They sent trusted emissaries—in this case, either the aforementioned Nick Nitti or Frankie Balistreri. I would hand over sealed envelopes from the bag. Eventually, I would become tight with future boss Tony Accardo, but Giancana was a ghost.

The envelopes had initials on them and were sealed, so I didn't know the sums of money I was giving away, but I recognized most of the initials on the envelopes. The bigger the name, the thicker the envelope.

After I made several trips to Vegas and Chicago, Mr. Costello expanded my area of responsibility. In addition to the stopover to feed the Outfit's coffers, I had begun making similar stops in Kansas City, where I'd deliver envelopes to mid-level wiseguy Corky Civella at a social club, and in New Orleans, where apparently protocol didn't mean much, because I'd personally meet with Carlos Marcello, the boss of the New Orleans mob.

Marcello was a tough guy, small in stature (often referred to as "Little Man," but not to his face) but big on reputation. He was around fifty when we first met, and he would reign as a powerful leader in the mob until his death, in 1993. The mob has always been big on loyalty and revenge, but Marcello would take both to a higher level later when Attorney General Robert Kennedy initiated deportation orders against him, and I would find myself right in the middle of the biggest murder conspiracy since the death of Julius Caesar.

Joseph P. Kennedy, JFK's father, was no stranger to the workings of organized crime. The Kennedy fortune was made bootlegging during the Prohibition years, and Papa Joe maintained his connections to the Outfit, as well as to East Coast mob families.

It was understood that JFK's 1960 battle with Richard Nixon for the White House was going to be a squeaker, according to the polls. To win the election, JFK had to take Illinois, which, coincidentally, had Chicago as its biggest and most populous city. If his son could take Chicago, he'd win the state, and old man Joe would have a son in the White House.

A deal was made with the devil—in this case, in the form of Sam Giancana, boss of the Chicago Outfit, whose predecessor, Al Capone, once said, "Vote early and vote often." Giancana would deliver Chicago, with a promise that the new administration would lay off the mob, *and,* as an added bonus, invade Cuba, where that Communist son of a bitch Fidel Castro had seized all the mob's casinos when he took over the country.

Giancana kept his word by voter intimidation, stuffing ballot boxes with votes from dead people, and multiple votes from the same voters.

But Giancana could not work this miracle alone. There was a nationwide effort by the mob's major players to swing the election to Kennedy. The Kansas bosses got the Teamsters on board, Carlos Marcello used his power in the South, and Santo Trafficante wielded tremendous political juice in Florida and, on Joe Kennedy's promise, was readying Havana for a return to the pre-Castro days of mob-run casinos.

Frank Sinatra was the go-between with the mob and the Kennedys. JFK and Sinatra were great pals, with the crooner supplying the horny married Kennedy with all the women he could handle, plus all the cocaine he could shovel up his nose. It was Sinatra who guaranteed that once the young senator from Massachusetts became president, he'd let the mob run their operation without any interference from his administration. And the wiseguys had better brush up on their Spanish, because they'd be back in their Cuban casinos and puffing on island cigars in no time.

The mob was ecstatic. For the second time in American history, an American president was going to be in the mob's pocket.

Life was grand.

All these promises had been made by Papa Joe and Frank Sinatra, but no one had bothered to get personal reassurances from John Kennedy, who, as it turned out, was using the mob to further his ambitions, and supply him with women and drugs, without the slightest measure of loyalty to the men who were expecting a free hand in running their "thing" once he got into office.

The election came and went, with Kennedy the victor (no surprise there), and the mob waited for its reward. Not only didn't the wiseguys get their payback; they knew they were had when JFK appointed his brother Bobby attorney general. Now America's top cop, Bobby vowed to destroy the Mafia.

The bosses were apoplectic. Fury doesn't begin to describe the feelings of every mob family in the country. I'd never seen Frank Costello angry. The perfect gentleman, he was the mob's poster boy for being cool and composed under stress. But now? The gentleman-gangster veneer gave way to a fury in Mr. Costello that I'd never seen or wanted to see again.

After hours of venting to anyone who would listen, Mr. Costello spent a few days off the grid with trusted subordinates. I knew I'd wind up getting involved in whatever these guys agreed upon as a next step. Whatever was being planned, it would undoubtedly take the form of revenge.

I didn't have to wait long.

I hadn't seen Mr. Costello in four days, a long time, given the usual daily meetings between us. He summoned me to Peacock Alley on day five.

He was grim and got right to the point.

"You know Cal Neva?"

I nodded. What I knew of Cal Neva I'd gotten from Marilyn Monroe during our many chats. Cal Neva Resort and Casino was located on Lake Tahoe, on the California-Nevada border. It was supposedly owned by Frank Sinatra and Dean Martin, but Outfit boss Sam Giancana was the major (silent) owner. Giancana's reputation as a mob boss precluded him from stepping foot anywhere in the entire state of Nevada, but he was a frequent "guest" of Frank Sinatra's at the resort, where he would hook up with his mistress, Phyllis Maguire, of the singing Maguire Sisters.

It was a major partying location for the Hollywood crowd, with opulent cabins reserved for celebrities. Marilyn had told me she had cabin number 4, Sinatra number 5, and the Kennedy clan occupied number 3. The Kennedy brothers, most notably John and Bobby, would go there often and be treated to a platoon of hookers, courtesy of Sinatra.

"Well, there's gonna be a meeting there," Costello said, "and I want you to be my eyes and ears. I won't be attending."

Bosses stayed away from events where they could be photographed, and anything going on at Cal Neva might attract media, although this meeting was supposed to be a secret. The resort was chosen because it wasn't in Vegas, which was a magnet for wiseguys, and that meant the FBI had a big presence there.

While Mr. Costello didn't share anything about the meeting with me, I picked up the particulars from less discreet wiseguys.

The object of the summit was to ensnare the Kennedy brothers in a situation where they could be blackmailed. If the mob bosses couldn't get the new president to keep his word, they'd extort their way into compliance. Bobby and John thought they were going to Cal Neva for a sex- and drug-fueled few days of fun. The mob used their father, Joe, to convince his sons to go away for a few days to unwind. Papa Joe was forced to lure his sons to Cal Neva under penalty of death for both boys. They didn't go, they'd die, and so would daddy. Both brothers were supposed to attend, as would their dad, who by this time was confined to a wheelchair after having had a stroke, supposedly suffered when the mob told him to play the game or everybody would die.

He wasn't the only one threatened. Frank Sinatra was also told that if the Kennedys didn't show, Frank would be crooning his next tune from Hell.

I arrived at Cal Neva three days ahead of the Kennedys, during the last week in July 1962. In attendance was Sinatra, Sam Giancana (who wasn't in a good mood), along with bodyguards, and Marilyn Monroe. I was told to stay away from Marilyn; she was part of the plan.

I'd been a huge fan of Sinatra's from the day Delores gave me a radio during my extended stay at Bellevue Hospital's polio ward. There was nothing I would've liked better than to talk to Frank, tell him about our shared birthday, and shoot the shit—just two guys from the block talking about growing up Italian. Well, it wasn't going to happen, at least not this time.

Everyone was grim, especially Sinatra, who might have been looking at a permanent resting place in a car trunk if things didn't work out. I did my job, kept my mouth shut, looked, and listened.

I hadn't seen her for a while, but Marilyn wasn't the Marilyn I'd remembered. She was either high on pills or booze, or a combination of both, for my entire stay there. She was bloated and spaced-out. Plus, she was being traded back and forth between Giancana and Sinatra, who were banging her like she was the last woman on earth. I felt sorry for her.

I found out about the plan after Marilyn was informed of her role in the plot, and she went ballistic. She was to have sex with both brothers (she was doing both of them anyway, only not at the same time), and the session would be filmed and used to extort the Kennedys to conform to the demands of the mob.

Marilyn was having none of it. Bobby and Daddy showed up without John, who begged off due to "government business," which everyone thought was bullshit. He was smart enough to distance himself from anything Sinatra. He was thinking with his head, not his dick, unlike his brother. Marilyn lit into Bobby in front of me and anyone else within earshot. She was through with the Kennedys. She was being used, had always been used by them, and she'd had enough.

She wanted out of Cal Neva and phoned her ex-husband Joe DiMaggio, with whom she was on good terms, and told him to come and get her. She was obviously in need of serious help. DiMaggio phoned Sinatra and asked him what was going on, but he was told, "Don't ask," and instructed not to come to Cal Neva. DiMaggio never showed.

JFK had promised Marilyn that once he was elected, he would divorce his wife, Jackie, and marry her. Marilyn believed it at the time, but now she wasn't falling for anything involving the Kennedys. And not only that; she was going to the press to tell them what the Kennedys were *really* like.

The extortion plan was a bust. For her part, Marilyn shouldn't have mentioned going to the media, because within three days, she was dead. Depending on which media source you believed at the time, she either committed suicide or died of an accidental drug overdose.

There were conspiracy theorists over the years who blamed her death on the mob. The mob bosses loved Marilyn, and if anyone came close to treating her well, it was the mob, involving her in the extortion plot notwithstanding and her assignations with Sam Giancana the exception. Giancana was a loose cannon and all he cared about was himself. His own men thought he was a scumbag.

If Marilyn didn't want to go through with the scheme, so be it; the mob wasn't going to push it. In fact, they'd thought she would like the idea because she could finally stick it to the Kennedys, who had used her since the day they had met. Truth be told, most everyone used her, but when she was with the wiseguys, she knew what to expect. The Kennedys, on the other hand, came across to an adoring public as the personification of a great American dynasty. She knew better, and wanted them exposed for the disingenuous, poor excuses for human beings that they were.

According to my mob sources, Marilyn was given an injection of air through her pubic area, hiding the needle mark, and directly into a vein by a doctor, on orders from Bobby Kennedy, who viewed Marilyn as a loose cannon. Bobby could not afford even *thinking* about having the Kennedy name dragged through the mud. The injection of air caused an embolism and she died. An autopsy revealed her body to be loaded with a variety of drugs, which were assumed to have killed her.

Knowing the Kennedys and their duplicity, I believe the story of Bobby Kennedy's involvement in Marilyn's death, as told to me by reliable sources. I also believe Marilyn would have survived if DiMaggio had grown a pair of balls, had not listened to Sinatra, and had gone to Cal Neva to get her out of there. Had this occurred, I sincerely believe Marilyn wouldn't have broadcast her intention of going to the media. DiMaggio was her lifeline and he deserted her. Only then, in desperation and anger, did she mention the press, which led to her death.

4

MY INVOLVEMENT IN THE CRIME OF THE CENTURY

The depressive cloud that spread over Cal Neva after the aborted Kennedy sex-tape plot spread like the mist in a horror movie. Within days of Marilyn's death, the mob went into cloak-and-dagger mode. No one was saying anything about the Kennedys, Marilyn's death, or anything that had occurred at the resort.

The normally visible Frank Costello was making himself scarce, and when I did see him at the Copa, it was from a distance. We didn't meet for business purposes, but I'd still see Blackie under the clock at the Waldorf during the week to get my assignments for the day. Even Blackie, not the most talkative person, usually had a smile and a good word. Now it was just business. "Here, kid," he'd say, then hand me instructions and be gone.

Something was in the air, and my guess was that plans were being made to deal with the sudden downturn in good fortune. The mob couldn't leave things as they were; the entire organization had been conned by the Kennedys and something had to be done. My guess was another blackmail scheme.

There was precedent behind my supposition; the mob was good at using extortion. A good example of cunning and a successful blackmail plan was leveled at FBI director J. Edgar Hoover, arguably the most powerful law-enforcement figure in the United States, if not the world.

Hoover denied the existence of the American Mafia through the mid-1960s, when a low-level New York Mafia soldier named Joe Valachi kept the nation captivated as he laid out the inner workings of the mob before a congressional committee, a hearing that was broadcast live on radio and television. A new name for the Mafia emerged: Cosa Nostra, Italian for "our thing."

There was no denying the existence of organized crime after that, and even Hoover had to acquiesce to its authenticity.

There were several reasons why Hoover denied the reality of the Mafia for over thirty years. For one, he didn't want his beloved Bureau to investigate organized crime, for fear his agents would become corrupted (think James "Whitey" Bulger corrupting elements of the Boston field office of the Bureau for over twenty years after Hoover's death), but the primary reason was that he had been photographed by the mob in a well-orchestrated plot to catch America's toughest lawman wearing a dress at a staged party of gay men in Chicago.

It has long been rumored that Hoover was gay. His close relationship with his second in command, Clyde Tolson, was cited. The fact that they're buried in adjoining cemetery plots, that they were virtually inseparable in life, and that neither Hoover nor Tolson ever married provides, of course, only circumstantial evidence, but pictures of Hoover prancing around in a dress sort of confirms the theory (and no, it wasn't Halloween).

The pictures were entrusted to Chicago attorney Sidney Korshak, a longtime lawyer for the Outfit, for safekeeping. I've never seen them, but I've heard they provided great laughs among the Chicago bosses over sambuca and espresso. The FBI boss was referred to as "Miss Hoover." In exchange for Hoover's hands-off policy, the damning photographs were kept in a safe place, virtually buried forever. Hoover had no choice but to acknowledge the Mafia after Joe Valachi's testimony, but the bosses kept their word and the damning pictures never surfaced. They didn't necessarily do this for altruistic reasons; Frank

Costello had Hoover in his pocket because of the director's gambling habit.

Hoover loved to gamble, horse racing being his sport of choice. Mr. Costello would take all his bets personally. It was the only time that I'm aware of that Mr. Costello broke his rule of not getting directly involved with "civilians." Hoover was too valuable to the mob, even after he was forced to admit that the Mafia was, in fact, real.

Costello still had him locked into compliance, because Mr. C. never went after Hoover for money for wagers that Hoover lost, but he paid J. Edgar off when he won. In essence, Hoover was being paid to cooperate with the mob even after he'd had to come around and deal with the fact that the Mafia existed.

Hoover wasn't above calling upon the mob when he needed them, most famously in 1964, when he dispatched Mafia capo Greg "Grim Reaper" Scarpa to Mississippi to help investigate the disappearance of three civil rights workers. Scarpa used the interrogation techniques that helped get him his nickname, and had confessions from the suspects in the case in short order.

It was my feeling that another honeypot trap was being planned for the Kennedys in order to get them into the fold. Sinatra had come close to dying after a similar plan with Marilyn went bust, but it was reasoned that the negative publicity of a Frank Sinatra murder wasn't worth the revenge motive for the crooner's falsely guaranteeing a cooperative Kennedy administration. Sinatra, it was determined, was duped by JFK, so he got a pass. Stupid doesn't make you dead, or there would've been more people whacked over the years.

It turned out that I was incorrect about another mob sex plot, and I had no idea I was about to become an unwitting player in the crime of the century.

On November 18, 1963, Frank Costello summoned me to a meeting at Peacock Alley in the Waldorf.

He had remained aloof for a few months prior to that, but I didn't comment on it when I entered his favorite booth. He was alone, dressed in a black pinstripe suit. He didn't mention his lack of contact with me and got right to business.

He slid a sealed envelope to me across the table.

"I want you to take this to the Little Man." From another pocket, he produced airline tickets. "You're going on a trip."

I don't recall whose name the tickets were in, but it wasn't mine. The Little Man was familiar to me from my courier trips to New Orleans as Carlos Marcello, boss of the New Orleans faction of the Mafia. He was called that because of his height, not his stature in the organization, which was exemplary.

Mr. Costello was unusually dour, none of his usual light banter.

"You'll get a reply, nothing written," he said. "You fly back the next day, see me personally with that message. I'll meet you here at seven."

Up until then, I hadn't said a word. "Yes, sir."

He was already sliding out of the booth when he said, "Questions?"

Obviously, he didn't expect any. "No, sir."

And he was gone.

The next day, I grabbed a cab after I landed at Moisant Field, outside New Orleans. My destination was Mosca's Restaurant, located in Avondale, a suburb of New Orleans. The Creole eatery was a well-known, popular family-run restaurant that had opened in 1946, but it was rumored to have Carlos Marcello as a silent partner.

The restaurant was empty; it was hours before the dinner crowd would begin arriving. Marcello was seated at a table by himself in the rear of the dining room, a mountain of pasta in front of him. He was facing the door; mob guys always face an entrance in a public place. There's nothing worse than that unexpected bullet to the head when you're enjoying your *linguine con le vongole*.

Marcello was sharply dressed in a gray suit and tie. I was surprised that he was alone. Marcello was a powerful guy, and bosses rarely appeared in public without security. Later, when things began to happen, I realized why he was solo: plausible deniability.

He recognized me right away and beckoned me to his table.

On the way, I passed the men's room on my right. A skinny guy, who looked to be around twenty-five, chose that time to exit the john and nearly collided with me. I sidestepped him, thought nothing of it, and made my way to the table while the beanpole mumbled something and made for the door.

Marcello was all business. He nodded toward a chair. I sat.

"You doing well, kid?"

"Yes, sir." I'd learned a while ago that I wasn't important to bosses at this level. I was there for a reason, and Marcello didn't care how the hell I felt.

"You got something for me?" he asked.

"Yes, sir." I handed him the envelope, which had been boring a hole in my pocket since I'd departed from La Guardia Airport in New York. It was fairly thick, undoubtedly had cash in it, and who knows what else, and I was glad to get rid of it.

While Marcello took the envelope, hefted it, and put it in his pocket, I took the opportunity to gaze around me, attracted by waves of food aromas coming from the kitchen, and reminded myself that I hadn't eaten since that morning in New York.

"Don't get comfortable, kid," Marcello said, but the statement wasn't malicious. He was smiling. "You need to leave here now. Tell Frank it's on."

I just stared at him. All this distance for a two-word message? I waited for more.

Marcello stared right back at me. "That's it, kid. Safe trip home." He went back to his meal.

Well, okay, then. It would turn out that I'd have more interaction with Marcello in the future, and we became friendlier. He was a very nice man, as long as you didn't cross him. The Kennedys would learn that lesson the hard way.

I was back in New York by 8:00 A.M. the next day, exhausted, but I had to meet with Mr. C. He had his routine; he would be at Peacock Alley at 11:30 A.M., like clockwork, then go off the grid until he showed up at the Copa at 8:30 P.M. We rarely spoke at the Copa and I didn't think he'd want me to report back to him there, so I had to hustle and get to the Waldorf before he left. I just had enough time to shower, change, and get to Peacock Alley by the appointed time. Mr. C. was there, same booth, different suit.

I'd flown three thousand miles in two days, hadn't gotten much sleep, and felt like an idiot for what I was about to tell the boss.

I sighed. "It's on," I said. "That's it, sir."

He nodded resignedly. "Thought so."

He didn't seem pleased or displeased; apparently, I'd accomplished the mission, whatever it was. What he did do was reach into his jacket pocket and produce another envelope.

I groaned inwardly. Another trip.

I took the proffered envelope. "Thanks."

"For what?" he asked, a slight smile on his face.

"I dunno. I'm being polite."

"That's good," he said. "Never hurts to be a gentleman. There's a ticket in there."

I knew it. Where to now?

"Barcelona, Spain. You leave this Friday on the *Independence*." He rattled off a West Side dock number and departure time.

Given the years I'd been working for Mr. Costello, nothing really surprised me anymore. Until now. "A boat?'

"The Staten Island Ferry is a boat. This is a ship, a luxury liner."

I knew I couldn't ask why I was going to Spain, but I thought asking how long I'd be there was a reasonable question. "When do I come back?"

"When do you think? When I say you can come back, that's when."

He wasn't angry, just stating a fact. He was Frank Costello. I should've known.

"Listen," he said as he leaned in closer to me, "it's gonna be a while, a year, maybe more. Here's some spending money; everything else is taken care of."

It turned out I'd be in Europe for close to two years.

A second envelope materialized. "There will be more if you need more. A guy named Vito will meet you when you get there. Stick with him; he's a good guy and can be trusted."

Mr. C. saw the confusion on my face.

"This trip is for your own good. You'll understand why in a few days. Things'll be clearer then." He slid out of the booth.

I stood up and he shook my hand. I couldn't recall the last time he'd done that.

"You're a good kid," the most powerful Mafia boss in the country said. He touched my shoulder and left. He hadn't done that in a while. I guess he needed luck.

I jammed the envelopes in my jacket pocket and didn't check how much money he'd given me until I got home.

It was jammed with hundred-dollar bills, thirty thousand dollars' worth.

It was going to be a helluva trip.

I was assigned a suite on the U deck, which turned out to be almost as big as Marilyn's suite at the Waldorf, complete with terrace and located next to the captain's quarters. This was one helluva boat . . . ship, whatever.

The purser, an efficient guy name Pennington, couldn't do enough for me. Apparently, he'd gotten the word that I was to be given special treatment.

After the purser left and the ship got under way, I sat alone in my palatial digs for a while, wondering just what the hell I was doing there. For about five years now, I'd been making good money, had built a decent wardrobe, been to the best clubs and restaurants in New York. But this?

It was Friday, November 22, 1963, and I was embarking on a journey, the reason for which has haunted me all my life.

While I had nothing to compare it to, I was in awe of the opulence and grandeur of the ship. The passengers, at least on U deck, were rich; those traveling with kids had nannies in tow and enough luggage for a cruise to the moon. While I was trying to figure out the reason for my good luck, a lifeboat drill was called. Immediately after that, everyone headed to the bar. I followed. Even though it was barely noon, I needed a drink.

The bar was packed with well-dressed passengers, all looking to begin their vacations by tossing back a few. No one was paying attention to the two televisions at either end of the bar.

That changed as the ship began passing under the Verrazano Bridge. A little after 12:30 P.M. the word BULLETIN flashed on both screens.

A hush fell over the room as an obviously distraught Walter Cronkite broke the news that President John F. Kennedy had been assassinated in Dallas, Texas.

Almost immediately, gasps and wails of anguish could be heard throughout the room. Passengers called for quiet as we all stood, enthralled by the calamity that was unfolding in Dallas.

A truism of the day is that everyone who is old enough remembers where they were and what they were doing on the day JFK was murdered. What stands out most in my mind about that exact time was that quite a few middle-aged men began running for the exits, and shortly thereafter, pilot boats began tying onto the ship. Those well-dressed men, Wall Street types, were boarding the pilot boats for the short journey back to Manhattan, their family vacations cut short by a national emergency, which translated into their need to be home when the stock market would undoubtedly begin a downward tumble.

Those of us who remained sat transfixed in front of the TVs for hours. Later that afternoon, I witnessed an event that would forever be burned into my memory: Lee Harvey Oswald, the suspected assassin, was paraded past reporters at the Dallas Police Department's headquarters.

My jaw dropped. Oswald, or his twin brother, was the same skinny guy I had seen exiting the men's room at the restaurant where I'd gone to meet Carlos Marcello.

The scene of a battered and bruised Oswald, who, allegedly, had also just killed a Dallas police officer, was replayed on the bar TVs numerous times. Each time I saw the images, I was convinced that the guy I'd seen exiting the men's room in New Orleans was Oswald. Over fifty years later, I'm still convinced of it, particularly when I realize that the rush of conspiracy theories surrounding the assassination included the theory that the Mafia had had Kennedy clipped. The reason? Pick one; there were a few, not the least of which was that JFK had gone back on his word to the mob after the election. And at the center of the mob conspiracy theories firmly sat Carlos Marcello.

Within weeks, bodies would begin dropping all over the country, and most of them had some connection to one or more of the alleged assassination theories. I came to the realization that Frank Costello had gotten me out of the country to save my life.

If my errand to Marcello was involved in the master plan to assassinate Kennedy, I had played a role, small as it was. While I was literally only the messenger, I was a connection between Mr. C. and Carlos Marcello. If the Commission was giving orders to kill anyone involved in the planning of the assassination, no matter how small a role had been played, and if I'd actually seen Oswald, it would stand to reason that I would eventually be put on someone's shit list.

I knew I'd be permitted to go home when things calmed down. What bothered me then, and bothers me now, was that I was involved in the plot. It still haunts me. Wiseguys get hit all the time, and I never gave it much thought. Someday my time might come, but Kennedy, as warped as he was, was still the president, had a family, and wasn't part of our thing.

I tore myself away from the televisions. A constant repetition of funeral dirges was being played by the ship's band. I was on the trip of a lifetime and I felt as if I were at my grandmother's funeral. Passengers were literally crying in their beer, and while I was just as depressed as the rest of them, I wasn't about to spend a week at the world's biggest floating wake.

I cracked Mr. Costello's envelope and approached the bandleader, a Latin type who had shoe-polish slicked-back hair and a mustache so thin, I wasn't sure it was there.

"Listen," I said, "can you pump up the music a bit? You keep playing what you're playing and you may be responsible for a couple of suicides."

The second-rate Ricky Ricardo gave me a condescending look and actually sniffed. "Sir," he said, dragging out the one-syllable word, "it's fitting we should pay tribute to President Kennedy."

I held three hundred-dollar bills against my chest so no one could see them but him. "Kennedy loved 'High Hopes.' It was his campaign song. Sinatra sang it. Try not to butcher it. Here." I jammed the bills into his cummerbund.

The mood was almost immediately enlivened with the song. It was bittersweet, but it brought back better times.

I ate at the captain's table every night. The food was great and I met interesting people. Remember those Wall Street guys who deserted the ship after we got news of the assassination? They had left their wives and girlfriends behind, and I had a new lady to dine at the captain's table with me every night.

It was with mixed emotions that I left the ship in Barcelona. I'd had a great time on the crossing, but it was over now, and I'd probably gained ten pounds, despite my best efforts to work them off.

I was met on the dock by a human fireplug, dressed all in black. His name was Vito, and he looked to be about fifty. He was holding up a sign with my name on it.

After a brief introduction, he said, "Okay, let's go." He had an Italian accent, which didn't come as a surprise. What did surprise me later on was that he spoke numerous languages and was quite the intellect. We'd need those language skills, because we'd be on the move for a while.

"Go? What do you mean, 'go'? I've got my luggage on the ship, all my clothes—"

"Fuck the clothes," he said, interrupting me. "We'll get you new clothes. Whatever you want."

I sized up Vito's wardrobe. He might have been dressed from head to toe in black, but it was expensive black, right down to his shoes. The man knew his clothes.

I shrugged. "Sounds good to me." And off we went.

I was Vito's responsibility, and he took the job very seriously. We weren't going to stay long in one place, at least for the immediate future. I got the impression that he wasn't concerned so much for my safety as he was about keeping us moving so that the law wouldn't lay eyes on me. The last thing Mr. Costello needed was for me to be questioned by the police, sure as he probably was that Carlos Marcello had an FBI tail and I'd been made coming and going from Mosca's Restaurant.

After a long drive, we stopped at the Monaco Beach Club in the south of France, where we had lunch. I don't remember what I ate, but I do remember the topless beach that abutted the restaurant. Literally everyone was topless, regardless of age. Most of the sun worshippers were in their twenties, however. Vito saw I was disappointed when we got up to leave after he paid the check.

"Everyone's topless in France. After a while, you won't even notice," he said.

"Yeah? I doubt that. I'm used to Coney Island, where the only things topless are the seagulls." He didn't crack a smile, something I'd get used to.

We toured Italy for the first month. Vito would be on the phone several times a day—reporting in to someone, I assumed. The first few times he'd leave our restaurant table to go and look for a phone, he'd always say, "Don't go anywhere without me."

Where was I going to go? Half the time, I didn't even know where I was. Besides, Vito was showing me a great time. Whatever city or town we were in, we frequented the best restaurants, and he knew many women.

I couldn't spend any money; Vito sprang for everything. He had a helluva an expense account. I was getting fine custom-made clothes, bought my first pair of custom shoes, and by the time we left Italy, I'd shipped most of it back to New York. If I got caught short for a silk shirt while I was traveling, I was sure I could find one.

Next stop Palermo, Sicily, where we stayed at the elegant Igea Illa Hotel. My suite overlooked the bay, which had the clearest water I'd ever seen—azure blue, and it sparkled like an aquamarine gemstone.

A day after checking in, we went to the palatial mountaintop home of Ugo Buffa, the boss of bosses of the Sicilian Mafia. Buffa was short, like most everyone else in Sicily (I was a giant in Palermo, and I'm five foot ten). His skin was very tan and weathered, and he had a face like a beat-up suitcase. He was very friendly, telling me that he would see to it that I was happy. Anything I needed was mine.

Buffa's right pinkie fingernail was very long, at least an inch. He saw me staring at it, and he offered an explanation: One long fingernail was a sign of aristocracy. I didn't think it wise to mention that I'd seen Sammy Davis, Jr., at the Copa with a similar fingernail. He used his for scooping coke.

My new best friend, Vito, and I hung out, partied, and worked on our tans for the next sixteen months. One day, Vito came down to breakfast, sat down, and said, "Things have calmed down. You're going home."

Gianni's excellent adventure had come to an end. I flew home, anxious to get back to New York and find out what exploits awaited me.

It turned out that I had been living in a fantasy world in Sicily: the best food, gorgeous women, and beautiful weather, with no cares or concerns.

I deplaned at what was now called Kennedy Airport—when I'd left, it was Idlewild—and walked straight into an antiwar demonstration on the sidewalk outside the International Arrivals Building. The Vietnam War was heating up, and a mob of weirdly dressed people were cursing and spitting at soldiers coming home from the war. Cops were pushing back, making arrests, but it was pandemonium.

Welcome to America.

Things seemed status quo in midtown, however. My wire-room home was still there, it hadn't been busted by the cops, and there was a present waiting for me in my top dresser drawer—twenty-five grand in an envelope with "Welcome Home" scrawled on it. I added it to the cash I'd taken with me to Europe, most of which I hadn't spent.

There's no place like home.

No one contacted me for two days; then I was summoned to meet Mr. Costello at Peacock Alley.

It was like I'd never left. Mr. C. was in his usual booth and greeted me warmly.

"Nice to have you back, kid. Did you find that envelope in the apartment?"

"Oh, yes, sir. Thank you." I'd thought he was the one who'd left me the money, but I hadn't wanted to assume anything and mention it until he did.

"Nah, that's okay. You did a good job."

I did? All I'd done was hang out and get laid. But who was I to disagree?

"Thank you."

"How'd you like Sicily?"

I smiled. "What's not to like?"

He nodded. "I got a good report from Ugo Buffa about you. He says to keep you close to me. He sees promise in you, and the old man's not easy to please. He sees a lot of your uncle in you." He lowered his voice an octave and put his hand on my shoulder. "Listen, kid, you've been with me a while and it appears you like what you're doing. Is that right?"

I nodded like a woodpecker. "Absolutely, Mr. Costello."

"Well, seeing as how it looks like you're in this thing of ours for the long haul, I want to explain something to you." He reached into his pocket and came out with a yellowed newspaper clipping. "You see this here? It's from *The New York Times,* and I've had it since the day it came out. Here, read it."

I unfolded it gingerly. It was a pretty long advertisement looking for laborers on a construction project. Nothing much else. The ad didn't have a date.

I looked up after I'd read it.

"That ad is over forty years old, and I kept it because I looked into that job when I was young . . . younger than you. That job paid Italians less than anyone else on the site, and it pissed me off." He took the clipping back and carefully returned it to his pocket. "The point I'm trying to make here is Italians were treated worse than dog shit when most of the immigrants came over. A lot of that prejudice still lingers today. This thing of ours was started as a matter of survival . . . to be able to compete.

"My point is, what we do isn't all about money. It's about equality, respect, and power. Never lose sight of that as you get older and become more involved in what we do. Do you understand?"

I got it, and I also understood why Mr. C. had gotten to where he was today. This man wasn't a thug; far from it.

"Looking to get back to work?" he asked.

"Absolutely, sir." Where I really wanted to be was back in Palermo, deciding where I wanted to go to dinner.

"Okay. I want you to go to Miami, meet with the Little Guy, and give him this."

Another envelope, what else?

The "Little Guy" was not to be confused with the "Little Man" (Carlos Marcello). The Little Guy was Meyer Lansky, the legendary "accountant" for the mob. Lansky was one of the original members of La Cosa Nostra, formed back in the early 1930s. Charles "Lucky" Luciano (who put together "our thing"), in his infinite wisdom, surrounded himself with only the best and the brightest, Italian or otherwise. Meyer, a Jew, was a perfect fit. He was a financial genius who literally never wrote anything down, keeping the day-to-day financial shenanigans of the mob in his head.

I wanted to ask Mr. C. how long I was going to be in Miami, but I knew better. But he answered my question without my asking.

"You'll be down there for a while," he said. "Keep your ear to the ground, enjoy yourself. The little guy is expecting you next Monday at ten A.M." He gave me the location of a bench on Lincoln Road and Collins Avenue. "He walks his poodle every day, sits on that bench to people-watch. He looks like every other old Jew. Guy could get lost in a crowd of two people. He'll be expecting you."

Anyone could deliver a message, and I got the impression that Mr. C. wanted me nowhere around him because of my visit to Carlos Marcello in Louisiana. I was the only connection between the Little Man and the big man just prior to JFK's assassination. I liked New York, didn't want to go to Florida, but I knew I had no choice. I would do a complete 180 as soon as I got down there.

I loved it.

As soon as the plane glided onto the runway, I knew I'd found a new home. It was February, and I had left New York with snow on the ground, then landed in Miami, to be greeted by a blast of eighty-degree warmth. Even the clouds looked different—billowing, copper-streaked, white soaring clouds against a blindingly blue, sun-drenched sky.

A room had been reserved for me in the Fontainebleau Hotel on Collins Avenue in Miami Beach. South Florida, Miami Beach in particular, was the hot spot for nightlife, the Fontainebleau the mecca for everyone who was famous or infamous. It was a beautiful eleven-story building located right on the beach, shaped, as one of my Vietnam veteran buddies would later describe it, like a Claymore mine—a concave white structure that would become the symbol for Florida decadence. It would hold that dubious distinction until the resurgence of the South Beach section of Miami Beach and the cocaine explosion of the 1980s.

I had a few days before my meeting with Meyer. I settled in quickly, registering under the name of Dr. Jay Adams. Miami Beach was also the vacation destination of choice for rich Jewish families, and I figured what Jewish mother wouldn't want to set their daughter up with a nice doctor? To that end, I had myself paged at the pool from day one. At the sound of "Paging Dr. Adams, Dr. Jay Adams," I'd leap from my overstuffed pool chair and make a big show of complaining good-naturedly to those around me that my patients couldn't get along without me. I guessed I'd score my first Jewish princess in short order, never figuring on someone corralling me when their elderly wife got sick.

I got paged almost as soon as my ass hit the pool lounge chair on my second day in the hotel. This wasn't part of the plan; the very generously tipped pool honcho was supposed to give me at least half an hour to get noticed before he paged me. I went to the house phone a bit pissed off; I'd instruct my shill how to tell time later.

The deal was that I'd talk to myself on the phone for a few seconds, then go back to sun worshipping. This time, a frantic voice greeted me.

"Dr. Adams? My name's Arthur Birnbaum. My wife, she's throwing up!"

I was all set to tell him to call a doctor, but I was a goddamn doctor. "How'd that happen?"

There was silence on the other end for a few seconds. "Uh, I was hoping you'd tell me that, Doctor."

"Oh, yeah, right. What's your room number? I'll be right up."

He gave me the room number. "And hurry. She's in bad shape."

Great.

The old lady was suffering all right; she looked like death. Her blue hair even looked pale. She was sprawled out on a couch, wearing a pink muumuu, with a pail next to her.

Her husband, who looked to be about the same age—ancient—hovered over me as I took her pulse, just like I'd seen Ben Casey do on TV. She had one, but that's about all I could tell. I took a shot: "What'd you have to eat last night, honey?"

Between groans, she told me she'd had lobster and some kind of soup I'd never heard of.

"Hmm . . . you got Pepto?" I asked the husband.

He gave me a quizzical stare. "Pepto? Aren't you gonna write her a prescription?"

I thought fast. "I'm on vacation, left my prescription pad back in the office." I led him away from his wife: she was making me nervous with all her retching. I put my arm around his shoulders.

"Listen," I said, "she's got a little agita . . ."

"A little what?"

"You know . . . agita." I tapped my stomach.

A light went on behind his eyes. "Oh, food poisoning!"

"Yeah, right . . . food poisoning, but it's a mild case. Give her the Pepto, two tablespoons twice today, once when she gets up tomorrow. She'll be fine."

He looked leery. "You think?"

I feigned being insulted. "Hey, pal, twelve years of medical school. I know agita when I see it." I prayed she wasn't having a frigging stroke.

"Gee," he said, "you look so young."

I was twenty-two "Yeah, well, I take care of myself."

The next day, I was on my way to the pool when Arthur Birnbaum corralled me in the lobby. He grabbed my hand and began pumping it as if filling a bicycle tire.

"Dr. Adams, I can't thank you enough. My wife is great, her old self! You're a miracle worker!"

I faked humbleness. "Just doing my job." This doctor stuff was pretty easy.

I met with the legendary Meyer Lansky at the appointed time and place. He was sitting on the bench when I got there, a gray miniature poodle on a leash by his side.

I'd seen pictures of Lansky over the years but couldn't put him in perspective physically. He was in his early sixties but looked older—balding, gray, thin, and short (about five foot five), with a paunch, wrinkled from sun and worry, and stooped a bit even when sitting. He looked like he'd been born old. But his eyes told a different story. Sharp and focused, they were the gateway to a remarkable brain, one that kept the mob bloated with cash for forty years.

I sat down next to him, just another tourist taking a break.

"What's your name?" he asked without turning toward me.

I told him. He placed a newspaper between us. I slipped the envelope Frank Costello had given me between the fold.

"So, you like Miami, Gianni?"

I know small talk when I hear it, but the little guy seemed genuinely curious. I would come to know Meyer very well, and he treated me with respect, although he didn't have to. In the beginning, we'd meet on business, but it morphed into a friendship and we'd meet for dinner (an early one) often. When he died, in 1983, the media reported his net worth at between $400 and $600 million. Meyer's second wife, Thelma, told me he died nearly broke, most of his money lost when Castro seized the mob's casinos in Cuba. "The Cuba thing, it ruined him," she said.

I don't know whether she told me the truth, or didn't know where he'd stashed his money, if, in fact, he had any. The feds hunted for the Lansky fortune for years. Nothing was ever found.

I lived in the Fontainebleau for six months and never paid for anything. I was also turning a good profit in a gin rummy game held in one of the cabanas a few times a week. A few made Genovese guys,

Carmine Black and Charlie Alaimo, also played in the game with rotating hotel guests who were also mobbed up.

One day, I was on my way to the cabana when I spotted a stunning beauty by the pool. She was about twenty years old and was with what looked like her grandparents. You couldn't swing a dead cat in Miami Beach without hitting a beautiful woman, but this one was exceptional. Best described as a cross between Sophia Loren and Angie Dickinson, this woman had the best attributes of each. Tall and raven-haired, she glided instead of walked, and gave every man whiplash as she made her way to the pool.

I was with Carmine and Charlie and a few vacationing mobsters from New York. We all gaped at her. Right then and there, the six of us threw a thousand dollars each into a betting pool, wagering who would get a date with her first.

Her name was Jessica Wexler, and her family owned a car dealership in Chicago with multiple locations. I'd made some calls about the family, and they were filthy rich. No skeletons in the closet that I could find; anytime I heard of a big Chicago business, I'd immediately think Outfit affiliation, but the family appeared squeaky-clean. Two of Jessica's uncles had been murdered in their dealership a few years back, but the police had deemed it a robbery gone bad.

What better catch for Jessica than me, a nice doctor on vacation?

The money in the dating pool was nice, but I really wanted to get to know her. I was going to make a move first and beat the other guys to the punch. But how to do it? She obviously got hit on by numerous men; therefore, I had to have a different approach.

I made small talk with her at the pool. She lived in Miami and was entertaining her grandparents while they visited from Chicago. I told them I was Jewish, which got me approving glances; Grandma was already planning the wedding—I could see it in her eyes. Jessica was warming up to me, but that wasn't a date. I needed to impress her and get her to go out with me.

I invited her to dinner at the new Doral Hotel, which had a restaurant on the roof. Getting a table there was next to impossible . . . except for me. She accepted! This was a date by anyone's definition and I was about to become five grand richer.

In her next breath, she said, "Can I bring my grandparents?"

Nope, this was not a date.

"Certainly," I said, "I'd love to have them join us."

Son of a bitch!

I was very gracious and showed the three of them a good time. The dinner was exquisite and of course I never got a check. Wiseguys never got a check.

After dinner, I got Jessica alone. "Would you like to take a ride tomorrow, find a nice empty beach somewhere?"

She thought about it. "Well, okay."

We agreed to meet in the lobby at noon.

Jessica drove a six-year-old yellow Corvette, which was nice, but I had a plan that was going to make me golden in her eyes.

If she had looked gorgeous the few times I had seen her, she looked like a goddess upon arriving in the lobby the next morning. She was wearing a short white sundress, which showed off her tan and her flowing hair. I was in love. So was everyone else within ogling distance. Jessica was the type of woman that drew stares from other women . . . straight women.

As we exited the hotel, I said, "Can we take your car? I've been taking cabs wherever I go." After all, what kind of a phony rich doctor drives his nonexistent Jaguar to Florida from New York?

"Sure," she said cheerily. She told the valet parker to bring her car around. The valet and I had already made arrangements for what was about to happen.

We waited a few minutes, making small talk. The valet stopped a *brand-new* yellow Corvette in front of us, got out, and tossed me the keys.

Jessica hesitated for just a moment. "Uh . . ." She tried to attract the valet's attention, but he kept on walking. "Excuse me? That's not my car . . . sir!"

In my coolest, unaffected voice, I said, "Yes, it is."

Her head snapped to me. "Huh? No, it's not. My car . . . huh?"

I looked her right in her gorgeous eyes and said, "No one as beautiful as you should be driving a six-year-old car. This car is yours."

Her jaw dropped. "You bought this for me?" There were tears in her eyes.

"Yes, I did. I don't want you to break down in that thing you're driving." I opened the door for her to get in, but she hugged me for a long while. I felt tears on my neck.

A friend of a friend owned a Chevy dealership in Fort Lauderdale. A new Corvette coupe at that time went for about $4,500. I got it for $3,700, which was at cost. I got the girl, plus made a profit of thirteen hundred dollars on the bet from the money pool. Jessica and I became a couple and would move in together in a few months. But down the road, disaster loomed.

I made up some bullshit story that I was in the process of selling my practice in New York. To that end, I bought a house on the Intracoastal Waterway outside Miami. I was genuinely in love; the game playing was over. While Jessica felt the same way about me, her grandparents were getting suspicious about the "doctor" from New York. Carmine Black had called me by my right name from across the hotel lobby, and Grandpa had heard it.

They began to ask pointed questions about my schooling, practice, and bounced medical terminology off me; I had no idea what they were talking about. I could fake just so much. If the Internet had been around back then, I'm sure I'd have been able to pull off the scam—research being only a click away—but for now my medical expertise depended on what Ben Casey and Marcus Welby were doing on their TV shows.

I decided to come clean about my not being Jewish—but I stuck to the doctor cover—confessing I'd said it to impress Jessica, but I said I had intentions of converting and marrying their granddaughter.

"Convert?" Grandma asked suspiciously. "So, when are you going to convert?"

Good question, and I came up with a good answer. "I start classes for conversion to Judaism tomorrow."

Granny's eyebrows shot up. "Oh, really? And who is the rabbi helping you in the process?"

I was ready, and whipped out a business card. "This rabbi," I said, and handed her the card, which read "Rabbi Henry Ellison," and gave contact information.

You see, I *really was* converting. I was on the road to becoming a Jew.

Like I told you, I was in love.

Jessica got pregnant, and we were both thrilled about it. Her family, not so much. We were still unmarried, but that was about to change as soon as my conversion process was complete. If visuals meant anything, I had taken to wearing a yarmulke, the traditional headpiece for men (I had seen my father wearing one when I was a kid, apparently to impress a woman, and now I was doing the same thing). Before any marriage could happen, however, the family must've hired a platoon of private investigators to check me out, and my doctor cover melted away. What I had told Jessica and her family was that I'd sold my practice, and, rich as I was, had decided to retire to Florida with my new family. My real plan was to continue my mobbed-up ways and wind up making more money than any doctor could dream of.

Jessica's family had other plans. The family convinced her that I was a scammer and flew her to Puerto Rico for an abortion. I was very upset, because I really did love her and very much wanted the baby, but my web of lies had snowballed into something I couldn't control. I had painted myself into a corner.

Jessica vanished from Florida; I heard her family sent her to

Chicago directly from Puerto Rico and put her somewhere I couldn't find her. But I had contacts in the Windy City, all of them with access to more information than the FBI. Within a few days, I had an address and phone number. My calls and letters went unanswered.

Jessica was out of my life, and I was crushed. The yarmulke gone, I went back to what I knew best: making money.

Frank Sinatra began appearing at the Fontainebleau for two-week stints several times a year. Frank and I had been acquaintances for a while—since before the Cal Neva fiasco. I'd run into him during his visits with high-level mobsters in New York and Chicago, but we began to connect more as friends during his Fontainebleau gigs. That relationship would grow and he would become the godfather to my son Carmello in later years.

Frank had a nightly table for ten right by the stage for all his shows. He could invite anyone he wanted, but he chose to entrust me with the arrangements.

"Do anything you want with the table, Gianni," Frank told me. "Make yourself a few bucks, too."

And so I did. I sold the ten seats at that table for every Sinatra performance and made thousands of dollars. Frank didn't care, just as long as I didn't put just any asshole at that table. I was careful; only well-heeled, properly dressed guests got the nod.

When he wasn't performing, Sinatra was in demand by the wealthy members of Miami society. If someone was throwing a gala social event, they wanted Sinatra there. I was the buffer between these people and Sinatra, who, at the time, was very involved with actress Mia Farrow. They hadn't married as yet, but that was coming.

One night, a wealthy—and well-connected—lawyer, Al Malnik, asked me if I could get Frank Sinatra to drop by the reception for Malnik's son's bar mitzvah. I cleared it with Frank, and told Malnik, "No problem."

The night of the bar mitzvah arrived, and I assumed Frank had gone; he was a man of his word. About 7:00 P.M., I got paged at the Fontainebleau bar. It was Meyer Lansky.

"So, Gianni, I'm at the reception for Al's boy. Where is Sinatra?"

Meyer didn't raise his voice—Meyer never raised his voice—but I knew he was pissed. He and Malnik were good friends.

I was flustered. "You mean he's not there?" My mind was racing. What the hell was going on?

"Listen, kid, would I be asking you where he was if he was here? I'm assuming he's on his way, yes?"

"Oh, sure. Absolutely, Mr. Lansky. I'll check and get back to you."

I raced upstairs to Frank's suite and banged on the door. No answer. I identified myself, banged some more.

Mia Farrow answered through the door. "He's not available, Gianni."

Huh? "What do you mean, 'not available'? He made a commitment to be somewhere and he's not." I was getting pissed, feeling that Mia had something to do with Frank's blowing off the party. She was a whiner, a complainer, and a control freak. She wanted Frank with her at all times when he wasn't performing, even took to changing his wardrobe to that of a sixties tie-dyed hippie. Frank was decades older than Mia and looked like a fool with bell-bottoms and a silk scarf around his neck.

"Mia, goddamn it, open the door. I've got to talk to Frank."

No response.

"Fuck this," I mumbled to myself, then backed up and charged the door, hitting it full force with my shoulder and blasting it inward.

Unfortunately, Mia was standing behind the door, and it hit her full in the upper body and face. She was on her ass on the carpeted floor when I burst into the room. There was some blood on her forehead, but she just had a scratch. Being a bit disoriented didn't stop her from cursing up a blue streak.

Sinatra, hearing the commotion, came out of the bedroom wearing a white terry-cloth robe and stopped short.

"What the fuck?" He stared at the shattered door, then at his girlfriend.

"Sorry, Frank. I didn't have a key." I got right to it. "Malnik's party?"

Frank looked at me like I had two heads. "What party? That was canceled." Now he looked confused.

"Canceled? Says who?"

Frank jerked a thumb at Mia. "Says her." Mia, for her part, was looking sheepish.

Mia had told Frank the party was off, so she could have him to herself.

Frank shot me a glance. "Give me ten minutes." He didn't say a word to Mia, who got up off the floor and vanished into the bathroom.

Sinatra knew better than to disappoint Al Malnik, who did a lot of work for the mob nationwide. Malnik was a lawyer by trade, but no one except those in the upper echelon of La Cosa Nostra knew exactly what he did, but whatever it was, he worked closely with Meyer and his expertise was highly valued. The who's who of the American Mafia was at that bar mitzvah reception, and Frank Sinatra had to be there.

We were at the party within the hour.

Don't misread what I'm relating. Frank Sinatra was no pushover. He got the highest respect he deserved; no one disrespected Frank Sinatra. Don Rickles is the only person I knew who could insult Frank and get away with it, because Frank loved him and he knew it was all in good fun. But let some half-assed comedian try something similar, and he'd find himself at the mercy of Sinatra's ire, which meant trouble for that comic.

Don Rickles called Frank "Skinny Guinea" in his act, and Frank loved it. Even back then, when Rickles was breaking in, he and Frank were great friends, and they remained so throughout their lives. Another outstanding comedian of the era was Shecky Greene, a very talented comic, singer, and storyteller. Shecky was at the peak of his career in the 1960s when he took to calling Frank "Skinny Guinea," too. I guess he figured if Rickles—a newcomer to the scene—could rib Frank Sinatra and get away with it, why couldn't he, a major star?

Frank didn't take kindly to Shecky and his "Skinny Guinea" rap and told him on numerous occasions that such talk was rude and disrespectful, and to cut it out. Shecky kept it up until the night Shecky liked to call "the night Frank Sinatra saved my life."

Shecky had just finished his act in a Vegas nightclub and went outside in an alley to have a smoke, when three goons came out of nowhere and proceeded to beat the shit out of him.

After a few minutes of a horrendous pounding, Frank walked into the alley and said, "Okay, that's enough," and the muscle drifted away.

Shecky Greene never mentioned Frank Sinatra in his act or in mixed company again.

Sinatra was also a great practical joker and had a great sense of humor. He could get away with almost anything because he was . . . well, Frank Sinatra.

Frank was invited to two separate fund-raising events in one night in Miami Beach. The first one was for the Italian American Anti-Defamation League, mob boss Joe Columbo's brainchild, which didn't work out very well for him, but more on that later. The other one was for the state of Israel, with guests Sammy Davis, Jr., and Moshe Dayan, the Israeli defense minister and war hero. While Frank couldn't be in two places at once, he was going to appear at both, dividing his time, so as not to offend either man; both were his friends.

"You want to come along?" he asked me.

"Sure, why the hell not."

"Invite says wear a tux," Frank said.

Two hours later, I was waiting for Frank in front of the Fontainebleau, spiffy in my tuxedo.

Frank stared at me. "Where's your fucking shirt?"

Couldn't slip one past Sinatra; I wasn't wearing a shirt, just a black designer tuxedo, patent-leather shoes, and a bow tie neatly fastened around my neck.

"Invitations says a tux, nothing about a shirt."

Frank rolled his eyes.

"C'mon, we'll have some laughs," I said.

Frank mulled that over. "Okay, you want laughs, we'll have laughs." We got into my Caddy. "Go to Ballew's Jewelers," he said. Ballew's jewelry store on Arthur Godfrey Road was the bling store to the stars and anyone else who could afford its prices.

Wherever Frank went, he was treated like royalty, and Ballew's was no different. We were ushered into a back room, where Frank made his request.

"You got opera glasses?"

"Of course, Mr. Sinatra," the owner said, and he took off and returned in less than a minute with several pair of miniature binoculars with a grasping handle jutting out from one side.

Frank examined them. "Which are the best?"

"These, Mr. Sinatra. Gold-plated, very well made."

Frank hefted the glasses and looked at me. "Whaddaya think?"

I didn't know opera glasses from shot glasses. "They look great, Frank. Who are they for?"

"Sammy and Moshe."

The owner of the store chimed in. "You want two pair, Mr. Sinatra?"

Frank shook his head. "Uh-uh. Just the one pair. Cut them in half."

"Sir?"

Frank smiled. "You heard me. Cut 'em in half. Wrap the halves separately."

I was confused, but the jeweler just nodded, "Yes, sir, Mr. Sinatra."

Back in the car, I just had to ask. "What's with cutting the glasses in half, Frank?"

"Relax, baby, you're not the only one who's gonna get a laugh."

For those of you who haven't figured out the gag, both Sammy Davis, Jr., and Moshe Dayan each had only one eye, and each got half a pair of opera glasses to accommodate his good eye.

Sammy would laugh at anything Frank did; they were great friends. But how did General Dayan take Frank's weird sense of humor? He loved it! All he could talk about was the gift he'd gotten from Frank Sinatra. I would bet if I'd pulled that stunt, I would've been buried up to my neck in sand in the Negev Desert.

General Dayan told Frank that he was proud that the Israeli fund-raiser netted over $300,000.

"Oh, yeah," Frank said, "I just came from an Italian benefit where we raised the same amount, but with a difference."

"What's the difference, Frank?" the general asked.

"Ours was in cash; yours was in pledges."

Dayan thought that the stereotypical reference to cheap Jews was hysterical. Only Sinatra could get away with something like that.

Every now and then I had to work for my keep.

A friend of ours, Jay Weiss, was the owner of Southern Wine & Spirits, which supplied booze to many bars and clubs, and had gotten stiffed by some guys who owed him money.

"These fucking mutts," Jay said, "are into me for twenty-five grand. Told me to go fuck myself." He was seething. "I'll give you fifty percent if you can get it for me."

"Fifty percent? Where's your profit?" I asked.

"Fuck my profit. That'll break me even, and that's okay. I don't want these assholes to think I'm a pushover. You can take care of this for me?"

"Yeah, sure. No problem."

"Well, there may be," Jay added. "These are tough guys . . . Cubans."

I thought about that, and was formulating a plan. "Not a problem. I'll take care of it."

I bought two plastic water pistols, a pair of rubber work gloves, and a five-gallon jug of muriatic acid. I made a fifty-fifty mixture of the acid with water, and conducted a few tests on a deserted road near the Everglades.

The next day, I donned a three-piece silk suit, jumped into my new Eldorado (a present to myself after the breakup with Jessica), and made my way to Little Havana. The guys I was looking for owned several bars, but the one I was headed to was their flagship gin mill.

I arrived at the joint a little after noon and was greeted by three men hanging out in front of the place.

After a short introduction, I established that these were the guys who owed Jay the money. These were mean-looking hombres.

"I'm here for the twenty-five grand you owe Jay Weiss," I said calmly.

The three Cuban stooges looked at me as if I were crazy. And they laughed. That pissed me off.

One of them said, "We'll pay him when we're good and fucking ready."

"No," I said, smiling, "you'll pay him now."

Now they were hysterical. "What, you gonna make us?"

I sighed. "Which one of you is the badass?"

"Huh?"

"You heard me," I said. "Which one of you guys thinks he's the toughest?"

The guy who had been doing most of the talking puffed out his chest. "That'd be me, motherfucker."

I nodded. "Uh-huh." I pulled the rubber gloves from my waistband and snapped them on. The Cubans were exchanging glances, obviously thinking I was a nutcase. "Excuse me," I said, and walked a few feet back to my car, where I retrieved the orange-colored water pistols.

One plastic squirt gun in each hand, I faced off the Cubans, who by this time were laughing so hard, I thought they were going to hyperventilate.

"You, José or whatever the fuck your name is, pay up the twenty-five grand . . . now." I leveled the two water pistols at his crotch.

My target regained his composure and gave me a hearty "Fuck you."

I shrugged, then squirted the prick in the groin with both guns. Almost immediately, his pants began to billow acrid fumes. The acid was doing its job. He began screaming and beating his hands against his crotch. The other two guys hesitated for a brief moment, then drenched him with beer to stop the acid from eroding his privates. That tactic didn't work, and more fumes were created.

The target got up and went for the door, unbuckling his pants as he went. I was on him, grabbing him by his greasy hair and pulling him to the ground. He was screaming when I jammed one of the pistols into his eye socket.

I looked at the two amigos and said in my most menacing voice, "Get me my fucking money now, or this guy's dick is gonna shrivel up like an overcooked tamale and I'll take his eye out."

Pants on Fire's buddies froze, not knowing what to do.

Until he yelled, that is.

"Get him the fucking money! Now!"

I had a bag of cash in less than five minutes, grabbed it up, and backed up to my car, my water pistols at the ready. "Take his pants off and douse him with water, not alcohol. He'll be fine." I got into my car and got the hell out of there.

The acid trick was taught to me by an old-time loan shark in New York, who said, "Some jerkoff owes you money, give him a squirt on his balls. He'll pay up, trust me. Dead guys don't pay; scared ones do." Words to live by. Full-strength muriatic acid can peel paint off a house, but watered down it burns like hell but causes no permanent damage.

I met Jay Weiss back at the hotel with his money. "I took twenty-five percent," I told him.

"Huh? I told you fifty. . . . It's okay; I just wanted to send them a message."

"No, Jay. It's too much." Don't get me wrong: I'm not averse to taking too much money—in fact, it's my favorite thing to do—but Weiss was a very well-connected guy and he'd be sure to get the word around that I wasn't a greedy bastard and could be depended upon to get the job done.

I needed to get my mind off Jessica, but it wasn't easy at the Fontainebleau Hotel, where I was easily reminded of her. There were plenty of other women around, but at that moment I wasn't interested in getting back in the game. What I needed was a good business venture to keep me occupied.

The Seventy-ninth Street Causeway connects Miami to Miami Beach, via North Bay Village and Harbor Island. Some of the hottest clubs and restaurants reside on the causeway, all of them moneymakers. I wanted to become part of the scene.

I scouted a few properties, and settled on a cavernous building, which I thought would make a great club. This was the dawn of the disco era, and I envisioned a club that would become the in spot for the beautiful people.

I had a few bucks saved, but not nearly what I would need to get rolling. Clubs, and, for that matter, restaurants, too, were high-risk businesses, which banks shied away from. Ninety-five percent of restaurants and clubs close within the first year, and as such they are not a good loan risk for banks. Fortunately, I had access to the best bank in the world, the National Bank of La Cosa Nostra, with no branches, no advertising, but plenty of loan officers. I would have no problem getting the money from my New York connections, but first I needed to make sure I took care of my obligations to Meyer Lansky.

Since I'd been in Florida, I was the conduit between Frank Costello and Meyer. I couldn't interrupt that flow, but I was about to get extremely busy with club business. I'd still meet with Meyer, exchange and pick up what he gave me, but I now needed someone trustworthy as a courier to get messages and money back and forth to New York.

I knew a made guy in Miami Beach who had a sister who worked as an airline stewardess, flew the New York–Florida route, and agreed to deliver envelopes and packages to someone at La Guardia Airport who would make sure they got to Frank Costello and would carry envelopes back to Florida. The woman was trustworthy (as vouched for by her brother), and everyone agreed to the plan.

That taken care of, I focused my efforts on building the new club. I had two partners, Genovese soldiers Carmine Black and Charlie Alaimo, my gin rummy buddies from the Fontainebleau. While we all ran the club, they would be operating mob-related mischief—for example, high-stakes card games in the back room, money laundering, and anything else that would generate an illegal but sanctioned buck. There's no better business to launder money than the club or restaurant business. Profits were mostly in cash—the use of credit cards wasn't as prevalent then as it is now—and the IRS had no idea how much money we were making; they had to take our word for it. We certainly weren't stiffing Uncle Sam out of club-profit taxes; quite the contrary, we were declaring more than the club actually made in order to "clean" ill-gotten gains from the mob.

The building had housed a failed club before we got it, so all we had to do was paint, hang mirrors, and put down carpeting. The fire chief of Miami Beach, Don Hickman, was an old friend of the family, and he pushed through the necessary paperwork. After ninety days of construction, Le Disc was born.

The club became an instant hit. Sammy Davis, Jr., was there opening night, and every star appearing in Miami Beach wound up making the club their second home. Along with Frank Sinatra, Dean Martin, Liza Minnelli, Lainie Kazan, Shecky Greene, and Don Rickles, numerous other celebs would become fixtures in the place.

We ran a clean club, or what I thought was a clean club, but more on that later. There were no drugs allowed on the premises, and we had enough bouncers to quell any type of disturbance. Anytime booze, women, and men are in one location, there's bound to be trouble, but at Le Disc problems were kept to a minimum. As soon as a disturbance started, the combatants were overwhelmed with bouncers who looked like refrigerators. Rarely were any punches thrown; the bouncers' presence was enough to keep the peace.

The club made national news when Richard Nixon and his running mate, Spiro Agnew, decided to hold their nomination victory party after the Republican National Convention at Le Disc. The Secret Service was at the club, vetting our employees for three days, and I was glad Carmine's and Charlie's names weren't on the liquor license. Two made guys would've been a major red flag, and I'm sure the Secret Service would've vetoed the club as a victory party location, even though it was no secret that Nixon was heavily mobbed up, which is why he chose my club to celebrate his win. It was a "suggestion" by my partners, Black and Alaimo, through channels, and Nixon went along with the idea.

Nixon had come through for the mob when called upon. Teamsters boss Jimmy Hoffa had been serving a lengthy federal-prison sentence when, to everyone's dismay, President Nixon commuted his sentence after he'd served less than five years of a thirteen-year sentence. Nixon was pressured by the mob to do it because Hoffa had found religion while locked up and was talking about exposing the current Teamsters boss, Frank Fitzsimmons, as a conduit of union pension money to the mob, unless he was released. Hoffa was a loose cannon, and he began talking about unseating Fitzsimmons a few years after he got out, and the mob knew that he'd bring up the looted pension funds. Bye-bye, Jimmy. He would vanish on July 30, 1975.

During the victory party, which included big-bucks Republican donors, celebrities, and captains of industry, one of the Secret Service agents came up to me and said, "A member of our party has taken a shining to that lady over there," and he pointed out Stephanie Clark, a dynamite blonde, daughter of a cop, and a friend of mine. The "member of our party" was none other than Nixon himself, who started breathing heavily in Stephanie's presence.

Arrangements were made for Nixon and Stephanie to meet, and it was an immediate love connection, at least on Nixon's part. He would wind up moving Stephanie into her own condo in Virginia. It wasn't long before Nixon's wife, Pat, found out about the affair and put a halt to it.

The club had been in business for about six months when my partners, Carmine and Charlie, were summoned to New York for a meeting.

"What's it about?" I asked.

Carmine shrugged. "Probably gonna get an attaboy 'cause we're doing so well."

Made sense. Le Disc was making fistfuls of money, and that always made the bosses happy.

"Okay, see you guys when you get back," I said.

They never came back.

It turned out that Carmine and Charlie were dealing coke from the club, which was strictly against mob rules. Not that the mob was averse to making money, but selling drugs carried major jail time, which might make it attractive for the dealer to talk about mob operations rather than go to prison for decades. The fact that drugs were a dirty business had nothing to do with the bosses' refusal to get involved or have anyone within the organization involved. It was a matter of survival.

Carmine Black took a header from a six-story tenement in Brooklyn, and the cops were unable to determine whether it was an accident, suicide, or murder. To me, it was obvious. Charlie Alaimo vanished, never to be seen or heard from again.

While I wasn't suspected of being involved in the drug deals with them, I was asked by Mr. Costello if I knew anything about what they'd been doing. I denied it, which was true. While I might always have been looking to make a score, dealing drugs was, and is, strictly out of the realm of consideration for me. To me, drugs, either using or selling, always lead to self-destruction, and dying for a few extra bucks held no appeal. I also didn't want to disappoint Mr. Costello, who had always been good to me.

Charlie, Carmine, and I had successors' insurance, which meant that whichever partner died first, his share of the business went to the surviving partners. Since Carmine was dead and Charlie presumed dead, I was now the sole owner of Le Disc.

I wasn't happy with my newfound fortune. The club was now on the Bureau of Narcotics and Dangerous Drugs' (BNDD) radar, and I, as the surviving owner, was under constant surveillance because of the conduct of Carmine and Charlie. I decided to quit—not sell—the club. I spoke about my decision with Mr. Costello, who, while he didn't come out and say it, admired my decision.

To be successful in the mob, keeping a low profile was imperative. While I might have been walking away from a lucrative operation, my decision was good business for the mob and certainly for my future.

In March 1970, I padlocked the door of Le Disc and walked away.

5

THE GODFATHER

It took me about two days after I unloaded my house for me to decide that I wanted to go out west; L.A., maybe Las Vegas. Start over again. Of course, I couldn't just pick up and go. I needed to clear it with Mr. Costello. I'd go where I was needed, and wouldn't have much say regarding my eventual destination.

"I think it's a great idea," Mr. C. said after I told him about my plans. "Pick one, but if it were me, I'd go to Vegas. More opportunities. We have more people there. I'll need you in L.A. from time to time, too." He went on to explain that I'd still be acting as his liaison, and that I'd have to clear any business ventures I might come up with through him.

"I want you to stop in Chicago first," he said. "Introduce yourself around. I'll tell Tony you're on your way. He might have something for you. Whatever he wants you to do, do it. It's like you were talking to me."

"Tony" was Anthony Accardo, boss of the Chicago Outfit and a close friend of Mr. Costello's. Accardo was an old-time mafioso who had started with Al Capone in the 1920s, was highly respected, and ran a tight organization.

I arrived in Chicago a week later and met with Johnny Roselli in a downtown hotel restaurant. Roselli was in his mid-sixties, a sharp dresser with movie-star looks, and one of Tony Accardo's trusted soldiers. Roselli was pleasant enough, made small talk about everything under the sun except mob business, and told me that Tony Accardo, the boss himself, would be joining us shortly.

Accardo, a big guy, maybe sixty, and solidly built—also a sharp dresser, as was fitting a man of his stature—arrived with only one bodyguard.

Accardo asked about New York, Mr. C. in particular, then made what he called a "request."

He produced a manila envelope. "Drop this off for me? You are going to L.A., right?"

I was now. The envelope was for a big shot in the stagehands' union, which Accardo controlled. Al Capone had been behind the union since its inception, and the baton was passed to Accardo upon Al's passing, in 1947.

"Stick around for a few more days," Accardo said. "Johnny here will show you anything worth seeing in Chicago. Where're you headed after L.A.?"

"I was thinking Vegas," I said.

"Yeah, good choice. Tell you what . . . when you get there, go to the Las Vegas Country Club. I'll have some calls made; you'll be expected."

The offer was appreciated and very gracious. Mr. C. must've asked Accardo to take care of me, and that's what he was doing.

After dinner, Accardo took off and Roselli and I hit a few clubs. Three days later, I was in L.A., dropped off the envelope, hung out for two days, and got on a plane for Las Vegas.

Las Vegas would be my home, off and on, for the next thirty years.

The glitter and glitz of Vegas impressed me from day one . . . still does. Even during the day, the hotels and casinos are like sleeping giants waiting for the sun to set before exploding in a massive light show that's almost as entertaining as the acts in the casino lounges.

The Las Vegas Country Club was a sprawling property that boasted an eighteen-hole golf course, a swimming pool, six tennis courts, lounges, complete health facilities, a dining room, and beautiful views of the city.

Moe Dalitz, Jack Entrata, Carl Cohen, and Hank Greenspun were waiting for me at the club. Dalitz and several partners were original owners of the club. The Moe Greene character in *The Godfather* was based on Moe Dalitz. Entrata was the paper owner of the Sands Hotel—Frank Costello was the actual owner—and Greenspun was the owner of the *Las Vegas Sun*, the biggest newspaper in Vegas, and a prominent real estate developer, much of his seed money coming from the mob-controlled Teamsters Union. Carl Cohen was one of the owners of the Sands Hotel and a former member of the Mayfield Road mob out of Cleveland, Ohio.

They made me feel comfortable in my new surroundings and gave me good advice on how to start making money.

"This is Vegas, kid. A one-eyed transvestite dwarf can get rich here and get laid more times than he can count," Moe told me. "You shouldn't have a problem."

Hank followed that up by saying, "Anything you need, just call."

Jack just nodded. "What he said."

Carl Cohen volunteered a room at the Sands. I'd divide my time between there and a room at Caesar's Palace. These guys were heavily involved with Frank Costello, and they were going to do everything possible to make my transition from New York to Sin City a greased road.

So far, my life had consisted of temporary housing—aside from the house I'd purchased for Jessica and me, which came and went—because I was always on the road. The room at the Sands would be no different, and my life would be nomadic for a while because I'd be splitting my time between Vegas and L.A. I was fine with it. I was still young, and having permanent housing was something I didn't think much about. I had plenty of cash and was looking to start a business, not buy a house, but that notion changed pretty quickly.

In a rare moment of self-reflection, I decided to mend fences—to a degree—with my parents. While I still harbored some resentment toward them for not maintaining contact with me while I was in the hospital being treated for polio, I felt it was time to have them come to Vegas for a visit. I had no intentions of changing anything regarding our relationship, but keeping in touch seemed like the right thing to do. I probably had Italian guilt to some degree, and wanted to do what was expected of me when it came to my parents. Honoring family was an Italian tradition, and I felt the least I could do was extend an invitation to my home—with me picking up the cost, of course.

On Father's Day, 1968, my parents arrived for a one-week visit, a time frame that I created. My mom was still gorgeous, but she was beginning to look her age. I'm sure living with my father accelerated the aging process. My dad hadn't changed. When I told him that I'd gotten them a suite at the Sands, he asked if they could extend their stay.

"For how long?" I asked.

My father shrugged. "I dunno . . . a while."

Once a freeloader . . .

I vetoed that idea. "Nice to see you and Mom, but no. I've got plans and I won't be around," I replied, lying. Why hurt their feelings?

We made plans to meet for lunch at Caesar's after they got settled in.

Two hours later, I was walking through Caesar's Palace on my way to meet them, when I bumped into a hot blonde who introduced herself as Susan Casino, her real name by the way. She was with someone who looked like a madam in a whorehouse, heavily made up and dressed to shock, but who turned out to be her mother. They were on vacation from Rhode Island and were at Caesar's, hoping to run into Frank Sinatra to snag an autograph and picture.

"Forget Sinatra; he's not a guy who likes to sign autographs or take pictures," I said. "Why don't you ladies have lunch with me and my parents? I'll tell you Sinatra stories."

Susan's eyes went wide. "You know him?"

"I do," I said, smiling.

Susan and her mom joined my parents and me for lunch. My father morphed into his usual charming self when he was around women, and wowed them with his bullshit. When it was determined that both our families came from the same region in Italy, it prompted the following exchange.

"Wow, that's wonderful," my father said. "She comes from good Neapolitan stock," he said to me. "You two ought to get married. You'll have great kids."

I turned to Susan, and shocked the hell out of everyone by saying, "I think that's a great idea. Will you marry me?"

After the initial shock and absorbing the absurdity of my request, Susan said, "I'll think about it."

Susan and I hit it off. She was just nineteen, but after a short time I was smitten. I realized that I barely knew her, but I would marry her if she was up for it. She accepted and began planning the wedding, which was going to be held two months to the day that we met.

To say I was young and irresponsible was putting it mildly. I was more in love with having kids—lots of them—than I was in love with Susan. She was an afterthought.

I got introduced to her family. Vincent Castaldi, her stepdad, was a made guy with the Patriarca family in New England (I couldn't escape the long reach of the mob—not that I was trying to). Her mother, Maria, I'd already met. Susan's brother, Steve, was a decent guy, but he didn't talk much.

Of course, Susan and her mom were excited to plan the wedding. When they asked for my input, I handed Susan's mother fifteen thousand dollars and told her, "Here's my input; spend it as you see fit." No one can say I wasn't involved.

The Castaldis (Susan's stepfather's name) were from Providence, Rhode Island, where the wedding was to be held, so I flew back east a few days prior. Susan and her parents told me they were taking me to dinner at the Cantina, one of Providence's fanciest eateries. Susan's dad told me all his buddies from the Patriarca family would be there and he wanted to introduce me around.

"You don't know these guys, Gianni, so be respectful."

I hadn't told Susan's dad about my mob connections, and kept my mouth shut in general regarding my personal life. The Mafia, after all, was a secret organization, and while John Gotti might have been unaware of that, I wasn't. Someone once told me you can never get in any trouble by keeping your mouth shut. Profound advice.

I decided to have a little fun with my soon-to-be father-in-law.

I knew many of the guys in the Patriarca family, having been introduced to them in my travels for Mr. C. To this end, I called a few of the Providence crew and told them I'd be in the Cantina the next day and would look forward to seeing them if they were available to stop by.

When we walked into the Cantina the next night, I was greeted, hugged, and cheek-kissed by a bunch of made Patriarca family men. My new best friend, Vinny, stood there with a dropped jaw.

"You know these guys?" he asked me.

"Yep," I said, and left it at that.

The wedding was rapidly approaching when Susan asked me how many guests were coming from my side.

"Two . . . my parents."

She was incredulous. "Two? You know so many people. Two? I don't get it."

Truth be told, I wanted to spare my friends, the few I had, from another boring wedding. Hell, I didn't even want to go, but I had little choice, being the groom and all.

"Susan, honey, my friends are busy and scattered all over the country. I'm saving them travel time."

She looked at me like I had three heads. "Okay, then, what about a best man? You need one of those, you know."

"I'll use your brother. What's his name again?" I replied.

Susan rolled her eyes. "Steve."

"Steve, right. Tell him he's my best man."

I got another eye roll, and she walked away.

I barely knew Steve, but the person closest to me was Frank Costello, and I wasn't about to ask him. He avoided notoriety like the plague. He famously refused to be photographed when he testified before the Kefauver committee on organized crime in 1951, which were televised. After his first day of testimony, he absolutely refused to reappear the next day if a TV camera was going to be trained on him. When his lawyer reminded him that he was under subpoena, he said, "Fuck a subpoena. I'll fight it until the committee is in the history books." For his next appearance before the committee, all the cameras were able to shoot were his well-manicured hands. Such was the power of Frank Costello. He liked his privacy. It wouldn't surprise me if Mr. C. didn't show up for his own funeral.

Something was telling me that this marriage was getting off to a bad start.

Steve stood up for me and the wedding was great, what I remember of it.

I bought a house I wouldn't even have considered buying just three months earlier—it was in Cold Water Canyon, in L.A.—and rented an apartment in Vegas in a complex behind the Riviera Hotel. I'd be shuttling between the two. Susan would be staying in Vegas.

I partnered with Susan's father in the jewelry business, opening up Russo & Castaldi Jewelers on the Strip. Always looking to make a quick buck, we came up with a foolproof scam, which was more unethical than illegal.

We needed showgirls and hookers to be part of the con, but that wasn't a problem, since they were everywhere. These women were beautiful and could get any men they wanted. Most of their guys were wealthy, married and had children, and came to Vegas to get away from their wives and let loose with gorgeous girls.

We got the girls to bring their boyfriends to the store and buy jewelry for them. Within a week, the girls would dump the guys, return the jewelry to us, and we'd give them half of whatever their short-term boyfriends had paid for it. These women had revolving-door boyfriends, and it wasn't rare for a single showgirl/hooker to ensnare three or four different marks a month. Everyone was happy, and the boyfriends never knew they'd been ripped off. We must've sold the same pieces at least fifty times.

With the excess money, I opened up Gianni's Wig World—wigs bought, sold, cleaned, and styled. My limited time at Wilford Academy had paid off. Within two years, I had six stores and they were all thriving. Who knew that wigs could be this popular?

My name was becoming known, which was a good thing. The notoriety came because I was a success at such a young age and had been interviewed by the media numerous times. The press ate it up. I was still working with Mr. Costello—that would never change—but my new legitimacy was a good way to send my illegitimate profits to the Laundromat. For the first time in my life, I wasn't concerned about where my next buck was coming from. I was making a steady income.

By mid-1968, I was buying a lot of TV time to advertise my businesses. I would purchase hour segments and appear as my own spokesperson. A local network approached me with an offer to host my own television variety show while I pitched my own products. It was called *Welcome to My Lifestyle*. By this time, I knew practically every celebrity worth knowing, because they all appeared in Vegas and guests were easily booked. Dean Martin, who also had a TV show at the time, got himself into hot water with his network, NBC, for appearing on my show, which was on a competing network. My show had decent ratings and ran for almost two years.

The new three-thousand-room International Hotel had just opened, with a fifteen-hundred-seat showroom, the biggest in Vegas. The owner, Kirk Kerkorian, and I were friends and I had a stageside booth reserved for whenever I wanted it. Barbra Streisand performed for the first two weeks after the grand opening, followed by Elvis Presley, who did fifty-eight consecutive shows over a two-week period. The room was packed every night.

I had met Elvis on a few occasions, but we hadn't spent any time together. One night after a show, I went backstage, where Elvis was with a group of his buddies—known as the "Memphis Mafia"—discussing where they were going to eat. He spotted me and called me over.

"Hey, man, you ever have a peanut butter and banana sandwich?" he asked, then added, "On white bread. It's my favorite."

I thought he was putting me on, so I played along. "Love 'em," I said. I wondered if an angioplasty came with it. The thought of combining peanut butter and bananas and slapping them between two slices of white bread really didn't appeal to me, but I was being polite. This was pregargantuan Elvis; he was still pretty lean, but the junk food was beginning to show.

"Great, man! You're coming with us!" He introduced me to his friends and we started to leave.

I knew you could get any kind of food in Vegas, but I had no idea where he was going to find a place that had this junk on the menu. But, hey, he was Elvis, and if he wanted a peanut butter and banana sandwich, I felt sure no restaurant was going to turn him down.

"Where we going?" I asked.

"San Francisco, brother. Plane's at McCarran."

We flew out of McCarran Airport on Elvis's private jet, landing in San Francisco about an hour later. It turned out that the dive diner we went to had the best peanut butter and banana sandwiches in the country. Had to be true; Elvis said so.

There were eight of us, and Elvis did the ordering. An initial round of sixteen sandwiches was sucked up in minutes, washed down by gallons of lemonade. I had one. Not bad, but I wasn't about to add it to my favorites list. Ten more of the buggers were ordered and polished off quickly.

After the gourmet meal, we got back on the plane and flew back to Vegas and the International. Once we were in Elvis's suite, he decided he wanted to watch a Western movie. A projector was set up and a 1930s oater with Hoot Gibson began.

Elvis and his crew were whooping it up like real cowboys, and I wondered what the hell I was doing there. These were a nice bunch of guys, but I was used to the pinkie ring, silk suit crowd. I have to admit, however, that I was having laughs. Then the guns came out.

Elvis packed a gold-plated .45 Colt semiautomatic pistol, which had been given to him by some starstruck general when Elvis got out of the army. His Memphis Mafia pals all had revolvers.

Elvis fired a shot into a wall, and everyone followed suit. They were following the action in the movie, where Hoot was chasing a bunch of bad guys and trading shots with them.

I thought a couple of rounds would've been it, but then Elvis started overturning furniture, and the guys divided up into two sides. I ducked behind a couch as everyone hid behind cover and traded shots. They aimed high, but bullets can travel through walls, and who knows where they could've wound up.

Within a minute, the Gunfight in Suite 3000 was over and everyone repaired to the bar to get loaded, pun intended. I stayed a while, but I couldn't hear a damn thing because I was temporarily deaf from the gunfire. Only in Las Vegas.

Frank Sinatra performed in Vegas sixteen weeks a year—two eight-week gigs. He entertained in mob-run hotels and he worked for free. Either Frank was still paying off his Kennedy dues or he got off being around wiseguys. I think it was a little bit of both.

Frank and I saw more of each other and became closer friends. I met him at the Sands one night after one of his shows; I'd walked in while Frank was having an argument in the casino with owner Carl Cohen, whom I'd known since arriving in Vegas. Frank wanted a fifty-grand gambling credit and Cohen refused to allow it.

Sinatra could be a good friend, but he was a worse enemy. When he didn't like you, he could get down-and-dirty mean. He called

(Above) Vito and Theresa Russo, taken in Naples, Italy, c. 1919. (Private collection of Gianni Russo)

(Left) The historic gate to the Bellevue Hospital grounds. (Library of Congress)

(Below) Parade of Italian-Americans on Mott Street in New York City at a flag-raising ceremony in honor of neighborhood boys in the U. S. Army, c. 1942. (Library of Congress)

(Above) The Park Avenue foyer of the Waldorf-Astoria Hotel in New York City. (Library of Congress)

(Left) (Left to right) Frank Costello and Blackie. (©Sueddeutsche Zeitung Photo / The Image Works)

(Below) A postcard from Frank Sinatra's CalNeva Resort and Casino, illustrating the border between Nevada and California. (Public domain)

(Top) The Rat Pack (from left: Dean Martin, Sammy Davis Jr., Peter Lawford, Frank Sinatra, and Joey Bishop) perform at the Sands in Las Vegas. (©Bill Kobrin, Globe Photos /ZUMAPRESS.com)

(Left) Carlos Marcello (left), alleged rackets boss in Southern Louisiana, is shown as he appeared before the Senate Rackets Committee. In center is Marcello's brother, Vincent, and at right is West Coast gambler Mickey Cohen, who was summoned as a witness, March 24, 1959. (Public domain)

(Bottom) Mosca's Restaurant, just off Highway 90, between Avondale and Boutte, Louisiana. (Public domain)

(Above) Gianni Russo as Carlo Rizzi and Marlon Brando as Vito Corleone on the set of *The Godfather.* (Mary Evans/PARAMOUNT PICTURES/Ronald Grant/Everett Collection)

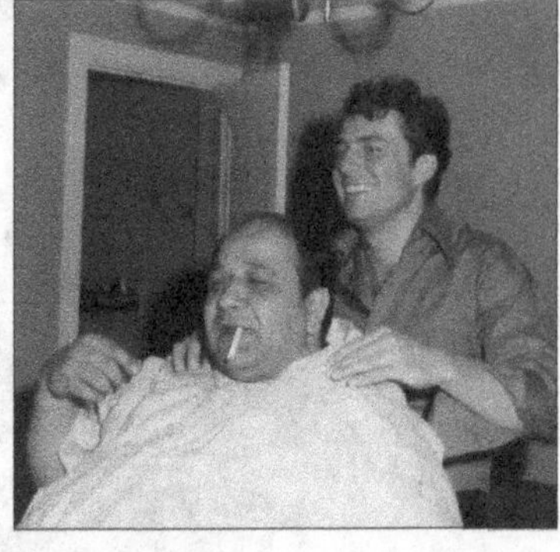

(Right) (Left to right) Richard Castellano, as Peter Clemenza, and Gianni Russo joking around on set. (Private collection of Gianni Russo)

(Below) (Left to right, foreground) One of Joe Columbo's enforcers (seated), Richard Conte, and Gianni Russo (standing) on the wedding set. (Private collection of Gianni Russo)

(Below) (Left to right) Gianni Russo, Al Pacino, and director Francis Ford Coppola discuss the baptism scene. (Private collection of Gianni Russo)

(Left to right) Yolanda Nitti, Gianni Russo, Sandy Nitti, Nicky Nitti, Air Pilot Captain Ferarra, and Nick Nitti seated at the Trevi Fountain in Rome, Italy, c. 1978. (Private collection of Gianni Russo)

Gianni Russo, seated on a black Ferrari parked in front of his State Street Club, poses for the cover of his album, *Live from State Street.* (Private collection of Gianni Russo)

A mug shot of Pablo Escobar, taken by the regional Colombia control agency in Medellín in 1977. (Public domain)

(Left to right) Lorna Luft, Gianni Russo, and Liza Minnelli. (Private collection of Gianni Russo)

(Above) Meyer Lansky walking his dog. This photo appeared in the *Miami News* on November 10, 1979. (*Miami News* Collection, HistoryMiami, 1989-011-21877)

(Right) The cake at the groundbreaking party for the Renaissance Hotel and Casino, April 1, 1980. (Private collection of Gianni Russo)

(Above) Gianni Russo with Pope John Paul II. (Private collection of Gianni Russo)

(Left) Frank Sinatra holds his godson, Carmello Russo, at his baptism. (Private collection of Gianni Russo)

(Below) (Left to right) Old friends Tony Accardo (aka Joe Batters) and Nick Nitti caught one of Gianni's performances with their wives at the Marriot O'Hare's Blue Max Room. (Private collection of Gianni Russo)

(Top) Elizabeth Taylor and Gianni Russo. (Private collection of Gianni Russo)

(Left) Gianni Russo with Senator Ted Kennedy. (Private collection of Gianni Russo)

(Below) (Left to right) *The Family Man* cast members Tom McGowan, Nick Cage, Gianni Russo (standing center with trophy), Jeremy Piven, and Joel McKinnon Miller celebrate a bowling victory. (Private collection of Gianni Russo)

Cohen every Jewish epithet imaginable, and cursed his mother loudly enough to draw a crowd.

Cohen was no pushover—to get to his position in mob-controlled Las Vegas, he had to be tough—and he got up in Frank's face.

"What did you call me?" Cohen asked Frank, an obvious threat in his tone.

"You heard me, you kike mother—"

Cohen gave him a solid punch to the mouth, and one of Frank's caps from a front tooth went airborne and he got knocked on his ass.

End of discussion. Frank never asked for credit again.

Frank could be petty at times, too. His daughter, Nancy, had cut a major hit record, "These Boots Were Made for Walkin'," in late 1966, which had gone gold, and Frank was throwing a huge party for her at Caesar's Palace. Everybody who was anybody was invited—major celebrities, heads of state, politicians, mob bosses, literally who was who in Vegas and beyond. Everyone, that is, except me.

I looked for my invitation in the mail. After a few weeks without getting one, I thought maybe it had gotten lost—these things happen—so I called his publicist, who informed me that I wasn't on the guest list. An oversight? I didn't think so.

I made some calls, and discovered that Frank had intentionally left me off the guest list because he thought I might steal some of the attention from his daughter. While I was now known all over town due to my TV show and businesses, and could charm a dead person, I was nowhere near the caliber of guests that could *actually* take the focus off Nancy. With Frank, though, you never knew what was going to piss him off, real or imagined.

I decided to have some fun with the snub, and *really* get Frank pissed at me.

I found out that the only invited guests who hadn't RSVP'd were Aristotle and Jackie Onassis, and I assumed they never would. I called Frank's office, disguised my voice, and RSVP'd for them, confirming their appearance at Nancy's party. I added that the Onassises would be arriving by helicopter.

I was planning a prank to end all pranks.

Dr. Elias Ghanem was a well-known doctor to the stars in Vegas. Among his patients were Liberace, the Osmonds, Ann-Margret, Tim Conway, Johnny Cash, and Glen Campbell. His most famous patient, Elvis Presley, nicknamed him "Dr. Feelgood." Elvis always looked forward to seeing Ghanem because the good doctor shot him up with so much meth, he could function for days without sleep or food. Dr. Ghanem also owned Air Avia, a local charter fixed-wing and helicopter airline. In a few years, it would be one of Ghanem's planes that was transporting Frank Sinatra's mother, Dolly, when it crashed into a mountain, killing all aboard.

I prevailed upon the good doctor, who was a frequent visitor to my jewelry shop, to let me borrow one of his helicopters and a pilot for about an hour on the night of Nancy's party.

"What do you need it for?" he asked.

"A surprise."

I had a replica of the Onassis logo made in a local print shop and slapped it on the chopper. The night of the party, I bought two dozen roses and had them gold-plated and placed in a long gift box. After donning an outrageous leather outfit complete with cape—I looked like someone out of a Victorian-era movie—I scooped up the roses, boarded the chopper, and made for the party. I was going to be fashionably late.

I had previously called Angelo, the maître d' in the room at Caesar's Palace where the party was going to be held, and told him that Ari and Jackie Onassis required a ringside table. "And make sure it's as close to the stage as possible," I'd said.

D-day had arrived.

The pilot hovered over the Caesar's Palace parking lot briefly before landing.

Two hotel security men were standing under the rotating helicopter blades when I got off the aircraft with six of my own security people.

"Where're the Onassises?" one of the hotel guards asked.

"On the way. We're security. Gonna do a quick sweep, make sure everything's jake."

They didn't bother to ask why I was dressed from head to toe in leather and sporting a cape that Batman would have been proud of.

My entourage and I made for the hotel entrance amid a throng of press and fans who were waiting to get a glimpse of someone famous. They'd have to settle for me and my goons.

I draped the cape over my forearm and brought it in front of my face, looking like Dracula. I cradled the box of roses in my other arm.

I barged into the party room as my security fanned out by the door. There must've been over a thousand people there, and my timing was perfect. The festivities were about to begin.

Everyone's attention was riveted to the front as Frank Sinatra escorted his daughter across the stage to a blinding explosion of camera flashes.

The cape still shielding my face, I leaped onto the "Onassis table" and jumped onto the stage, no more than three feet from father and daughter. Frank looked as if he'd been caught with his pants down in a convent—wide-eyed, his jaw dropping. Nancy just stared at me.

I showed my face, smiled broadly, and handed Nancy the flowers. She said something, but that has been lost to the years.

I thought Frank was going to have a stroke when he saw my face. His eyes bulged and he took a step toward me. I had just enough time to take a bow to the now-cheering audience before jumping off the stage and running like hell toward the exit, where I was encircled by my guards.

As I broke out of the hotel and out into the night air, my security team scattered, as instructed, while I jumped into the first cab in the queue and went back to the Sands.

Frank wasn't the type to call me and give me hell; if he was pissed at you, you were frozen out of his inner circle, his rationale being that to be shunned by Ol' Blue Eyes was the kiss of death socially and financially. Frank could blacklist a person with a few phone calls. I didn't think that was going to happen to me, so I waited for his ire to dissipate.

I was passing through the Galleria Bar in Caesar's a few weeks after Nancy's party, and I saw Frank sitting at a table with his New York buddy Jilly Rizzo. Frank would hold court at the Galleria after he rose at the crack of noon, conferring with friends. Spotting me, he said, "Hey, asshole!"

Frank could have a vicious temper when confronted, and I didn't want this chance meeting to escalate into another Carl Cohen scenario, so I went up to him and played the friendship card.

"Hey, Frank . . . we've been friends for a long time. You gonna let my half-ass prank ruin that?" Truthfully, if I'd known he'd hold a grudge for that silly prank, I'd never have done it.

Sinatra was cordial after my mea culpa, but I knew he was still aggravated with me.

Frank and I would remain friends, but it took a while for him to get over my little joke. Frank was a practical joker himself, and I'd assumed he'd handle my antics better, but I guess when it came to his daughter's special night, he had thin skin.

I was spending at least half my time in L.A. seeing to mob business, most of it involving the stagehands' union. I hung out in the Candy Store, which was a run-of-the-mill candy store until 11:00 P.M., when it became a private club until sunrise. Sinatra, Dean Martin, and Sammy Davis, Jr., among other Hollywood heavies, were also fixtures there.

I'd get warmed up for the nightlife at the Beverly Wilshire Hotel bar. It was there that I met the infamous Swifty Morgan, aka "the Lemon Drop Kid" (he was never without a bag of lemon drop candy).

Swifty was a con man, thief, and robber of legendary reputation. When I met him, he was well into his sixties, and was always dressed nattily—custom suit, shirt, and shoes. His ties were hand-painted and

Italian in origin. All this splash on a guy who might measure five foot two hanging by his thumbs. But his physical stature came nowhere near his reputation as the best at what he did, where he soared.

Swifty made his name ripping off none other than Al Capone when Al was the most powerful, ruthless gangster in the country. Swifty borrowed two thousand dollars from him and never paid it back. He should've just shot himself in the head after he took the money, because Capone was pissed—not because of the money, but because he had been made a fool of. He was Al Capone and no fucking dwarf was going to rip *him* off.

Capone ran into Swifty a few years later, and he was still fuming. When Capone asked Swifty why he'd stolen the money from him, Swifty said, "Because I could."

Capone burst out laughing, saying he admired the balls on the little guy, and from that day forward, Swifty Morgan couldn't spend a dime in Chicago. He had free run of the city, courtesy of Al Capone.

The legend of the Lemon Drop Kid grew, and when he got old and too well known to apply his trade, he was taken care of financially by the likes of Frank Sinatra, who would fly him to all his shows, and Lew Wasserman, top-tier talent agent and the president of MCA. Wasserman took care of Swifty because Chicago told him to; Wasserman and the Outfit went back to the Capone era. Swifty would hold court in the Beverly Wilshire, where he lived for free until the day he died.

I've been a movie buff all my life. When I was hospitalized with polio as a kid, I missed out on going to the movies because I was basically held captive at Bellevue. Upon my release, a whole new world opened up for me; the movies drew me into a fantasy world where I could lose myself for a few hours, and I would attend as often as I could.

The old Paramount Theatre on Broadway between Forty-third and Forty-fourth streets was open 24/7, showing movies around the clock except when live shows were scheduled. After leaving the Tommy Dorsey Orchestra in 1942, Frank went with the Benny Goodman Orchestra and made his debut performance at the Paramount. It's still being talked about. He did eleven shows a day, beginning at 8:30 A.M. in the morning and finishing up at 2:30 A.M. the next day. The Paramount and Sinatra are synonymous.

It was a huge theater, with over 3,500 seats. I'd go to see a picture at all hours, whenever I had a chance. It didn't even matter so much what was playing; I admired the acting craft, and I'd fantasize of one day becoming an actor. Even as a kid, I knew the odds of that happening were next to zero, but the fantasy got me through some hard times.

Then I read *The Godfather*, by Mario Puzo.

The book took the publishing world by storm when it hit the stands in March 1969. I devoured it. I saw people I knew in real life portrayed as fictional characters in the story. The Godfather: Frank Costello; the fictional Johnny Fontane: Frank Sinatra, and most of the other characters were familiar to me as guys I'd known since I'd been in the life.

Then I read somewhere that Hollywood was going to make the book into a movie and that they were looking to cast unknown actors in major parts. In the acting trade, I was so unknown, I was damn near invisible. I had a new goal in life: I was going to make it my mission to get a part in that movie—no matter what it took.

I had opened up a club in the Frank Costello–owned Tropicana Hotel in Vegas. Called Tiffany's, it operated from midnight to 6:00 A.M. I'd lock it down at sunup and head to the airport for the short flight to L.A. to work on getting in the new *Godfather* movie. Sometimes I'd stay a few days, but there were times I'd make the round-trip in a day to be back at my club when I had to be there.

I was seeing less and less of Susan, which added to an increasingly tumultuous relationship. I should never have gotten married, and I'd done so impetuously. I wanted kids, and I was about to have one; Susan was pregnant. But right now, my focus was on getting a part in *The Godfather.* Maybe my soon-to-be-born child might have an Academy Award winner as a dad. I was always a person who went for the gold.

With every one of my business ventures a success, my ego grew, unabated. I didn't think landing a role in a highly anticipated movie would be a problem. An ego is good, unreasonable expectations not so much, but I never was able to admit that anything I went after was unreasonable, and I think this was what led to many of my business successes. When I wanted something, I was a pit bull; once I grabbed ahold of a goal, I never gave up until I realized it. I wanted the role of either Michael or Sonny, the sons of Don Corleone, or that of Carlo Rizzi, the evil son-in-law who was instrumental in getting Sonny whacked, and I had a master plan to land one of those parts.

I decided to film my own screen test. To that end, I put together a nonunion film crew, hired a film editor, and a guy I knew contributed a can of 16mm film.

A star is born.

We filmed in the studio where I did my TV show. The first scene I shot had me in the Michael Corleone role, reacting to his father—the Godfather—being shot while grocery shopping. In the next scene, I was Carlo Rizzi, getting the crap kicked out of me for beating up the Corleones' sister, Connie. In the final scene, I was Sonny, sitting in on a meeting with the drug dealer Sollozzo, who was trying to convince Don Corleone to invest in his drug business.

I thought I'd done a pretty credible acting job, but I'd have thought that even if I'd done the scenes with a bag over my head. My ego told me I was a natural; what could possibly go wrong? Plenty, it turned out.

When I viewed the edited scenes, I saw everything was tinged in a mild brown hue. I was pissed. I'd spent a ton of money putting the reel together and now I was looking at what appeared to be an amateur attempt. I sought out the guy who gave me the film and played the reel for him.

"What the fuck's with the brown color?" I asked.

"That's sepia," he said.

"What?"

"Not brown . . . sepia. The film was older than I thought, I guess," he said sheepishly. "But, hey, it looks cool, no?"

"Brown, sepia, who gives a rat's ass? And cool? Whaddaya mean, 'cool'?"

"Look," he said. "The scenes are supposed to take place in the 1940s, right? After the war? The sepia tone gives them a retro look. I think it looks great."

I thought about it, and viewed the reel again. "I dunno, but you may be right. I'll let you know how I make out."

Pookie Newman was a friend of mine, and she was also legendary director Darryl Zanuck's secretary, and as such she knew everyone worth knowing in Hollywood. One such contact was Betty McCart, who was Al Ruddy's secretary. Ruddy was the producer of the hit TV show *Hogan's Heroes*, but he had just been tapped as a producer of the new *Godfather* picture.

Betty called and told me that Ruddy was getting bombarded with requests from actors who wanted to be in the movie, and that I needed to make myself noticed to bring my name to his attention.

"The screen-test reel isn't enough? Which unknown actor does that? Shit, which *known* actor does that?" I said.

"This movie is breaking all the rules," Betty said. "We've got actors showing up in zoot suits, Spencer Tracy fedoras, and with toy machine guns. You've gotta do something different to get Al's attention."

I thought about this for a moment. "What're his favorite things?"

"That's easy," she said. "Flashy cars and Asian women . . . preferably Chinese."

The wheels in my head began to spin.

I already had the flashy car, a four-year-old Bentley. Everywhere I went, the car turned heads; it wasn't a stretch to think it would impress Al Ruddy. As far as the Chinese girl, I lived in Vegas, where pretty girls were the rule rather than the exception. I found a gorgeous Chinese showgirl at the Tropicana named Chyna, who made knockout actress Lucy Liu look like Keye Luke, the actor who played Charlie Chan's number-one son. I gave her five hundred dollars and her marching orders.

On the day in question, Betty McCart got us a drive-on pass to the Paramount lot, where Al Ruddy maintained an office. My Chinese beauty, Chyna, behind the wheel of my detailed Bentley, drove to Ruddy's office dressed in clothes skimpy enough to have gotten her arrested in a Las Vegas whorehouse. Betty arranged a quick meeting between my China doll and Ruddy, who gladly accepted the package with my screen-test reel, which was wrapped in the *The Godfather* book cover, along with Chyna's phone number.

The next day, I got a call from Al Ruddy, who was extremely gracious and flattering before I even had a chance to get past "Hello."

My bad-news meter was on full tilt.

"Listen, Gianni," Ruddy said. "Your tape was excellent. I can see you went through a lot of time and expense making it"—I saw a *but* coming here—"but I'm sorry you were given erroneous information."

"What do you mean?" My heart had already sunk below my testicles.

"Whoever told you we were looking at unknown actors was mistaken. . . ."

"I read it in one of the trades," I said.

"Well, believe less of what you read or hear in this town, unless it comes from the horse's mouth, and in this case, I'm the horse. You'd have been great in this movie in any role, but we're looking for union actors with . . . well, some experience. The budget for this movie necessitates we get proven talent for the major roles as a draw."

Some small talk followed, but when all was said and done, I didn't get *any* part, let alone one of the three that I had wanted. My grand plan collapsed like a day-old soufflé, and I was depressed. The last time I recalled feeling like this was when I was dropped off at the polio ward at Bellevue Hospital by my mother in 1949.

Just when I was psychologically accepting the fact that I was never going to be the next Humphrey Bogart, the mob blew up the main gates to the Paramount lot, and I saw another opportunity.

The mob, in the form of Joe Columbo, the boss of the crime family that bore his name, had created the Italian American Anti-Defamation League in the spring of 1970, after one of his sons was arrested on a federal extortion charge. Columbo formed the league as an action group against what he saw as unjustified labeling of Italian-Americans as gangsters. For a guy who was attempting to debunk the Mafia "myth," he seemed to be going about it the wrong way. Columbo structured the league like a Cosa Nostra crime family; the more money you raised for the cause, the higher a position you attained in the league. For example, if you sold a mountain of league buttons at a buck apiece, you were made a capo, which is the mob rank of captain. There was a mob book out at the time by *New York Daily News* reporter Jimmy Breslin, entitled *The Gang That Couldn't Shoot Straight.* I called the league "The Gang That Couldn't Think Straight."

The league soon gained national attention, and the ire of the bosses of the Commission, who reminded Columbo that La Cosa Nostra was a *secret* organization and to part company with the league. Columbo ignored this sage advice and would live to regret that decision. For now, however, the league latched onto the new *Godfather* picture as an example of the stereotyping of Italian-Americans.

While I was self-absorbed and trying to land a role in the picture, Columbo was telling executives from Paramount Pictures to cease and desist with their plan to bring *The Godfather* to the big screen. Some low-level wiseguys, not connected with Columbo, had Coppola's custom Cinemobile stolen right off the streets of Little Italy as a message, which in part was "You have some balls coming into our neighborhood without permission and shooting your fucking movie." The oversized vehicle was jammed with millions of dollars' worth of film equipment, plus both sides were emblazoned with the *Godfather* movie logo and was in the neighborhood scouting potential locations. No one saw anything; the vehicle just vanished. It was returned a few hours later, and it was thought that the movie people had gotten the message, which was that certain people in the neighborhood would have to be paid before Coppola would be allowed to film in Little Italy. Apparently, the studio big shots didn't take what they considered a prank seriously and were proceeding with preproduction.

Since the vanishing Cinemobile stunt didn't work to solve the problem, someone in Joe Columbo's crew sent a different message—a loud one—by having the iconic mammoth steel gates at the entrance to the Paramount lot blown up. In the middle of the night, a box loaded with dynamite with a short fuse was attached to the gate, and the resulting explosion reverberated throughout the neighborhood. The studio got this message this time and woke up; they knew something had to be done to salvage their picture.

Enter Gianni Russo, negotiator extraordinaire.

After the bombing, mob bosses summoned Joe Columbo to a suite at the Waldorf. The bosses were incensed that Columbo, a boss himself, had allowed the bombing, knowing full well that Tony Accardo had been controlling the film industry for years, and in that role had promised labor peace, guaranteeing that everything in Tinseltown would run smoothly. I think some low-level associate, or more likely a league flunky, blew the gates on his own to impress Columbo. Joe, not being stupid, wouldn't have done something so foolish. Regardless, the assembled group held him responsible because the league had been his idea and he ran the day-to-day operations.

Accardo, indignant due to the breach of etiquette, had called Frank Costello, inquiring as to why Mr. C. couldn't control his people.

In attendance were high-ranking bosses, including a rare appearance by Frank Costello. Mr. C. shied away from publicity and meeting with mob bosses except in the most extreme of circumstances, this being one of them. I attended with him.

This time, they weren't going to try to convince Columbo to distance himself from the league; they were going to order it.

Aniello "Neil" Dellacroce, a highly respected elder statesman with the Gambino family, sat Columbo down and spoke to him like a father.

"Joe, you're going to hand over the day-to-day operation of the league to someone who's not with us. This is not a request. This bombing, it's no good; your people are running wild. You're bringing heat. Every time I turn on a TV, I see your face in front of the FBI building, leading pickets. Today it stops."

Everyone else at the meeting echoed Neil. This was as close to an intervention, mob-style, as I would ever witness.

Costello told Columbo, "Remember how you got here, Joe. You're a boss. You should lead by example. This league is an embarrassment, and worse, it's not how a boss should conduct himself."

The drubbing went on for over an hour, and Columbo sat and took it; he had little choice. He was respectful, saying he would take care of the problem, but I could see in his eyes and tone that he had no intention of giving up the league. He was getting more attention from the media than anyone deserved and he was loving it, saying in his latest TV sound bite that the FBI acronym stood for Forever Bothering Italians.

Joe Columbo didn't enjoy a very good reputation in mob circles. He was a captain in the now-nonexistent Profaci family when he went to Carlo Gambino, telling the Gambino boss that family boss Joe Profaci and the Genovese family boss, Vito Genovese, were going to make a move on Gambino and take over his family.

The Profaci family was broken up, Genovese backed off with his tail between his legs, and, as a reward, Joe Columbo was given permission to take over what was formerly the Profaci family.

While Carlo Gambino, boss of the biggest family in the country, was grateful for the heads-up, the bottom line was that Joe Columbo had betrayed his own boss by coming forward to Gambino. Being a rat doesn't sit well for someone's reputation.

No one was happy when the meeting broke up. It was evident to me that Columbo had chosen his path and wasn't going to back away from it, despite having said he was going to take a backseat in the league.

I didn't know what the bosses were going to do, take a "wait and see" stance, or take more drastic measures. Whatever decision was going to be made, it was well above my pay grade, and I did what I did best: kept my mouth shut and went with the flow.

Betty McCart told me that the movers and shakers behind *The Godfather*—Stanley Jaffe (president of Paramount), Robert Evans (producer and head of production at Paramount), Gray Frederickson (producer and investor in the movie), and Charlie Bluhdorn (controlling stockholder in Gulf & Western, of which Paramount Pictures was a subholding)—were flying to New York as she spoke to try to straighten out the burgeoning problem with Joe Columbo.

"Who are they meeting with?" I asked Betty.

"Barry Slotnick, the lawyer for Columbo's league, invited them to New York for talks." Betty said. "They're in panic mode; too much money already spent preproduction and they can see it all going to shit. They'll be in the Gulf building tomorrow morning, hoping someone will come up with some kind of plan. Bottom line is, they wanted to get out of L.A. and go to where the problem is."

I was on the red-eye flight to New York right behind them.

I went straight from LaGuardia Airport to the Gulf & Western Building on Columbus Circle, on the southern end of Central Park. I had a plan, albeit a risky one, that would make both sides happy.

Bluhdorn's office was on the thirty-third floor, but I decided to wait in the lobby. Eventually, I figured, someone from the group would pass my way. Going to Bluhdorn's office didn't seem appropriate. Let them frustrate themselves for a few hours before I came to the rescue.

A little after eleven o'clock, I saw Al Ruddy getting out of an elevator.

To say he was surprised to see me would be an understatement.

"Hey, Gianni. What the hell are you doing here?"

I ushered him aside and sat him down in a lobby chair.

"I'm here to save your investment."

"What?"

"You want to make this movie?"

"Of course," Ruddy said.

"Well, you need to cooperate," I said.

"That's why we're here. We're trying to reach out to Columbo through Barry Slotnick."

I shook my head. "You need to cooperate with labor, carpenters' and electricians' unions, not only Columbo. This is New York; all the unions are mobbed up." I was making the problem worse than it was, and I could see Ruddy go pale at the thought of dealing with a bunch of people with their palms outstretched. He was out of his element.

"Jesus," he said. "What the fuck are we going to do?"

Just the response I was waiting for. "I can bring everyone together," I said matter-of-factly. A bold statement, to be sure. While I knew most of the players on the mob side, I had very little juice, because I wasn't a made guy and had never belonged to any one particular family. I was going to take a flier on sheer balls, appealing to the mob's greed.

"You can do that?"

"Hell, yeah," I said. "I guarantee it."

I worked the phone for hours, dropping names of people I didn't know and getting past secretaries by mentioning Betty McCart's name. I was exhausted, still on West Coast time, but catching some sleep was out of the question. I had to strike and strike fast, convincing both sides I knew the other side well enough to pull off a settlement that would make the side I was currently talking to come out ahead.

The next day, I brought both factions to the table in Bluhdorn's office. Bluhdorn was willing to talk with anyone who could help get the picture made, and I told him I fit that description.

On the mob side was Joe Columbo, his top lieutenant, Fat Anthony, and two capos: "Butterass" DeCicco (so named because his ass was as big as a cow's) and his brother "Boozy" DeCicco (so named because he liked the occasional drink). With them was attorney Barry Slotnick, who had coaxed the movie honchos from L.A.

The debate went on for hours. Columbo was adamant that terms like *guinea, wop, greaseball,* and the like would not be mentioned in the movie. Also, the names Mafia and La Cosa Nostra were verboten. The movie people envisioned their gritty, authentic script would wind up sounding like an episode of the Hardy Boys Meet Nancy Drew.

As the talks dragged into the afternoon, we were looking at an impasse.

Finally, someone called for a break and I corralled Columbo on the side. After listening to his bluster for hours, I thought I knew how to handle him.

"Joe," I said, "you're in control here. You can make this movie happen, and go down in history as a great American."

"You think?"

Playing to Columbo's ego was definitely the way to go. "Absolutely, and I'll tell you what else. I'll arrange to get prints of the picture ahead of time and you can have showings across the country at private venues and make a ton of money."

I held no sway in the industry, but it sounded like a reasonable proposal. Columbo could look like a big shot in the Italian community in a few cities across the country and have *his* premiere before the official one. I was playing to Columbo's greed and ego. Columbo was pondering all this as the meeting reconvened, but I was confident a deal would be made.

In the end, the movie people promised that nothing derogatory regarding Italians would be in the movie (I had to explain to Columbo what the word *derogatory* meant), and that Columbo would get advance prints to bolster his reputation among the Italians he'd been championing with the league. He would also show his constituents that he had enough juice to make a movie that was fair to the Italian heritage.

I'd get some advance prints myself and hold screenings on Staten Island for a Down syndrome charity, and one at Marlon Brando's son Christian's school.

Any disagreements as to content during filming would be rectified before the shooting continued, which meant Columbo would have to see the shooting script. He would have a few complaints, particularly regarding the scene where Carlo beat up his wife, Connie Corleone. And, of course, there would be parts for any wiseguy who wanted one, but it would be up to the director as to who got what part. I knew these guys could be placated with roles as extras—something they could brag about to their grandchildren. There were also some parts that would go to professional actors who were connected by blood, marriage, or friendship to the mob.

The Godfather was going to be made. Everyone shook hands, and chairs started to shuffle as the parties got ready to leave.

I leaned into Columbo. "Hey, Joe, what about me?"

"Oh, yeah," Columbo said, almost as an afterthought. He raised his hand like a schoolkid. "Hey, before we go . . . what're we gonna do for my boy here?" He jerked a thumb in my direction. "Wasn't for him, you wouldn't be making your picture."

Bob Evans, in motion and almost at the door, said, "Yeah, we'll give him something."

I wasn't about to let anyone out of the room until I got what I wanted.

Rising quickly from my seat, I said to Evans, "Hold it up, Bobby. No one goes anywhere until it's decided here and now what part I'll be playing."

You could've heard a dead body drop. The movie people didn't want to make a fuss and upset the wiseguys, and the wiseguys seemed to like my display of testicular fortitude because it showed "our side" to be in charge.

Everyone sat down. And the debate began.

At this point in preproduction, the part of Michael Corleone had just gone to an up-and-comer named Al Pacino, who had appeared, to rave reviews, in the picture *Panic in Needle Park,* and whom Coppola pushed hard for the part, on the premise that the Michael role should go to someone who didn't fit the Mafia stereotype (*"Michael's a fucking war hero, not a gangster!").* The part was originally supposed to have belonged to James Caan, but after Pacino got it, Caan was given the part of Sonny. Carmine Caridi, a veteran character actor, who was supposed to play Sonny, was now booted from any major part in the picture that would have him in the same scene as Pacino. Caridi was very tall and would make Pacino, who was on the short side, look like a midget. Caridi was tossed a bone, a part in the new movie *The Gang That Couldn't Shoot Straight,* an adaptation of the Jimmy Breslin novel.

"So, there's still the Carlo Rizzi part, right?" I said.

I know the producers agreed to this grudgingly, but they had little choice. Joe Columbo said, "Either the Kid gets the part or you'll be shooting your fucking movie on the moon."

The deal settled, I needed to get my Screen Actors Guild (SAG) card, which would allow me to appear in a union-sanctioned picture. Most actors wait years for their coveted SAG card; I got mine in about two hours

I was beyond thrilled. I had pulled off the deal allowing *The Godfather* to be filmed with nothing more than sheer bravado. Now I had to prove myself. I had no professional acting experience, but I had survived on the streets of New York, and made my way into the inner circle of the mob without getting myself killed, which required acting ability and a cool head.

A police officer friend of mine once told me, "You guys are like us;

we both need to be consummate actors to survive on the street or we're fucking dead."

I wasn't facing death on a movie set, but I'd have to convince some well-respected actors that I deserved to be in the picture, and I knew that wasn't going to be easy.

6

ON THE SET OF *THE GODFATHER*: ALWAYS LOOKING TO MAKE A SCORE

All the main actors, myself included, moved into the Park Lane Hotel, located on Central Park South, except Marlon Brando, who chose the Hotel Elysée on East Fifty-fourth Street. It wasn't because he thought he was special—well, maybe a little special—but because he liked the Monkey Bar, which was located in the hotel.

I had driven cross-country in my Bentley with Chyna, the Chinese bombshell I'd used to deliver my screen test to Al Ruddy. She was too hot to send back to the Tropicana chorus line and would make a great roommate. Susan and I were practically strangers. My daughter, Carmen, had been born and I doted on her, but Susan and I weren't going to make it. We both knew we'd done the wrong thing by getting married when we hardly knew each other. Susan was a nice person, but there was no love there. I'm sure she felt the same about me.

The word had gotten out that the cast of the picture would be staying at the Park Lane, and once shooting began, we were greeted every morning by a mob of fans in front of the hotel. *Godfather* fever was gripping the city in a big way. Anything *Godfather*-related was getting stolen daily, the most prized items being anything emblazoned with a *Godfather* logo. Clothing used in the picture and other personal items got feet. If it wasn't nailed down, it was gone.

During preproduction, we would meet for full-cast table reads to acclimate ourselves to one another and the story, and work through any problems. These were informal readings, set in an informal location.

The director, Francis Ford Coppola, chose Patsy's Pizzeria on First Avenue in East Harlem for the table reads. It had been at the same location since 1933, when the area was predominantly Italian, and deserved its reputation as a premier neighborhood pizza joint. And most important, it had a private back room, where we wouldn't be disturbed. What better joint to rehearse an epic gangster movie?

So, what does one wear to a table reading? It really made little difference to me, because I was always well dressed. That first day, I was wearing one of my many Brioni suits. Why bring this up? Because I was in the company of people who, no matter what their acting reputations or wealth, dressed liked they had just rolled out of bed, except for Diane Keaton, who looked like a bag lady. Sterling Hayden's uniform of the day consisted of dirty jeans, a T-shirt, and engineer boots, with unkempt hair down to his shoulders. The rest of the cast was equally "informal." I felt like a tuxedo in a sea of brown shoes, but I cared little. Being well turned out is who I am, and always will be. I did get some odd looks, however.

There was a long table set up, and seating was arranged by order of character importance, with Brando at the head. Francis had everyone introduce themselves by name and character, beginning with Brando. Next, Francis asked that we begin reading our parts in order as they appeared in the script.

"No acting at this point, just read," he said. "Except you genuine Italians. I want you to exaggerate your speech, colloquialisms, and hand gestures. Everyone else pay attention."

There was a pizza break, and most of the actors wanted to talk to Brando, who was a living legend. All the featured players would go on to become huge stars, but at the time they were just kick-starting their careers. To be able to corral Brando for a little acting advice, and to brownnose a little, seemed to be the order of the day. I held back out of respect. I might have landed the plum role—and first role—of my life, but I was under no illusions as to my acting ability. I felt grateful to be in the picture, and I was there to soak up everything I could. To that end, I was going to keep my mouth shut and observe.

Marlon Brando had other ideas. Instead of commiserating with his fellow thespians, he cornered me and hit me with a bunch of questions.

"You're a big movie actor?"

I shook my head. "Nope."

"Television?"

Again, I told him, "No."

"Who'd you study with?" Brando asked.

"Study what?" I had no idea what he was talking about.

Brando finally realized that I had zero experience in the acting game. I could tell he was upset. He turned to Francis Ford Coppola.

"Francis, this guy," he said, pointing at me, "marries my daughter, sells out the family, and is instrumental in getting my boy Sonny killed. This part needs to be given to an experienced actor. You should reconsider who has this part."

The room went silent. I was seething and I didn't give a fuck who this guy was, I was going after him.

I put my arm around Brando—which turned out to be something you didn't do, in addition to no eye contact—and ushered him to a corner.

I got right in his face but kept my voice subdued. "Who the fuck're you to try to do this to me? I'll cut your fucking heart out, you rat motherfucker. I'm part of this picture whether you like it or not, you cocksucker." I was this close to decking him. How humiliating would it be if I got dumped, particularly after the massive party my friends threw for me in Vegas?

Brando stared at me for what seemed like a minute.

"What?" I finally said in a threatening tone.

"Man, you're fucking good," he said. "I take back what I said. You've got great acting chops."

Holy shit, I couldn't believe it! Brando thought I was acting! This was the first day of a friendship with Brando that would last until he died. Full credit would go to Frank Sinatra, who would teach me how to sing and help me launch a singing career. And I will forever be indebted to Marlon Brando, who taught me how to act. He coached me every chance he got. I learned from the master.

"Hey, by the way," Brando said, "is that your Bentley out front?"

"Yeah," I said, my anger now totally deflated, "it's mine. You like it?"

"It's a Bentley; what's not to like? But I like your driver better." I'd come to learn that Brando liked exotic women.

Chyna was dutifully waiting for me behind the wheel of the car until the workday ended.

"Come with me," I said. "I'll introduce you." Chyna would wind up moving in with Brando at his hotel, and he would later take her to one of the Tahitian islands that he owned. She had asked me if it was all right to move into Brando's hotel room. I told her I was fine with it. To my way of thinking, beautiful women weren't a rare commodity, but there was only one Marlon Brando. He'd be more valuable to me and my future than Chyna would ever be. I got a new driver, Pat Ruffalo, an actor who played a wiseguy in the picture, and who welcomed the chance to earn some extra money.

From that day forward, until we wrapped the movie, I would pick Brando up at the Elysée every morning for the ride to whatever location we were shooting at that day, and he'd coach me on my part. We'd go back and forth, with Brando reading every part opposite me. He was invaluable to my learning the craft. In the evening, we'd go to the Monkey Bar at his hotel and we'd role-play for hours. We'd not only run through the script but he'd hit me with improvisational scenarios off the top of his head and we'd go with it.

Every day my confidence increased, until I felt as comfortable as I was going to get around the professionals.

One morning, Ruffalo and I picked up Brando and we headed to Patsy's. As we drove north on Park Avenue, Ruffalo said, "We've got company."

In the lane next to us was a station wagon with Robert Duvall and

Jimmy Caan in the backseat. The window was rolled down and Caan had his naked ass shoved out the window, shooting us a classic moon. It was still pretty early, but it was daylight and there was enough traffic on the road for everyone to see what was going on.

Both cars drove side by side up Park Avenue for quite a distance, with Jimmy Caan's naked butt as my visual. Mooning became the sport of choice during the filming, with actors trying to outdo one another with the audaciousness of their exhibitionism.

I was more comfortable as preproduction progressed. As the actors became more familiar with one another, we'd go out every night for a few—make that quite a few—drinks. Usually the watering hole of choice was the Monkey Bar, in deference to Brando, but we barhopped, too.

One thing I discovered about actors over the years: Despite their fame or wealth, they were the cheapest people I'd ever met. When the check came, they began to disappear or have sudden urges to go to the bathroom. I could give a pass to the younger actors in *The Godfather*; this was their first major picture and they had been struggling in their craft for years and had little money. They weren't making a helluva lot to appear in this picture, either. Brando's salary was one million dollars, but the rest of the cast got considerably less, myself included. I was only paid seventeen thousand dollars, but I figured I didn't deserve any more. But Brando never put his hand in his pocket—ever—reminding anyone who would listen that he was broke and the picture had bailed him out of some serious debt.

I picked up most of the checks and did it without bitching. I'd been overly generous all my life and enjoyed seeing people having a good time. There wasn't a morning I didn't get up when the first thought that came to my mind was how lucky I was to be in *The Godfather*. I spent money and enjoyed doing it.

The table reads went for over a week, after which we went into full rehearsal mode.

While this was going on, Frank Sinatra went on a crusade, calling everyone he knew in Hollywood and asking them not to accept the role of singer Johnny Fontane if it was offered to them, and certainly not to pursue the role. He was fighting mad, in that he considered the character a bad rip-off of himself, and used all of his considerable power to coerce, threaten, and cajole anyone even remotely thinking of taking the part.

When singer Al Martino read for and was offered the part, Frank was livid. When all manner of flattery and promises of Frank's help with Al's career didn't work, Frank resorted to threats. The threats had worked on Vic Damone, another great singer of that time, who had been offered the Fontane part, but Martino told Frank to go fuck himself, saying he was taking the part because it was the role of a lifetime.

Frank was desperate by this time, and decided to sabotage the entire picture. He called me, and began using the friendship card.

"You're a friend of mine, right, Gianni?" He didn't wait for an answer. "I'm asking you as a friend to bow out of the picture. I don't want it made. You'll do that for me? I'll get you any part you want, kid," he said, "just dump this part. I'll owe you big-time."

I was blindsided by the call, totally unprepared for it. In a moment of weakness, and with a desire to patch things up after I'd crashed his daughter's party in Vegas—which he was still seething about—I told him I'd quit the picture.

I regretted my decision. For the next three days, I ruminated about how I was going to tell Frank that I'd changed my mind, until I came up with what I thought was a reasonable explanation for doing so. I also knew it would piss him off at me even more than he already was, but I thought asking me to dump a chance of a lifetime to stroke his ego was selfish. I called him.

"You're a friend of mine, right, Frank?" I said, choosing to use his opening line from a few days ago. There was silence on the other end. I think he knew where this was going. "Suppose," I said, "I'd have called you when you got the part in *From Here to Eternity*, you know, the part that won you an Oscar?" I thought bringing that up was a nice touch. "Would you have quit that movie if I'd have asked you to?"

He hung up on me.

My refusal to bend to his pressure put a serious strain on our relationship, which had already seen a few bumps in the road after his daughter Nancy's party at Caesar's Palace.

With mob influence, the remaining cast was hired. Al Lettieri, who played vicious heroin peddler Sollozzo, was married to Thomas ("Tommy Ryan") Eboli's sister. Eboli was front boss for the Genovese crime family and had a lock on gambling machines on the East Coast. Lenny Montana, who played the slow-witted enforcer Luca Brasi, was a real-life enforcer and arsonist for the Columbo crime family, and a professional wrestler. The memorable scene where the Luca Brasi character is talking to himself, rehearsing the speech he is going to make to Don Corleone during his daughter's wedding, was actually a real rehearsal, with Montana going over his lines prior to his part being shot. Unbeknownst to Montana, Coppola had Montana's rambling rehearsal included in the movie.

Coppola, it should be noted, was afraid of the real wiseguys in the movie and steered clear of them. In fact, most of the antics in the wedding scene were ad-libbed, with Coppola giving total freedom for anyone and everyone to improvise. Or as he famously put it, "Do what you'd do at a real Italian wedding," which to everyone meant get loaded, be loud, and enjoy yourselves. Even Mama Corleone, played by singer Morgana King, broke into her wedding song, which wasn't scripted.

The results are movie history.

All the actors playing gangsters who are seated at Don Barzini's table during Carlo and Connie's wedding were, in fact, real Columbo soldiers who got their parts per the agreement between Columbo and Francis Ford Coppola to include real-life gangsters in the movie.

One Saturday night, I decided to go to Jilly's, an infamous watering hole on the East Side, owned by Sinatra's best friend, Jilly Rizzo. The joint catered to a diverse crowd: entertainers, wiseguys, politicians, and locals.

When Sinatra was in town, he was a fixture at Jilly's, and Jilly Rizzo often joined Frank on the road. I'd run into him often in Vegas. He and Frank were joined at the hip.

I was at the packed bar with wiseguys Tommy Bilotti and Boozy DeCicco, having a few drinks. Unbeknownst to me, Jimmy Caan was in the back room with Carmine "Junior" Persico, underboss of the Columbo crime family.

Jimmy Caan was a mob buff and wannabe tough guy. He loved hanging out with wiseguys, and would famously attend one of John Gotti's trials, giving sound bites to the press daily. Different strokes. I didn't really care what Jimmy did or how he inflated his substantial ego, and we got along fine until that night, when a lifelong feud was born.

Caan joined us at the bar and I introduced him to Tommy and Boozy.

"Hey, Gianni," Caan said. "Junior's in the back with his daughter. Come back and say hello."

I made my way to the back room. Junior Persico was there with a positively stunning brunette who looked to be about twenty. I was thinking if Junior has this knockout for a daughter, she must've been switched at birth, because the Persicos aren't exactly model-beautiful like this woman was.

I wanted to be respectful and polite, so I complimented his daughter. "Your daughter is beautiful, Junior. You must be very proud." Caan was standing a few feet from me, smiling.

An odd look came over Persico, but I thought little of it, excused myself, and went to the men's room. I was standing at the urinal when two of Persico's gorillas entered and locked the door behind them.

I figured they wanted to use the only urinal, so I said, "Be done in a minute, guys."

I turned to wash my hands, and one of the goons said, "What are you, some kind of fucking wise guy? You insulted Junior."

I was confused. "What the fuck are you talking about?"

"Whaddya mean, what am I talking about? The girl you called his daughter isn't his daughter; she's some fucking snatch."

Persico felt highly insulted that I'd called some random broad his daughter, and he wanted to make me pay for being disrespectful. These guys were going to tune me up. I was in a tight spot. That son of a bitch Caan had set me up, knowing that woman wasn't Junior's daughter. I was fuming. If this was Caan's idea of a joke, I wasn't laughing, and if I was going to get my ass kicked, I was going to do likewise to Caan—after I got out of the hospital.

There was a loud banging at the bathroom door.

"Hey, Gianni, you okay in there?"

It was Tommy Bilotti. Apparently, he'd seen the two goons follow me into the bathroom and he was checking up on me.

"Not really!" I said.

A second later, the door busted off the hinges and Tommy strode in, fists clenched.

One of the goons said to Tommy, "Get the fuck outta here; we're talking."

Tommy Bilotti was one of the toughest guys I knew. He didn't take shit from anyone. Without a word, he clocked the guy closest to him, and the guy hit the floor like a deadweight. He was out for the count. His buddy raised his hands in a defensive motion. "Hey, Tommy . . . no disrespect. The kid insulted Junior."

Tommy was confused. "Gianni? Bullshit. What happened?"

The guy who was still conscious told Tommy what had gone down. I was shaking my head.

"What?" Tommy said to me.

"That fucking Jimmy Caan. His idea of a joke. Lemme go back and explain this to Junior," I said.

While the conscious guy helped the unconscious guy, Tommy,

Boozy, and I went to the back room, where Junior was conferring with an associate. He turned to me with murder in his eyes.

Boozy, a Gambino underboss, said, "I'll talk to him." He and Junior huddled in a corner for a few minutes while I awaited my fate. While I'd been duped into the remark by Caan, there was no telling what Junior might do. He had a vicious temper and might make an example of me just for the hell of it. Finally, I heard Junior say, "Get that asshole Jimmy in here."

Caan was ushered to the back room from the bar. He stood by while there was a big sotto voce conference among Junior, Tommy, and Boozy.

Then Junior said loudly enough for everyone present to hear, "Ah, fuck it. Jimmy made a mistake. I'm gonna forget about it."

Tommy and Boozy wouldn't let it go.

"Hold it, Junior," Tommy said. "You were ready to fuck Gianni up for a comment he made innocently. Jimmy here instigated it. He needs to be taught a lesson."

Jimmy Caan was getting extremely uncomfortable, and I saw fear in his eyes, which were darting about the room, finally settling on the exit door to the bar. Was he going to make a run for it? Tommy wanted to beat the shit out of him and he was scared. It was showing.

It would've been nice to see him get his ass handed to him, because he deserved it, but in the end, I came to his rescue, and not because I was letting bygones be bygones. Jimmy Caan was a valued player in the movie, and if he was laid up in a hospital for a month, the picture might go belly-up, or I might get fired as the guy who'd caused it all. Jimmy Caan might have been an asshole, but he was an important asshole.

The drama came to an end after I spoke up for him, but I had to give him a well-deserved parting dig. "He's a fucking jerkoff," I told Junior. "Give him a break, or he'll shit his pants."

I tried to figure out Caan's motivation for doing what he did. Maybe it was jealousy because I had Brando's ear and he didn't? Or perhaps he was pissed because I'd gotten a major part in the movie with no experience? Maybe he just wanted to be a tough guy and show me he had juice with Junior. The bottom line was, he was made to look like an idiot with no balls.

While the incident was over, the repercussions would reverberate throughout the filming and would culminate in my being injured in a fight scene with Caan, and a grudge created that would never go away.

7

FILMING *THE GODFATHER*

Producer Al Ruddy asked me to go with him to Staten Island to scout locations for the picture's wedding scene. They were looking for a house that would mimic the Corleone compound, which was located on Long Island in the book. Since most of the street scenes were going to be shot in Manhattan, the producers wanted a house within city limits to save money.

Staten Island was the home to quite a few wiseguys, and I knew it well. The Todt Hill and Grymes Hill areas had the type of luxury digs that were built in the 1930s, which was what we were looking for. We found a house on Longfellow Road in the Grymes Hill section, right around the corner from Gambino boss Paul ("Big Paul") Castellano's mansion, known as the "White House."

The Longfellow Road property was perfect for our needs. There were three houses on the property, built by a former Staten Island borough president. Ruddy envisioned one house belonging to Don Corleone, one for son Michael, and one for Carlo after he married Connie Corleone.

I don't know what the production company was willing to pay for a two-week rental, which was how long it would take to shoot the wedding scene, but they got it cheaply. All the owner requested was that the production company pay for a new roof on the main house. He could've held up the producers for a lot more than that, but he certainly wasn't aware how big the budget was for the movie.

In the book, the house was a fortified compound, so the special effects people worked their magic and transformed the main house into a mirror image of how it was described in the book. To that end, an eight-foot wall was constructed of a lightweight plastic, which looked like stone, and encircled the house.

The rooms in the house were deemed inappropriate for what director Francis Ford Coppola envisioned the interior of Don Corleone's home would look like, so rooms were constructed in a studio on Long Island that was owned by comedian Alan King.

A band was needed for the wedding scene. I suggested the Nino Morelli Band, which, coincidentally, had played at my actual wedding, and the producers went for it.

I never realized what went into shooting a movie, but a picture the scope of *The Godfather* required significant logistical planning.

Security had to be tight because fans were trying to sneak onto the set by breaching the phony wall to steal whatever *Godfather* memorabilia wasn't nailed down, and to catch a glimpse of the stars. The NYPD did a great job of providing a hard perimeter around the block, so that problem was alleviated.

Some 750 extras were used in the wedding scene, with days of rehearsals before a final take. These people got thirsty. I worked a deal for myself where I'd sell soda and pocket the profits. I went to Staten Island Community College's theater department and asked for volunteers to serve the soda, and I got more people than I needed who wanted to rub shoulders with real movie stars. I was running through forty-five cases of soda a day, with a seventeen-dollar profit per case for the two weeks it took to shoot the scene. I made about ten grand.

Three wedding cakes were needed for the cake-cutting scene: a real cake, a fake cake, and one that could be sliced. I volunteered to find a bakery that could supply the cakes, and approached a local shop, La Rosa Pastry. I told the owner there was a contest among Staten Island bakers to see who would supply the wedding cakes for the picture. At first, he wasn't interested, but when I told him the winner would have bragging rights as the baker that supplied the wedding cakes for *The Godfather*, with pictures to prove it, he became interested. I told him I'd get back to him in a few days because other bakeries were in the running, too.

There was no contest and no other bakeries were approached. This was me, continuing on my never-ending quest to make money.

I waited a few days, then told the owner of La Rosa that after I'd spoken to the producers, his bakery had been chosen out of all the bakeries on Staten Island to supply the cakes. La Rosa commenced to make the cakes.

The bakery budget for the cakes was fifteen hundred dollars, which I pocketed, along with a two-hundred-dollar "stocking fee" I got from the bakery. I took Polaroids of the finished products, which the owner proudly displayed in his shop.

Obviously, I didn't believe in the starving-actor stereotype.

Finally, after countless rehearsals, the day came to shoot the wedding scene for real. Coppola wanted realism and requested that everyone enjoy themselves. To do that, we needed wine. I supplied that, too.

During the wedding scene, Don Corleone gathers the immediate family for a group picture. As the photographer is about to take the shot, Don Corleone notices that his youngest son, Michael, isn't standing with the group. He says, "Where's Michael?"

While Michael (Al Pacino) was walking into the picture frame, Brando took the opportunity to moon everyone, winning a bet for the person who mooned more people at one time than anyone else. Duvall, Caan, and Brando had made the bet. All the extras, including kids, had Brando's massive naked ass to remember for the rest of their lives. I'm wondering how many of those kids had nightmares, and for how long, and if there's a category of PTSD that includes being exposed to a wrinkled ass?

This was our acting intelligentsia, the cream that Hollywood had to offer.

Brando had a personal makeup man for years who traveled with him from picture to picture. The actor was in the chair between three and four hours a day, getting made up to look like an old man for the role of Don Corleone (Brando was only forty-seven years old when the picture was shot). During these makeup sessions, he'd have me sit next to him and he'd coach me in the fine art of acting, stressing the nuances in scenes that made a performance memorable.

"Let me give you an example," he said. "When we did the scene where Don Corleone is in his office the day of the wedding, and he's doing favors for people, catching up on business, I asked for a cat and a fish tank to be included in the scene. You know why?"

Don Corleone has a cat on his lap when he's talking business, and there's a clear shot of the fish tank. Brando had to put catnip in his pocket to keep the cat from jumping off his lap.

"Tell me," I said.

"Because"—he paused for effect—"it makes the fucking don *human*! I didn't want everyone to think he was a heartless killer. How can you dislike someone who keeps fish, and strokes a cat on his lap? The first rule of writing: Make the protagonist likable, even if only slightly. Did you know Hitler loved dogs? There's some good even in the evilest of people.

"You've got to show emotion. You've got to show fear," he said. "You've got to do what a real person would do under the same circumstances. Go off script if you have to."

Brando gave me excellent pointers in the pivotal scene near the end of the picture when Michael confronts Carlo with his duplicity, which resulted in his brother, Sonny, being killed.

Brando was present during that scene, just out of camera range. He had a tough time showing up on time for his own scenes, and would normally take off when he was finished shooting, but he arrived on time that day to make sure I gave my most effective performance in that crucial scene.

"When Michael accuses you of being a traitor," Brando told me just before the shoot, "you need to convey genuine fear. Think of something that scares you. And Carlo needs hope—he thinks he's gonna die, right?"

"Yeah, right," I said.

"Okay, so when Michael tells you your punishment for betraying the family is banishment to Las Vegas and he hands you a plane ticket, you've gotta glance at the ticket. This is important. You're looking to make sure the ticket is real. You see that it is . . . you have hope. Your mood elevates a little."

I was taking all this in, hoping I wouldn't screw any of it up, particularly with Brando a few feet away, watching me.

We took our places; the cameras began to roll. I am on the phone when Michael walks in. He tells me to hang up the phone. I detached myself from the moment and thought of the most terrifying time in my life . . . when I was taken to the Bellevue polio ward as a kid.

Michael sees Carlo is scared. The script called for him to go into accusation mode, but Pacino departed from the script and offered Carlo a drink to "calm your nerves." He was playing to the effectiveness of my fear and thought offering Carlo a cocktail would calm him down and make him think he was safe.

My death scene was complicated and there were many takes. When Carlo leaves under escort, supposedly for a ride to the airport for the flight to Las Vegas, he gets in the front seat of the car. Clemenza (Richard Castellano) is in the backseat, and he says, "Hello, Carlo." Carlo nods, and Clemenza wraps a garrote around Carlo's neck, and the death throes commence.

I had been outfitted with a pair of steel-soled shoes because I was supposed to kick out the windshield of the car while I was thrashing. Easier said than done. The windshield was originally scored with a fine gouge down the middle to make it break apart with a few kicks, but the gouge line was evident and would be seen by the camera. Two score lines were applied, this time at either side of the windshield, and they were off-camera.

With the garrote applied to my throat, I began my frenzied kicking. The windshield began to shatter, but I kicked so hard that one of my legs careened off the glass and landed square on the side of the stunt driver's head. I had knocked the poor bastard out, and the car shot forward into a pile of sand, stopping short upon impact. The windshield, already history, wasn't there to stop my forward movement and I slid out of the car, cutting the backs of my legs. No great damage done, but I was reminded how easily actors can get hurt while going for realism. The scene was reshot after the actor who played the driver came to. This time, it went smoothly.

Brando was just getting warmed up with his practical jokes.

Just prior to the scene in which Don Corleone is brought home on a stretcher upon his release from the hospital after the attempt on his life, Brando gathered the actors who were playing ambulance attendants.

"Listen up" he said. "Don't fucking drop me when you're carrying me into the house if you ever want to work on a picture again. You drop me, I'll be very angry. Trust me, you don't want to piss me off."

Unbeknownst to those actors, or anyone one else in the scene, for that matter, Brando had the stretcher mattress loaded down with hundreds of pounds of camera weights. The poor bastards struggled to get him out of the ambulance and didn't make it halfway to the house before they dropped him with a thud.

Pandemonium ensued, but Brando popped to his feet, laughing hysterically. One of the actors who'd dropped him took off running and we never saw him again.

It was funny, but I guess you had to be there to appreciate the twisted humor.

One of the crucial scenes in the picture was the fight scene between Sonny and Carlo, after Sonny seeks revenge for Carlo's beating up Sonny's sister.

Jimmy Caan had been avoiding me since being humiliated in Jilly's over the "practical joke" he played on me. I didn't need Caan as a friend, and didn't give a damn whether he was humiliated or not, and if he never spoke to me again, so be it.

The fight scene was to be shot in East Harlem, on 116th Street between Pleasant Avenue and the FDR Drive. A Budweiser beer truck was parked crossways at the end of the street to block the view of the FDR Drive, so modern vehicles wouldn't be seen driving through the scene. The producers also gave a pile of cash to a wiseguy known as "Cheesecake" for distribution to locals so things would run smoothly.

Caan and I had choreographed the scene for an entire day the previous day, just to make sure everything would go smoothly and no one would get hurt.

The scene begins with me (Carlo) on a stoop, talking to one of my numbers runners. As I say "Stop taking action on the Yankees," Sonny (Caan) jumps out of a car with a sawed-off billy club and charges me. At no time during our rehearsals had he been armed with anything.

I was thinking, Where the hell did the club come from? Caan threw it at me as I ran from him as scripted, and it connected solidly with the back of my head.

Coppola yelled, "Cut!" and I got in Caan's face as my head was examined by a medic. I was cut, but not badly.

"Hey, Jimmy," I said, "what the fuck?"

"I decided to improvise," Caan said. "Sorry I hit you."

I thought, Oh yeah? I smelled a rat.

Everyone regrouped and we shot the scene a few more times, until Coppola was satisfied. Caan threw the club at me with every take, but he didn't hit me. He knew better.

The fight started in earnest after that, and Caan came after me for real. The scene called for him to chase Carlo down and toss him over a low railing. So far so good; I was padded just in case I took a bad fall. Once Carlo is over the rail, Sonny jumps after him, picks up a garbage can cover, and smacks Carlo in the arm with it. Those were the days prior to lightweight aluminum garbage cans, and the lid Caan was wielding was heavy metal. He was supposed to barely touch me, but instead he hit me in my right elbow with everything he had, chipping a bone.

But he wasn't done. Carlo then winds up in the gutter under a fire hydrant sprinkler, at which point Sonny is supposed to kick Carlo in the chest, which Caan did, but he put enough power behind it to break two of my ribs.

Then Sonny breathlessly says, "If you ever touch my sister again, I'll fucking kill you!" and gets in a car and leaves.

It took me a few days to recover from the thrashing.

I believe Caan wanted to get back at me for humiliating him that night at Jilly's. He let it be known that my injuries were an accident, but I don't believe that. It takes significant power to break ribs. He was supposed to kick me with the top of his foot; he used his toe.

A question I'm always asked concerns the "phantom punch," when Sonny supposedly punches Carlo in the mouth during the classic street-fight scene. The punch wasn't supposed to connect, and didn't, but of course I reacted as if it had, as dictated by the script. The punch missed my face by at least four inches, and it's evident to anyone who has seen the movie that the punch came nowhere near me. Either no one viewing the dailies picked up on it or they thought the viewers wouldn't notice. Surprise, they did!

So why wasn't the fake punch cut after the picture's release?

The picture was nominated for numerous Academy Awards. Once a picture becomes eligible for an Oscar, *nothing can be changed*. So, the phantom punch will remain forever.

Another question I get asked often pertains to the significance of oranges in the movie. It seems that in many of the picture's crucial scenes, oranges appear. As an example, when Don Corleone gets shot, oranges spill from his bag of groceries. There are numerous other vital scenes where oranges appear, too. Fans have been speculating since 1972 as to the reasons for the fruit.

Now it can be told: There is no reason. There was no plan, no symbolism, no devil worship, no allegory. They're just oranges. Maybe the prop people had scurvy and needed the vitamin C.

The filming was running smoothly, with very little interference from attorney Barry Slotnick, who kept a running list of words or phrases in the script that Joe Columbo might find offensive. The rewrite people made the changes rather than deal with Columbo. The changes were minor and didn't impact the significance of any of the scenes, so no one cared.

Then there was the scene where Carlo beats up his wife, Connie, which is revealed later as a ruse to get Sonny killed. Slotnick pointed out a line in the script that Columbo would find unacceptable.

As part of that scene, I have the infamous line "Clean up the mess, you guinea brat!" when Connie has a hissy fit after talking to one of Carlo's bimbos on the phone, and breaks up the house, scattering dishes, clothes, and food everywhere.

Slotnick said, "Joe's not going to let 'guinea' in. He'll close down the set if the scene isn't rewritten, trust me."

This was a sticking point because the line was important to show Carlo's rage. He needed to show out-of-control anger, followed by his beating of Connie.

There were also problems with Carlo's beating the pregnant Connie with a belt during the same domestic-fight scene. It was thought to be too violent by some, not violent enough by others, and just right by the rest.

My plan was to let the suits come to an equitable agreement on the issues while I went back to the Park Lane, my day's work obligation completed. No sooner did I get into my room than the phone rang. It was Tommy Bilotti.

"Gianni, you going to the rally?"

Tommy was referring to a rally in Columbus Circle that had been long scheduled for that day, June 29, 1971—I could see the location from my hotel room window—organized by Joe Columbo as yet another event to promote his league's ongoing battle with the FBI.

Thousands of spectators were expected, and numerous celebrities and politicians were to be seated on a dais. I had a reserved seat—in the front row—alongside attorney Barry Slotnick.

"Yeah, I'm going." I was doing this out of respect for Columbo, *and* assuming he was going to have someone other than himself give the keynote speech. I didn't think he'd be crazy enough to give a speech at a rally that would be covered by every media outlet in New York. The bosses were already pissed at him; to have his mug plastered all over the network news was suicide.

"Well, you're not going," Tommy said.

"Huh?"

"Carlo advises against it. . . ."

Tommy wasn't referring to my character in the picture; he was referring to Carlo Gambino, the boss of the family that bore his name for forty years, and considered the boss of bosses, because the bosses of the other four crime families deferred to Carlo Gambino on all important matters.

"And when the man says you don't go, you don't go," Tommy said.

This was an order, and I wasn't going to question it to stroke Joe Columbo's ego.

"Sure, Tommy, not a problem."

One thing I wasn't going to do was hang out in my room and have someone from Columbo's crew come to get me when I didn't show. I decided to go to Angelo's, an Italian restaurant in Little Italy; no one would look for me there, and I was hungry anyway.

When I left the hotel, crowds were forming in Columbus Circle.

The media projected a crowd of 150,000, but now that Carlo Gambino had put out the word not to attend, I expected a smaller number.

I hadn't been at my table in Angelo's five minutes when a news bulletin interrupted a show on the TV above the bar.

Joe Columbo had been shot twice at the rally.

My mind was racing. Everything was falling into place. Carlo Gambino wasn't warning certain people away from the rally to boycott it; he did it so his people could have plausible deniability: *Shooting? What shooting?*

The shooter, a black man by the name of Jerome Johnson, fired two rounds into Columbo at close range. Johnson was immediately gunned down, shooter unknown. It was later determined that Johnson was the "lone gunman," a phrase that Americans had become used to hearing after the assassinations of JFK, RFK, and Martin Luther King, Jr.

Columbo didn't die at the scene, but he would remain mostly paralyzed—he was able to move a finger—for seven years, until his eventual demise on May 22, 1978. Columbo underboss Joseph Yacovelli would be named as acting leader of the family, but he was actually the front boss for Carmine Persico. A front boss is the guy who is recognized by the media and cops as the boss and will fall on the sword for the real boss should arrests come down.

The story behind the shooting unfolded pretty quickly, at least in our circles.

The mob was fed up with Columbo and his league, and the rally was the last straw. Carlo Gambino had ordered the hit, and the "honor" went to Joey "Crazy Joe" Gallo, who had just been released from prison and had been promised an important position in the mob after he clipped Columbo. Believing that Carlo Gambino would make that happen, Gallo set the assassination plan in motion.

Gallo recruited Johnson, with whom he'd served time in prison. Gallo gave Johnson the bullshit story that he would personally see to it that Johnson was made a big shot in the Mafia. How stupid was

Johnson? A black man in the mob? He'd have an easier time becoming the Grand Wizard of the Ku Klux Klan.

Gallo's plan, which worked out well, was to have Johnson pull the trigger, on what was surely a suicide mission, what with numerous armed Columbo soldiers in attendance. Johnson had been promised by Gallo that he'd be spirited away from the scene. In reality, Johnson barely fired the second shot before he was dead himself.

The Italian American Anti-Defamation League lived on under Columbo' son, Anthony, but without the bombastic leadership of his dad, Anthony ran it into the ground and it was defunct within a year.

I got very popular after the shooting. The Columbo family, which, of course, wasn't privy to Carlo Gambino's order to have its boss whacked, was suspicious of my absence at the rally, assuming I was either privy to or one of the masterminds behind the assassination attempt. The seat reserved for me in the front row of the dais—with my name prominently displayed on it—was glaringly empty on news footage before the shooting.

I used the excuse I'd use in numerous interviews with the FBI and the NYPD: agita, the Italian curse. Bad case of heartburn, or was it food poisoning? Who can tell the difference? When Barry Slotnick asked me why I wasn't at the rally, I told him the truth. He had been representing wiseguys for a while and knew the score. He just nodded.

The cops knew I was bullshitting them, but they couldn't do anything about it, at least not at the time. I knew they'd be back to talk to me at a later date, once they'd gathered more information during their investigation. The Columbos, on the other hand, assumed I was involved in the shooting plot because I was conveniently absent from the rally, and they put a contract out on me. Was I worried? You bet your ass I was worried. It was the FBI guys who told me their sources had told them that there was a contract on my life.

I had the protection of Frank Costello and Aniello Dellacroce, and while that meant a lot, there was always the nut wannabe gangster who would be making a name for himself, with possible induction into the Columbo family, by clipping a coconspirator in their boss's death. I stayed away from anything Columbo for years after the shooting, always mindful of a possible murder attempt.

Joey Gallo would meet *his* lone gunman on the night of April 1, 1972, when he was murdered in Umberto's Clam House in Little Italy. He was dining with his wife, Sina, and actor Jerry Orbach and his wife. They were celebrating Joey's forty-third, and last, birthday.

According to witnesses, a good and boisterous time was being had by the two couples, when at approximately 4:30 A.M., our friend the lone gunman burst into the nearly empty restaurant and dispatched Gallo. Joey made a gallant attempt to make a break for the street and safety, but that was not to be.

Gallo might have avoided death had not that Columbo associate been walking down the street at that hour and seen Gallo and company in Umberto's. The shooter ran home, got a gun, and the rest is history.

Gallo had to die for his involvement in the shooting of Joe Columbo. He undoubtedly felt safe in Little Italy, due to one of the rules of the mob: No one gets whacked in "da neighborhood." Rules are made to be broken, and when accidentally spotted at that late hour, Gallo became a victim of opportunity. Truthfully, I was a bit surprised that the shooter, while doing the mob a public service, didn't get clipped himself for breaching mob etiquette. I guess the outcome outweighed the faux pas.

As for *The Godfather*, without Joe Columbo bitching and complaining about what words we could or couldn't use in the script, the "guinea brat" line stayed in, but so the producers wouldn't draw the ire of what remained of the league, those words that had already been omitted stayed out. The league was without much juice in Joe Columbo's absence, and we didn't have problems with them again.

The Godfather filming wrapped up, and the requisite postproduction work began in earnest. Naturally, I wasn't part of that. I continued to keep a low profile, dodging cops who were still investigating the Joe Columbo shooting, and the Columbo crime family, which was still suspicious of my absence from the rally on the day of the planned hit.

The picture was going to premiere in two venues—L.A. and New York—simultaneously, with the New York premiere in the Paramount Theatre on Broadway. No expense was going to be spared, and it was billed as a black-tie event. After the showing of the picture, a gala after party was to be held on the roof of the St. Regis Hotel. The cast, about thirty of us, were the honored guests.

My ego was bigger than ever. I was rolling in money, and I was a featured player in the most anticipated movie in years. This was going to be a *Gone With the Wind* moment. A question presented itself: How best could I capitalize on the premiere? A plan began to formulate in my twisted mind.

The Columbos had it in for me; this was a well-known fact. The only thing that was keeping me from a dirt bath was my connection to Frank Costello and Aniello Dellacroce. But suppose there was an attempt on my life the night of the picture's premiere? I couldn't buy the publicity an attempted hit on me would generate. I'd go from "Gianni who?" to an internationally recognized name overnight. Instant publicity, and, I assumed, my path to Hollywood stardom.

After considerable thought, I devised a plan and put it in motion.

Tommy Bilotti's brother, Joey, a soldier with the Gambinos, was a recognized expert marksman. He had entered many shooting competitions around the world, and even counted Panamanian dictator Manuel Noriega as a shooting buddy.

I was going to ask Joey to shoot me at the premiere as I exited my limo onto the red carpet. I thought this was a great idea, which shows you the extent of my ever-ballooning ego.

Adhering to mob protocol, I contacted Tommy Bilotti first because of his standing with the Gambinos. We met in a restaurant where neither of us was known.

I laid out the scheme and asked him what he thought.

"You're fucking crazy," he said, without asking for details.

"No, Tommy, listen. Joey's a great shot. He could wing me, maybe a shoulder wound, thigh, something like that."

I'd known Tommy almost as long as I'd known Frank Costello. We were good friends and could talk about anything. My plan, however, wasn't one of the subjects Tommy cared to discuss. I pressed, cajoled, and eventually wore him out.

"Okay, I'll have Joey call you. You can hash it out with him, but for the record, you're a fucking lunatic."

Joey called me and we met in a coffee shop in Brooklyn.

I told him about my flesh-wound plan. "You could be across the street on a rooftop with a rifle. Whaddaya think?"

"I'm with Tommy," Joey said. "You're fucking nuts."

I was prepared for his reaction. Between the time I spoke to Tommy and had the meeting with Joey, I'd called a friend, Dr. Theodore Jacobs, and asked him to go with me to the premiere.

"What am I, your date?" he asked jokingly. "Run out of women who'll go out with you?"

I told him the plan. "I'd like to have you around to treat the wound on the spot. You know, stop the bleeding. Bring your doctor shit with you."

Dr. Jacobs was silent for what seemed like forever.

"Well, will you do it?" I asked.

"You're out of your mind," he said.

"That may be true," I responded, "but will you go with me?"

The doc did his best to talk me out of my ill-conceived plan, but when he saw that I was dead serious, he said he'd go. "Better I'm there than you have to wait for an ambulance." Then he recommended a good psychiatrist.

Joey wasn't about to go along with the program, and he spent considerable time trying to dissuade me.

"Doctor or no doctor, you never know where a bullet will wind up. Yeah, it's an easy shot with a decent scope, but lots of things can happen to a bullet when it leaves the barrel. First of all, the fucking thing is traveling at over three thousand feet a second—we're talking a rifle here, not a handgun. The longer the barrel, the faster the velocity. A gust of wind, a fucking raindrop hits the round, and it could deviate a fraction of an inch. That could mean the difference between a through-and-through wound—"

"A what?"

He dumbed down the ballistic jargon. "A bullet that goes in and out of your thigh, for example, without hitting anything vital, *or* if it's pushed by that raindrop, it could decimate your femoral artery. You could bleed out in less than a minute, doctor or no doctor."

"You mean the doc'd be no help?"

Joey sighed. "Gianni, a bullet going that fast could vaporize any flesh in its path. Your flesh will be liquified, and that artery—the femoral artery—will turn to mush, and not only where the bullet strikes it. You could lose a leg, or fucking die from shock, even from a minor wound. This isn't a fucking movie."

He talked me out of my master plan. Later on, I called Dr. Jacobs and told him his services wouldn't be needed.

"Fuck you, I'm going," he said. "And I should send you a bill for my services. Set me up with a hot starlet and you'll be off the hook for the bill."

The glitz and glamour of the premiere were impressive. I'd been used to Las Vegas flash for a few years, and the Paramount Theatre was lit up like a Vegas casino, with crisscrossing aerial lights like you'd expect to see at a golden age movie debut (or a nighttime Nazi blitzkrieg attack on London in World War II).

Crowds of fans and media pushed and strained at the wooden NYPD barriers as blinding camera lights made me wish I'd brought sunglasses. Most of the action was taking place in the lobby; for the media to attempt to interview any of the actors on the red carpet would have been difficult. It was just too noisy.

The Paramount Theatre brought back many memories for me, most of them pleasant. Tinged with nostalgic and heartwarming reminiscences were also recollections of loneliness and abandonment.

I'd go to the Paramount often after my release from the polio ward to escape the reality of the real world, in which I was trying to survive. The movies transported me to a fantasy world where I was the hero of the story and would survive what was thrown at me to continue another day. I always felt better after going to a movie.

I'd also just go to the Paramount to get out of the biting cold typical of New York winters. A day of peddling pens on the street, with the wind whistling through the skyscraper canyons in midtown Manhattan, would wear me out. The cocoon of warmth and security of a darkened theater made me forget my problems and discomfort, if only for a few hours.

My life had done a complete 180; I was entering the Paramount Theatre now as a featured actor in a picture that would be on critics' lists of all-time best movies. I'd also just been notified that I was up for an award at the upcoming Cannes Film Festival in France as the Best Newcomer in a motion picture (I'd eventually lose to Diana Ross for *Lady Sings the Blues*). I had money, a degree of fame, and good health. I should've been happy at this most important time in my life, but I wasn't. The sadness of my past enveloped me, and it was difficult to shake. Did I belong here? Did I deserve what I'd achieved? I was also concerned about a *real* attempt on my life by the Columbo crime family.

My sadness was increased by the nagging feeling that something was wrong with Frank Costello.

I'd seen him less and less over the last three months, and was dealing with Blackie, Mr. C.'s right-hand man, almost exclusively. Blackie was a man of few words, but I saw concern on his face, something that increased daily.

No one in my immediate circle had had any contact with Mr. C., either, at least not on our level. The other bosses must've seen him, but whatever was going on, we peons weren't privy to it.

After doing some interviews in the lobby, the lights dimmed three times, indicating it was time to take our seats. The actors were seated in the center orchestra and we were the last to enter the theater. The applause for us was humbling. After everyone was settled in, the gigantic screen flickered and the picture began.

I left the theater during the opening credits.

A combination of my dark mood and the fact that I had seen the finished movie several times made me not want to sit through it again. I told Dr. Jacobs I'd see him at the after party, and went for a few drinks at the Warwick Hotel bar. I kept to myself.

The roof of the St. Regis Hotel had been transformed into a beautiful, expensively decorated party scene. The entire ceiling was covered with red roses, and the best crystal and linen tablecloths covered tables that would seat the six hundred invited guests. As the guests began arriving, they were greeted by Andy Williams on a makeshift stage, singing "Speak Softly, Love."

There were wall-to-wall celebrities—not only the cream of Hollywood but also members of New York's elite society, politicians, captains of industry, and, of course, mob bosses. I stayed for a respectable amount of time but left early.

Being involved with *The Godfather* had been the experience of my life, but it was time to get back to Las Vegas to do what I did best.

8

MARKERS

While my wife, Susan, and I weren't getting along, we both doted on Carmen, our baby girl. Things weren't going great, but I thought we might make the marriage work for the sake of our little girl. That all changed rapidly when Susan told me she had been pregnant with our second child, had had an abortion, and had filed for divorce.

I was livid. Susan's reasoning for getting the abortion was that she didn't want to be my baby machine, and knew that's what was in store for her. On reflection, she was right about the baby-machine part. I wanted lots of children, and amid the arguing after the abortion and divorce announcement, I told her, "What did you expect? We knew each other for two months before we got married. I married you for kids."

I was sorry as soon as I said it, but the harm was done. My Italian temper got the better of me and I said things I shouldn't have said. I recall saying during one memorable outburst, "I hope you get cancer, you bitch."

Within a month, Susan was diagnosed with ovarian cancer.

The guilt kicked in immediately. While Susan and I would divorce, I paid for the best cancer treatment money could buy for her for the next ten years. I found an eminent oncologist in Paris who was willing to treat her. She was usually too sick to go to France, so the doctor came to her. The good news is, she survived. The bad news is, she survived.

Forty years later, she's still breaking my chops from afar.

I was back in Las Vegas, but the shooting in New York of Joe Columbo continued to haunt me. The NYPD and the FBI let it be known that they wanted to talk to me again, and I made it my business to avoid them. Despite what you see on TV, unless there's a warrant out for your arrest for a heinous crime, the cops don't do much to locate you. If they should run into me, I'd be their captive audience; other than that, I just had to avoid my usual haunts. The Columbos interest in me never waned, either.

Then, on February 18, 1973, Frank Costello died; the official cause was a heart attack, but I assumed he'd been sick for a while, given his unexplained vanishing act over the three previous months.

I was crushed. It was like I'd lost my father—no, it was worse. I didn't grieve for my father like I grieved for Frank Costello when my dad died years later. Mr. C. had raised me, guided me, had given me the best advice. As a kid, I'd felt safe around him and anyone he had introduced me to.

Mr. C. was larger than life; when he walked into a room, no matter how many people were present, you knew someone special had arrived. He was always low-key, quiet, respectful, and mannerly, especially around individuals who weren't part of our thing. I thought he'd be around forever. I also had to consider that half my protection from the Columbos was gone, but Aniello Dellacroce still had my back, for what it was worth. Loyalties in the mob were fluid; the star of today could be the corpse of tomorrow if he pissed off the wrong person, or stopped earning enough money for the family. It's all about money in the mob; forget loyalty and honor—that's all fiction. *The Godfather* was a phenomenal picture, but it was a fairy tale.

The funeral was held in the chapel of the Frank E. Campbell

Funeral Chapel on Madison Avenue in Manhattan. Campbell's was the funeral home to the elite; the last big name whose wake was held there was Judy Garland in March 1969, but the list of luminaries that passed through Campbell's is lengthy, beginning with legendary western gunman and newspaperman Bat Masterson in 1921.

Law enforcement officers, who were still actively looking for me, would have a big presence at the funeral to catalog the comings and goings of who was who in the mob when they came to pay respects. I also didn't want to embarrass Mr. C.'s wife, Lauretta, and the rest of the family by being led out of the service in handcuffs. And, of course, there was always the ominous threat of someone from the Columbos seeing me and making me a spur-of-the-moment hit victim like Joey Gallo.

I watched the proceedings from a school across the street, giving a janitor twenty dollars for the privilege. It was heart-wrenching to watch mourners coming and going without being able to thank Mr. Costello personally for all he did for me. I called Lauretta Costello after the service and told her how much I regretted not being able to attend, and the reason why. She understood.

Mr. C. didn't even lose his influence in death. He was buried in St. Michael's Cemetery in East Elmhurst, Queens, and in 1974, his mausoleum was blown up on the orders from mob boss Carmine Galante, who had just been released from prison. Galante was making a statement; he wanted the mob to know he was back in business, was planning big things for himself, and that the Costello days were over. Five years later, Galante himself would be slain in ambush in a Brooklyn restaurant. While Galante had many enemies, Frank Costello still had loyalists, and it is my belief that it was a combination of alliances from both camps that led to Galante's violent demise.

I was back in Las Vegas within the week, resuming my role as the conduit for the skim money traveling from the casinos to New York.

Casino cages are accessible to only a privileged few. Cages are where the money is kept, literally millions of dollars at any given time. In the Sands casino's cage room, there was a separate room labeled THE MORGUE. I had never asked what was in the room, until one day my curiosity got the better of me.

"That's where we keep the deadbeat markers, kid," a pit boss told me.

Markers are Las Vegas–speak for IOUs incurred by gamblers who ask for credit. Credit is provided to anyone deemed reliable and likely to repay the debt. Normally, such professionals as doctors, dentists, lawyers, and the like were extended credit with little fanfare; they asked for it, they got it. Most repaid their debts, but there were always the few deadbeats who didn't pay and never returned to Las Vegas. A little-known law back then read that collecting casino debt was unenforceable against those debtors who resided outside of Nevada.

Those of you who are mob aficionados are probably wondering why the wiseguys didn't go after deadbeats; it's done in the movies all the time. It had crossed their minds, because there were upward of four million dollars in markers in the Sands morgue, most from out-of-town gamblers. It was the mob's thinking that if they went after the deadbeats with threats—let's say a six-foot-five, three-hundred-pound late notice—that eventually people would stop coming to Las Vegas to gamble. It was a smart move; lose four million but make many times that yearly from the influx of gamblers who came to town.

My devious mind formulated a plan. What if I offered to purchase the markers from the casino for twenty-five cents on the dollar? They had nothing to lose; they weren't making any money on the markers as things stood. Of course, I'd be holding worthless paper unless I actively sought out the deadbeats and collected the money they owed—money that I could then legally keep.

At this point, I'd like to add that I'm not a tough guy, never was, never will be. I'll protect to the death my own life and the lives of those whom I love, but I never saw the rationale of violence as a means of intimidation. I knew I could use my intellect to extract the money from the debtors by making them think they were in serious trouble if they didn't pay up.

I ran my idea by the casino bosses. I didn't expect any pushback, because there was no downside for them—no money up front, no investing in muscle, and no travel expenses. They'd make a ton of money essentially for doing nothing.

They agreed, and I initially optioned $500,000 in markers for ninety days, after which I could buy the markers outright for the aforementioned 25 percent. This was a great deal, because I didn't have to lay out any money; if I collected a marker, the casinos got their 25 percent cut and I got the remaining 75 percent. I used my option only with money I had already collected. For the deadbeats I couldn't locate, the casino got those markers back. There was a minuscule number of those I couldn't find and collect from.

The markers were kept in index-card drawers—think old library card catalogs with small pull-out drawers in a large wooden cabinet. Each marker was signed by the debtor and stapled to an index card plainly listing the debtor's name, address, and phone number, as well as the date, time, and amount of the debt. Most of the markers were years old, and therefore I couldn't rely on the listed addresses as being accurate.

Those were the days before anyone had even thought of the Internet, so I had to rely on phone books to look for up-to-date addresses. I started with the California deadbeats, focusing on the Bel Air and Beverly Hills addresses of doctors and dentists. If they could afford to live and/or practice in those neighborhoods, they could afford to pony up what they owed.

All were still in business, although some had changed locations. I flew to L.A. and began making appointments to see the doctors first. I dressed like a businessman, not like the stereotypical mob money collector. The meetings would be cordial, but always with a looming aura of the possibility that some bad things could happen if they didn't pay up.

I'd arrive at their practices as a potential patient feigning an illness, and once in a room alone with the doctor, I'd tell him the real reason I was there. My first visit was to a doctor who had skipped out on a fifteen-thousand-dollar debt.

"So, what can I do for you today?" the deadbeat doctor asked.

"Doc, you and I have a problem," I said, and I produced the marker. Then I passed myself off as a casino employee and said that I was there to rectify the doctor's "oversight."

There was a look of terror in the doctor's eyes that I would see in virtually all the deadbeats as time went on. I'd come to find out that these people weren't afraid of me as much as they were frightened of their wives and their reputations if they were found to owe gambling debts. I'm sure most, if not all, of the debtors had also dallied with hookers while they were in Las Vegas and assumed I knew about it. I didn't, and I didn't care. I did, however, allude to the fact that "we" wouldn't want to have to "go public" with the debt, which, of course, would mean adverse publicity.

I worked the same deal with most of the deadbeats: They could either give me the entire amount up front or 25 percent down, with the rest to be paid off in a year or less. There was an interest rate of 1 percent a week, so it behooved them to pay off the debt as soon as they were able. Most gave me a lump sum so they wouldn't have to pay the interest (vigorish or vig in mobspeak). I would personally revisit those who were on the payment plan every month to collect.

No one got a break on the principal; everyone paid 100 percent of what they owed. I threw them a bone, however, by telling the payment-plan guys that as soon as they paid off 50 percent of what they owed, they'd be allowed to return to Vegas.

Money began to roll in.

I started traveling in earnest. Constantly on the hunt for the elusive deadbeat, I was flying so much, I had to think about where I was half the time. I'd make rounds in New York, Kansas City, Cleveland, Milwaukee, New Orleans, San Diego, L.A., Miami, and other large cities. After a while, I was overwhelmed with money, and the list of deadbeats kept getting bigger as other hotels joined the list of my clients when they heard about my success.

This was also a good opportunity to cement business relationships with other mob families across the United States. Right from the beginning of the marker project, I'd make sure I stopped by to see the local mob bosses of whatever city I was in and give them "tribute." In our world, the word *tribute* meant money. This was protocol. I didn't have to do it, and no one would've known if I hadn't, but it was the right thing to do.

I would stop by, introduce myself to those who didn't already know me, and pass along a cash-stuffed envelope. I was operating in their territory and the money was my way of saying "Thanks for the consideration in allowing me on your turf." I was also investing in my future by securing my reputation with powerful bosses. It was my insurance policy against treachery; no one turns on an earner, as it's not in the mob's best interest.

Then I had another brainstorm. Why do all the work myself? I had terminal jet lag, and while being weighed down with cash was a good feeling, the traveling was getting me down. I was also suffering from what I now realize was PTSD, which I got trying to find a decent Italian restaurant in Cleveland or Milwaukee. For me, that was traumatic.

I began working deals with local wiseguys. I'd pay them a percentage to follow up my initial visits to the debtors and collect the monthly payments, which they would then forward to me in Las Vegas.

I was building a strong allegiance with powerful mob bosses across the country, and my reputation as a person who could be trusted *and* was a huge earner began to take on legendary proportions. I was offered to get "made"—inducted into a crime family—by a few bosses, all of whom I turned down. Most mob associates like myself lived for the day when they got their "button"—that is, became an official member of a crime family, with all the benefits that went with it. I told the few bosses who had a sense of humor that I preferred zippers to buttons.

I didn't see much of a benefit in being made. Contrary to what you see in the movies or on TV, being made is a hassle. Soldiers (the incoming rank) have to run money up the ladder in the family every month. A portion of what a soldier makes from his crimes goes to pay his capo (crew boss), who, in turn, pays the family boss. There is a minimum amount you have to pony up. What, you had a bad month, didn't make much money? Too fucking bad; you still owe the bosses, and you'll owe that much more the following month.

By staying an associate, I'd be free to do—or not do—whatever the hell I wanted and didn't need to feed the bosses unless I had a big score. The petty family jealousies, the push to earn more money, and the friggin' family gossip were things I didn't have to deal with. Wiseguys gossip more than a busload of soccer moms.

I worked the marker racket for over four years. In the beginning, the rush was great. I was making money, cementing ties with friends of ours across the country, and building a good reputation. But then the tedium of seeing the misery gambling created began to get to me. The constant gloom of seeing families destroyed by the breadwinner with a bad gambling jones made me sick.

Some of the deadbeats were sorry excuses for human beings. They would rather gamble than feed their families or be with their kids. I dealt with degenerates who lost mortgage payments and their kids' college money. One guy, Frank DiMicelli, owned Rafters, a very prosperous steak house in Milwaukee. This poor bastard could never win a bet—he reminded me a lot of John Gotti in that respect—and was always going to Vegas. He had eighteen thousand dollars in markers, which took him over thirty years to pay off because he could never get near the principal; all he could afford to pay was the vig, and the eighteen grand remained unpaid until he married a rich woman, who paid off the nut. In the end, he lost everything—his family, his business, and, worst of all, his self-respect. At one point, I began collecting fifty cents on the dollar from him, releasing him from the balance, figuring I could help him pay his debt faster. He actually cost me money. And what did he do with my generosity? He gambled it away. He died broke a few years ago.

I eventually turned the marker business over to an associate. I don't like dealing with weak people; they can't be trusted, and you'll never find a weaker individual than a compulsive gambler. Plus, I was overdosing on wiseguys. I was meeting with them, dining with them, giving them money, listening to them complain about everything, and I'd had enough. I found myself yearning for the times when I mingled with normal people, or what passed for normal in my circle of friends.

I met the great Judy Garland in 1961, when she was dating a character named Jimmy Mack. She lived in an apartment on East 72nd Street and East End Avenue. Sinatra had a triplex apartment in the same building, which he occasionally stayed in when he was in New York. Judy's pad was much smaller but no less elegant, with a great view of the East River.

I had been out with some friends, and everyone was headed to Judy's apartment after she finished her last show. I had met quite a few celebrities, and while I was impressed with most of them, Judy was high on my list of people I wanted to meet.

Never one to go to anyone's home empty-handed, I took several dozen red roses with me. She was gracious and welcoming, and maybe a little buzzed. After she thanked me for the flowers, I watched her as she took them to the kitchen. I assumed she'd gone to get a vase, but after she didn't return to the living room, where about ten guests were drinking, curiosity got the better of me and I made my way to the kitchen. I figured that maybe she needed help with something.

Judy was cutting some of the roses off the stems and frying them in a pan with eggs and cheese. I just stared at her.

She turned abruptly, smiled at me, and said, "You don't know a frittata? What kind of Italian are you?"

Frittatas are an Italian food staple. When I was a kid, my mother would make frittatas with leftovers. Italian mothers never threw out leftover food. Any ingredient could be added, but a frittata usually was made with diced salami, eggs, cheese, artichokes, tomatoes, and mushrooms. I'd heard of people in the old neighborhood plucking daisies and dandelions from City Hall Park and frying them up for inclusion in frittatas, but roses? They were a new ingredient, but I was willing to try it. They were surprisingly good.

We were still partying it up when her kids, Liza and her younger brother, Joey Luft, joined the group at about 7:00 A.M. Liza was about fifteen at the time and had the same pixieish look she'd maintain throughout her life. Judy introduced her kids to the group, and I spoke with Liza briefly. Years later, we would reconnect.

Liza Minnelli would begin appearing at the Riviera Hotel in Las Vegas in 1970. By then, she was a big star, and I hadn't had any contact with her since the impromptu party in her mother's New York apartment nine years prior.

Back then, performers appearing in Las Vegas would have two- or three-week engagements, consisting of two shows a night. Currently the workload for performers is considerably shorter. Everyone worked harder in Vegas when the mob ran the town.

I went to the Riviera to see her last show of the night with some friends. Every show I saw in Vegas was from a ringside table, and that night was no exception. Liza was a dynamo, tireless and bubbling with talent. I wanted to go backstage to reconnect, and I had a friend, Eddie Torres, of Detroit's Purple Gang, do the honors.

I didn't think she would remember me, and I was right. But after a few minutes of chitchat, it was like we were old friends. Her mother had passed away the year before, and I expressed my condolences. I could see she was still feeling the pain. We began seeing each other after that night, but the relationship wasn't exclusive.

A few months later, I got a frantic call from Liza.

"Gianni, you've gotta help me out of a jam. I did something stupid," she said breathlessly.

"Yeah, sure, honey. What did you do?"

"I got engaged to someone I barely know, and after I wised up, I can't get rid of the guy."

I could certainly relate to that, as a mental picture of Susan popped into my head. "Tell me about it."

She had begun dating Eddie Albert, Jr., a few months before and had agreed to marry him in a moment of weakness, helped along by half a bottle of vodka. He was the son of acclaimed actor and war hero Eddie Albert. Apparently, Junior had none of his father's traits and turned out to be a bit of a pussy, in addition to being an actor and musician. I'd seen him around town—not a bad-looking guy. Liza, realizing her error when she sobered up, tried to get rid of him without hurting his feelings.

"He's a nice guy, Gianni, but not marriage material. He's weak. I don't like weak men. I've tried everything short of telling him to go fuck himself. He can't take a hint. He tries to be with me every second of every day, can't get rid of him. He's like a fucking summer head cold."

"What would you like me to do?"

"Come to my show tonight. He'll be seated ringside—he's there every goddamn night. I have a ringside table reserved for you. Every song I'll be singing will be directed toward you. I'll flirt, bat my eyes, stare at you every chance I get. He'll pick up on it. After the show, have a talk with him, tell him we're together."

"That's it? That'll work?"

"Jesus," she said, desperation in her voice. "It better. I'd hate to have to change my name and leave town."

That night, I was at the designated table, and at a table nearby sat Junior, staring googly-eyed at Liza as she made her entrance at the beginning of her act. Sure enough, every song out of her mouth was directed at me. She came up to my table, leaned over the stage, and blew me kisses. Can't get any more direct than that.

Junior, whom I'd been watching peripherally, was squirming like a worm on a hook. I was hoping he wouldn't come out swinging after the show, but if he did, I'd do what needed to be done to protect myself.

The show ended and the crowd began to dissipate, except for Junior; he just sat there looking like he'd just lost his best friend. Maybe he had. If he wasn't going to come to me, I'd go to him.

I strolled over and introduced myself. "Leave Liza alone; we're together now. I don't want to see you anywhere near her . . . or me, for that matter." I braced for an attack, angling slightly sideways to avoid that unpleasant kick to the balls.

Nothing happened for maybe ten seconds. Then, out of nowhere, Junior began to cry. And I don't mean a few tears; the guy was bellowing as if he were walking the last mile to the gas chamber.

I felt bad for him, but I could see why he didn't appeal to Liza. I didn't even know him, and he was embarrassing me. I wanted to offer a man-up lesson, tell him no woman wants a man who isn't at least a little tough. But it wasn't my place to do that. I just walked away.

Liza's plan worked; Eddie Albert, Jr., was out of her life.

After that, Liza and I would be spending more time together. She knew how to party, but I didn't know how much. I was going to find out.

I met Liza one night at 2:00 A.M. at the Stardust Hotel coffee shop. She had just finished a show and was holding court with some friends. I was with Nick Nitti, grandson of the infamous Frank Nitti of the Capone era, Nick's son, John, who was about twenty years old, and seven others. Liza and I began talking about cooking. She was bragging about her fettuccini Alfredo.

"No one makes better Alfredo than me," Liza said proudly. I felt a challenge emerging.

Liza did have a reputation as a good cook, but so did I. Sons in New York Italian families learn to cook before they learn how to play stickball, and I was no exception. I had expanded upon the rudimentaries my mother had taught me, and had become quite accomplished in the kitchen. Some of the best chefs in the world work in Vegas, and I was always picking their brains for their expertise. I still love to cook; I find it relaxing, and the praise from people who have sampled my dishes is appreciated, too.

A few drinks later, the gauntlet was thrown; Liza challenged me to a fettuccini Alfredo cooking contest.

Each of us would go shopping—right now, by the way—for ingredients and meet back at Dionne Warwick's house; she had lent Liza her digs at the Sierra Country Club while she was out of town, where we would do our cooking.

There were twelve of us in attendance, including Liza and me, and ten would be the judges. Two plates were marked "L" and "G" on the bottom, and the finished meals would be dished out by Liza and me onto our respective plates. This was a blind taste test; none of those sampling the pasta would know who had cooked what.

Alfredo sauce is relatively quick to prepare, and by sunup, Liza and I were ladling out the results while the judges waited in the dining room. We watched and waited as they dived in. After everyone had completed their taste test, they pointed to the plate they thought had the best sauce—the pasta was insignificant, as anyone can boil al dente pasta.

All except one person—probably Liza when no one was looking—voted for my dish. I dramatically took my bows, thinking that was the end of the contest.

Liza, fueled by more than a few cocktails, thought differently. By way of protesting the results of the contest, she dug her hands into her bowl of pasta and formed a ball with the gooey, heavy, sauce-laden noodles. For those of you who aren't aware, fettuccini Alfredo is sometimes referred to as "heart attack on a plate," due to its calorie and fat content. It's heavy with cheese, butter, and eggs; you can actually hear your arteries clogging up with every mouthful.

Liza hurled the pasta ball at my head, missing me by inches. What she didn't miss, however, was a really nicely framed painting suspended on a wall resplendent in light lavender wallpaper. Liza's unannounced attack left the assembled group speechless and temporarily frozen in place, which gave her time to reload. Another ball came my way, this one finding a resting place on my custom-made silk shirt. The tan shirt complemented the light yellow sauce quite nicely, thank you.

Naturally, I was pissed and wasn't going to let the ambush go. I dug into my bowl of pasta, rolled a fine ball, and let fly, catching Liza in the forehead. Liza began laughing as she made another pasta ball, and within seconds everyone in the house was in the battle. At first, Liza was the sole target, but in less than a minute we were throwing pasta grenades at one another.

By the end of the melee, we were all covered with pasta, with dripping sauce slithering down our bodies like drunken snakes, but this is why God invented dry cleaners; no big deal. The house, however, decorated in a classy, expensive ultramodern motif, now looked like something resembling a Salvador Dalí painting. We would find out later that the damage to the house and décor amounted to over fifteen thousand dollars. Liza got evicted and paid the damages. She was unconcerned, because her Riviera gig had only three days remaining, and she suffered the indignity of staying in a hotel suite without complaint.

The food fight became part of Las Vegas legend, and I was pleased to be part of history, however ridiculous.

Many of my friends were spontaneous like Liza, perhaps not prone to food fights, but with great senses of humor.

I appeared on *The Merv Griffin Show* twenty-three times over the years. Merv was a great guy, and a phenomenal businessman, having created a television entertainment empire that survives to this day, years after his death. If you like *Jeopardy,* you can thank Merv.

Merv had a great sense of humor, and it was difficult to insult the guy. He was gay and came on to me once, but I cut him off with a terse "Get your hands off me or I'll shove them up your ass." Anyone else in Merv's position of power might've had me banned from his show, or hurt my show-business prospects, but Merv thought my comment was hilarious, and we remained good friends until he died.

He phoned me one afternoon with a request. The movie *Mame,* starring Lucille Ball, was about to debut, and one of his friends needed a date for the Hollywood premiere. Would I be interested in being an escort to a "big star"?

Merv knew many Hollywood A-listers, and images of beautiful actresses ran through my head. Could it be Raquel Welch, Angie Dickinson, Loni Anderson? The list was endless, and I was definitely on board.

"Absolutely, Merv. Who are we talking about?"

"Zsa Zsa Gabor," he said unapologetically.

I was silent for a few moments. I've mentioned Merv's sense of humor, but he was also a great practical joker, and I assumed he was putting me on. No offense to Zsa Zsa, but she wasn't exactly a Hollywood heavy, aside from her weight, but that wasn't what was fueling my trepidation. I was thirty years old, and Zsa Zsa was fifty-seven. I thought we'd look a bit foolish walking down the red carpet together, and I knew our pairing would result in biting media comments.

"You're putting me on, right?" I replied.

He insisted he wasn't. "It would be a personal favor to me, Gianni. She's stuck for a date and I told her I'd find her one. Whaddaya say?"

Merv and Zsa Zsa went way back; everyone knew that they were close. Zsa Zsa, in her prime, had appeared in many movies and TV shows, and would continue doing so until the 1990s. In most of her TV appearances, she'd play a caricature of herself, a spoiled chanteuse with an over-the-top Hungarian accent, and repeating her famous tag endearment, "dahlink" (darling), as often as she could.

I didn't want to do it, but I liked Merv and he had been good to me and my career. I reluctantly agreed.

Zsa Zsa lived in reclusive billionaire Howard Hughes's former mansion in Beverly Hills. I arrived on time the night of the premiere in a chauffeur-driven limo, ready for whatever lay ahead.

Zsa Zsa answered her own door, which was surprising, because most people who lived in Beverly Hills had servants for everything. She was dressed and ready to go, but she looked like a lamp shade at my grandmother's house—garish gown, hair higher than the Pope's miter, and would look more at home on top of a wedding cake. But she was Zsa Zsa Gabor, and making heads turn was one of the things she was known for.

I got a "Hello, dahlink," and we exchanged compliments on our respective appearances and then were off.

The event was being held at the Cinedome on Hollywood Boulevard, which was about a fifteen-minute ride. We chatted about inconsequential bullshit, had some laughs. At one point during the ride, I placed my hand on her thigh. I know if I did something like that these days, I'd be locked up for sexual harassment, but back then it was part of my act—and a lot of others', too—and was accepted.

As I placed my hand on her leg, the first thing that hit me was that my hand was flat on her thigh. I've had my hand on numerous thighs over the years, and I expected my hand would naturally curve around her leg. What I experienced on Zsa Zsa's thigh was a level surface; my hand extended flat, as if I were Bruce Lee preparing to administer a karate chop. It just unnerved me; my hand would curve when I placed it on my own thigh. This was one large lady, but she hid it well under what she was wearing.

I was noticeably uncomfortable as the limo pulled up in front of the Cinedome. Paparazzi were everywhere, cameras rolling, lights blinding. The fans lined both sides of the red carpet, as is the custom in Hollywood.

There to greet us was a smiling Merv Griffin. He hugged Zsa Zsa, shook my hand, and waved at the crowd.

"Attention," Merv hollered above the din. "I have an announcement to make!"

What now?

The press gathered around us as Merv said, "It's my pleasure to announce that Mr. Gianni Russo and Ms. Zsa Zsa Gabor have become officially engaged." The crowd went nuts and the media people pressed closer, questions coming fast and furious.

I was like the proverbial deer caught in the headlights. Engaged? What the fuck?

Merv was busting a gut laughing and talking up the reporters. Any questions they asked regarding our "romance" were answered quickly by Merv with one lie after another. Then he turned and winked at me.

This was Merv Griffin's idea of a practical joke. Zsa Zsa, who would do anything for publicity, smiled and nodded a lot, but she didn't say much. She was obviously in on the gag, but she didn't dare expound on it because she was unsure of what my reaction would be. The engagement announcement would be covered by all the trade papers. Merv's joke would take me months to set straight.

Merv vanished to his seat, which wasn't near ours—good for Merv—and Zsa Zsa and I quickly became yesterday's news after Lucille Ball arrived fashionably late, and all media attention was diverted to her.

The event dragged on after the movie with the obligatory after party and interviews. I dodged the press, leaving Zsa Zsa to do what she did best: pose and spew forth a bunch of "dahlinks," while she responded to the questions of our engagement without really answering them.

The ride back home was a welcome respite from the madness that is a Hollywood premiere. We didn't talk during the trip back to her house, but as the limo pulled into her driveway, she said, "Why don't you come in for a drink, dahlink?"

I had to make a decision. "Stopping in for a drink" in anyone's language meant sex was a distinct possibility. I'd already had more than my share of cocktails, and my judgment wasn't the best. Would I politely beg off, like any responsible gentleman would, or would I decide racking up another notch on my belt by bedding a Hollywood icon was the way to go?

"Sure," I said, "why not." Not exactly a rousing endorsement of what I believed was going to happen, but I'm not a disciplined person when it comes to women, and with my judgment fueled by booze, I would've thought sword-fighting with Zorro would be a good idea.

We wandered through a darkened, and what I thought to be an empty house without uttering a word to each other.

A dim floor lamp was on in her massive bedroom. She said, "I'm going to slip into something . . . more appropriate, dahlink. Make yourself comfortable."

I felt like I was in a time warp, living in a 1930s Cary Grant romantic comedy. By the time I conjured up a clever Grant-like response, she was gone in a swirl of flowing fabric, switching off the lamp as she exited.

Booze coursing through me like the Colorado River fueled my next move; I got naked, threw back the covers on the aircraft carrier–size bed, and climbed in.

I was enveloped in total darkness. I literally couldn't see my hand in front of my face, but I assumed I'd gain some night vision as my eyes became accustomed to the inky blackness. I didn't believe I wanted to have sex using the braille system, but, on the other hand, I didn't know if I wanted to see Zsa Zsa Gabor naked, either.

I was staring at the ceiling for maybe a minute, my eyes getting accustomed to the darkness, when the door that Zsa Zsa had disappeared through opened. A faint outline of a female figure wrapped in some kind of graceful, long robe approached the bed. It was dropped to the floor as she crawled in beside me. I put my hand on her breast.

This person was not Zsa Zsa Gabor.

I was in bed with a young woman, with the emphasis on *young*, maybe twenty-five—but it was hard to tell her age in the dark. She had long, straight blond hair. She didn't say a word, just got down to business. I said something, but I forget what. The woman didn't respond. I know I didn't inquire as to where Zsa Zsa was. Who cared?

It was an unforgettable experience. Either this woman was a pro or she had talents beyond her years. As soon as we were done, she got up, swung long, slender legs out of the bed, scooped up whatever she was wearing, and glided out of the room.

Not a word had been exchanged between us. A few minutes later, the floor lamp was switched on as Zsa Zsa materialized, wearing a white chiffon robe, still made up, hair done. She was smiling.

"I think you should leave now, dahlink. I had a maahvelous time. Can you see yourself out?"

Before I had a chance to answer, she did a graceful about-face and left through the same door she had entered by.

Perplexed but happy, I got dressed and departed, the limo driver having waitied patiently, engine idling.

The next day, Merv called me and asked if I'd had a good evening. I detected a knowing inflection in his voice.

I gave him the rundown, paying particular attention to what had transpired when we got back to Zsa Zsa's house.

"Do you know who the girl was, Merv?" I asked for two reasons: Obviously, I was curious, and I wouldn't have minded seeing her again.

There was a moment of silence; then he said, "Yeah, I know who she is."

"So, what's the story? Did Zsa Zsa assume I'd think it was her in bed? That's ridiculous."

Merv never answered me; he wished me a good day and rang off. It was obvious to me that Merv would never share what he knew, and I never brought up the subject again.

I never saw Zsa Zsa Gabor again, and over forty years later, the reason behind the episode of what happened in her bedroom is a mystery, and with her recent death, it will remain so.

9

INTERNATIONAL MONEYMAN

In the spring of 1978, I was summoned to Tony Accardo's palatial home in Chicago. Accardo was the boss of the Outfit, and when he called, I dropped what I was doing—which in my case wasn't much—and flew to the Windy City.

Accardo's home was beautiful, complete with a bowling alley. Present at the meeting was my friend Nick Nitti, and an Alitalia airline pilot, who was introduced to us as Captain Ferrara.

Accardo was a very cordial, polite person, and in his position, he didn't have to be. He was also a very good cook, and he prepared a lavish meal for us before getting down to business in his soundproofed den.

The mob made tons of money—no surprise there—but it couldn't be spent initially because it didn't have a legitimate history. The purpose of the meeting was to explain a new venture that would launder the illicit cash and make it spendable.

Accardo laid out a money-laundering operation that was international in scope, using the Vatican Bank in Rome as a conduit for the mob's ill-gotten Las Vegas gains.

"Gianni," Accardo said, "I want you and Nick to be couriers to the Vatican Bank. You'll be carrying the Vegas skim on Alitalia, on flights flown by our friend here"—he nodded to Ferrara—"and delivered to Rome."

He went on to explain the details. The circulated, well-worn Vegas money would be exchanged for new, uncirculated hundred-dollar bills through Perry Thomas, a senior executive of the Valley Bank, which had branches in Nevada. These crisp new bills would be bundled tightly and transported by Nick and me in two engineer bags, which were about twenty-four inches in length. At least four million dollars could be jammed into the two bags, and we'd be making the trip at least twice a month. With Accardo's influence, we would be able to obtain government-courier licenses under assumed names to smooth things out at airports should problems arise. No one bothered to ask for our passports because we had the courier licenses, or maybe someone was greased to allow us through; I never found out which. This was long before the terrorist attacks on September 11, 2001, and enactment of the Patriot Act, which turned a spotlight on international travel. We would make so many trips to Rome under different names that I often forgot what name I was traveling under.

On the Rome end, we'd deliver the cash to Archbishop Paul Marcinkus, who ran the Vatican Bank. Marcinkus was an Illinois native and a friend of Accardo's of many years standing. The archbishop would invest the money for the Outfit at a 5 percent return, keeping 15 percent of that as the Church's end, which was on the high side for money launderers. Normally, it was around 6 percent, depending on the amount, and I was also sure that the 5 percent return on our money was only a portion of what the Church was actually making on the millions of dollars we gave the archbishop to invest. If we were gangsters, what was the Church? Both business models sounded similar to me.

The archbishop had been Accardo's buddy for years, and he offered a higher rate of return than would Swiss banks, which were the banks of choice for years for those wishing to hide income. Swiss banks, however, would offer 1 percent *negative* interest, meaning the money would be skimmed by the Swiss for the convenience of using their services. A bank customer would actually lose money, but it was safer than hiding the cash in mayonnaise jars and burying them in your backyard, and it kept you off the IRS's radar, which was worth the small fee. The Swiss would throw you a bone if you deposited really large amounts, offering a push—no interest charged or given—or maybe 1 or 2 percent on the plus side if the deposits were huge. In the world of illicit money transfers, our eight million dollars a month wouldn't fit that definition.

The major upside of the plan was that the Vatican was on our side; they'd been sympathetic to the mob for years and could be trusted, and the Swiss were just conducting business. In our world, friendship trumped business relationships any day. If the Swiss were called on the carpet by the U.S. government, they'd fold like a circus tent in a hurricane. No one would question the authority and power of the Catholic Church, although there have been investigations over the years delving into the Vatican's business practices. The investigations snagged a sloppy private banker or two, but the Vatican always emerged unscathed.

In case you're wondering, we were told that the Pope was on board with the fiscal shenanigans. This, however, wouldn't always be the case, as I'll explain shortly. I came to realize that those affiliated with the Catholic Church, long my savior and respite in hard times, were gangsters in their own right. Since there are bad people in any business—and the Catholic Church is a business—I accepted the fact, and it didn't have an effect on my strong religious beliefs. I was still attending Mass several times a week (even having it written into my contract that I could do so when I appeared in *The Godfather*), and continue to do so to this day.

Italian customs officials were involved, too. Nick and I would sail through their checkpoints like we were red passport–carrying ambassadors.

Archbishop Marcinkus was on hand to meet us in Rome most of the time. He'd send his limo with a priest chauffeur, and two additional priests as security, to the airport to pick us up. I'm assuming the priests were armed. I would never see any weapons, although they could've hidden rifles under their ankle-length garb.

Marcinkus was in his mid-fifties, slight of build, and spoke very little English to us. Most every conversation was in Italian. I remember one time as we handed over the cash-laden bags to him, he said in English, "We turn a blind eye." One gangster talking to his American counterparts.

The operation grew bigger and the Outfit also began using Alitalia pilots as couriers, but only when Nick and I were otherwise engaged in other mob business.

We would stay overnight in a palatial suite at the Ambasciatori Hotel in Rome and fly home the next day. Naturally, there were no U.S. Customs problems on the return trip because we returned empty-handed.

I met Pope Paul VI on one trip, which was indeed an honor, and had a photo taken with him, which I have proudly and prominently displayed in my home to this day.

I was back in the States for only a short period of time after the picture was taken when the news broke worldwide that Pope Paul VI had died of natural causes. Out of respect, on August 12, 1978, Nick and I flew back to Rome for the funeral and stayed for the inauguration of the new Pope, John Paul I.

We assumed it was going to be business as usual for the money-laundering business, just a changing of the guard, so to speak, but I was very much mistaken.

I noticed a mood of doom and gloom among Accardo and other mob higher-ups about a week after we returned from the funeral and inauguration. There was a lot of hushed talk, and many of the bosses suddenly became "unavailable," which to me meant that there was a major meeting of the Commission somewhere off the grid. The last time the bosses had gone into whispered conversation mode and vanished from their usual haunts was prior to President Kennedy's assassination. Something big was about to happen and it wasn't going to be good.

We also didn't make our next scheduled trip back to Rome. "We're gonna hold off for a while," a representative of Accordo's told us.

About three weeks after Pope John Paul I was inaugurated, he died in his sleep. The official cause of death was a heart attack. The world—not only Catholics—was shocked; the Pope's death was the main topic of conversation on every television news channel. People were talking about it on the street and special Masses were being held in the Pope's honor.

Nick and I flew back to Rome for the funeral, our second for a Pope in little over a month. There was an air of despondency at the Vatican, as was to be expected, but there was also secrecy emanating from Archbishop Marcinkus and his bank officials. No one in the Pope's inner circle was saying anything about the circumstances under which the new Pope had died.

Conspiracy theories abounded when we returned home: The Russians killed the Pope, the CIA did it, and other such theories, which just got more insane as time passed.

In our world, people began to talk. The story was that the new Pope hadn't gone along with the money-laundering scheme; he'd been adamant about not continuing it. A decision had been made on our end by the Commission that the Pope had to go; there was just too much money involved to end what we had going. The Vatican hierarchy had agreed. What's hard for the average person to wrap his head around is someone ordering a hit on a sitting Pope, but I believed that's exactly what had happened. The word on the street was that the Pope had been given a hot shot of an untraceable drug and died instantly.

If the mob could murder the president of the United States, is it such a big leap to have a Pope killed? My belief was supported by the temporary halt in courier flights to Rome after the new Pope had been inaugurated. The mob is all about money and power; they don't care who you are. If you stand in their way, you're history. There was just too much money at stake to walk away from the operation. Immediately after the funeral, our trips to Rome resumed.

I stayed with the courier runs for five years, then gave them up, lucrative as they were. I figured my luck would run out sooner or later, the gravy train cut short by either the feds or the mob. I had survived for years by not being greedy. It was time to move on.

Two months later, on November 22, 1978, the *Las Vegas Sun* ran a story by their business writer, Gary Thompson. It read, in part:

> *A young entrepreneur's dream to build a $54 million-dollar hotel/casino moved closer to fulfillment Tuesday.*
>
> *The board of county commissioners granted Gianni Russo's request for a use permit to build and operate a 650-room, 23-story structure on a seven-acre lot at Harmon Avenue and Koval Lane.*
>
> *The 34-year-old Russo said he plans 21 blackjack tables, four craps tables, a Big Six wheel, baccarat, keno and 750 slot machines in the 18,000-square-foot casino area of his project.*
>
> *Russo said he has obtained private financing for the project.*

For years, the federal government had been trying to shut down the mob's involvement in skimming profits from Las Vegas casinos. Additionally, they knew that service employees, such as waiters and bartenders, were cheating on their taxes by drastically underestimating their tips, which comprised the majority of their income. The government's investigations went nowhere, which led to frustration and the reorganization of the feds' efforts.

Enter Howard Hughes, billionaire businessman.

Hughes, who was always looking for his next billion, was approached by the feds with a deal. The U.S. government would award the Howard Hughes Corporation lucrative aircraft construction contracts if Hughes would begin buying Las Vegas hotels and casinos and help the feds rid Vegas of mob influence.

Hughes agreed, and he began by purchasing the Sands and Frontier hotels—there were more to come—into which the FBI infiltrated agents to work as service employees to spy on the tax cheats. The conduit from Hughes to the government were the numerous former CIA and FBI agents whom Hughes had on his payroll.

Add to this mix the rapidly diminishing cadre of old-school Mafia dons who had built Las Vegas and who were in the process of dying off, being replaced by younger men who weren't as steeped in the casino business as were men like Frank Costello, and you had the perfect storm of opportunity. I was beholden to no one, not being a made member of any one mob family, and I had no criminal record; I had never even been arrested. I was flush with cash from my Vatican Bank involvement and the marker business, some of which could be funneled through the Banca di Roma in Italy as a construction loan.

I had harbored dreams of becoming a Las Vegas hotel magnate for a while, and I decided to go for the gold. I'd carefully vet my employees—federal agents need not apply—and with the cooperation of a few well-placed friends, I'd be in business.

I locked up a ninety-nine-year lease on twenty-three acres of land behind the Aladdin Hotel and adjacent to a golf course, which would later become the site for the MGM Grand Hotel. With the unwitting cooperation of the Las Vegas Planning Commission, which made Paradise Lane and the Strip one-way thoroughfares leading to and from the airport and past the site of my projected hotel, I was on my way to fulfilling my vision.

I was focusing all my time on planning the new hotel when another opportunity I couldn't pass up presented itself.

On January 2, 1979, I received a call from a General Mobabba of the Iranian military. The name Mobabba was familiar to me, but I'd never met the general. My ex-wife Susan's gynecologist was Dr. Mobabba (the general's daughter), and was married to my friend Dr. Teddy Jacobs, who had gone with me to the premiere of *The Godfather*.

The general was very professional but vague as to the reason for his call.

"Can you come to Tehran as soon as possible to discuss business?"

With what little I knew about Iran, I was pretty sure the general wasn't interested in opening up an Italian restaurant.

"Can you tell me what this entails, General?"

"Not on the phone, but it will be worth your while."

Iran wasn't exactly an easy commute, and I hesitated, trying to think of a way to pry more information out of him before I committed myself. While I was pondering my next move, the general said, "I heard about your recent holiday at the Vatican. I'm a big admirer of the Pope."

Now I knew exactly what he wanted to discuss. It was no secret that Mohammad Reza Pahlavi, the Shah and ruler of Iran, was about to be overthrown by the Ayatollah Khomeini, a religious zealot who was close to knocking on the Shah's door as we spoke. It didn't take a genius to figure what the Shah wanted. Our job was to get his cash out and let the Vatican work their laundering magic. What I found a bit surprising was that my Vatican activities were known to the Iranians; they had an intelligence service, and apparently it was a good one.

"My partner and I could be there as quickly as you can secure the visas and whatever else we're going to need to get into your country." I said. I knew Nick Nitti would be on board with any new business deal, and he was one of the few people I trusted implicitly. We went back a long way. Nick owned a travel agency in Chicago and ran a lot of charters to Vegas. He was destined to be in the life because of his grandfather, the infamous Frank Nitti. Nick was a slim guy, on the short side, and one of the funniest people I've ever met. He reminded me of a computer geek or a librarian.

"Very good. It's as good as done," the general said. I detected a tone of relief in his voice.

I gave the general the information he needed for the travel documentation. After I hung up the phone, I realized what I had just committed myself to. I was going to a foreign country whose ruler was about to be overthrown at any moment, and I was doing it blindly. Certainly the prospect of making a big score was a huge motivation, but I can't deny that the intrigue of the whole thing got my adrenaline pumping.

I met Nick at McCarran Airport the next day for the flight to Tehran. Eighteen exhausting hours later, we landed at Mehrabad International Airport, a veritable armed camp, ringed with anchor fencing, barbed wire, half-tracks, and hundreds of armed soldiers.

I had expected hot, dry desert weather, but what we got was a frigid blast of cold air as we deplaned. It turns out that January in Tehran is like being in Denver during the winter. Nick and I had worn summer-weight suits for the meeting, which now looked like we'd slept in them, but they would have to do. We didn't plan on staying long.

We were met by six men in suits and ties and driven to an office building in Tehran in a three-vehicle caravan. The trip took less than fifteen minutes, and the highway was nearly deserted. Iranians were staying off the radar; there was revolution in the air.

General Mobabba looked to be in his early fifties, with a close-cropped gray beard. He tried to project an air of calmness and control, but I could tell he was frazzled; his eyes kept darting around the room, as if he was expecting to be arrested at any moment. He was wearing a well-pressed suit and gleaming shoes. In the third-floor office with him were two bodyguards, also in civvies, and armed with AK-47s.

After a short round of pleasantries, the general got right to it.

"You can get money out of the country?"

Nick said, "Sure. That's what we do."

The general nodded. "How much can you get out at once?"

"All of it," I said.

"Don't you want to know how much? This is the Shah's family fortune. It's extensive."

I shook my head. "We need to know weight and volume; the amount is unimportant."

We talked for what seemed like hours and a plan was formulated. Understanding that time was crucial—the general said the regime could topple within the week—Nick and I decided that we needed more help.

We flew to Sicily that afternoon to recruit a crew to help us carry the cash; there were literally hundreds of millions of dollars in Iranian rial waiting to be transported out of Iran. Our expertise wasn't necessarily needed to transport the cash, but to provide a new home for it was another matter. Anyone could load money onto a plane and take off, but where do you land with six dozen duffel bags stuffed with money, and how do you keep it safe?

We were exhausted, but we kept on moving, fueled by coffee and visions of how much money we were going to make *if* we were successful.

Our buddy, the Alitalia pilot, Captain Ferrara, was pressed into service. While he was chartering a plane to take us back to Tehran, Nick and I met with a Mafia boss, who supplied us with six guys who looked like they could strap the duffel bags on their backs and walk them out of the country.

The plan was to leave for Tehran as soon as Captain Ferrara got the aircraft. We would load the money the following day, fly back to Sicily, pay off the help, refuel, then fly to Rome to unload the cash to priest couriers, who would deposit it in the Vatican Bank. Then Nick and I would fly home.

What could possibly go wrong?

We slept fitfully on the plane ride back to Tehran, nervous as hell. The plan's success depended on getting all the money out of several banks simultaneously just before closing time, so as not to arouse suspicion that we were moving the cash out of the country. We would then meet up at the building where we had met the general initially, and make the fifteen-minute trip to the airport. A government was about to fall and we were sure that there were some members of the Shah's military in on the coup. No one could be trusted, save for General Mobabba, and maybe he was just a few million rial away from betraying the whole scheme. Nick and I didn't trust anyone; there was just too much money involved. What was to stop the general and his cronies from relieving us of the money once we got back to the building, killing us, and taking our plane and dough to parts unknown?

I had never been so tired in my life, but sleep eluded me the night we spent at the Hilton Hotel back in Tehran. So much depended on the general's loyalty and perfect timing.

We assembled with the general and his men at noon in the office building. At 2:00 P.M., we were divided into three teams, then sat waiting for it to be exactly 3:00 P.M., when each team would be assigned to pick up cash at two banks. The money would be waiting for us because it had been prearranged with the banking officials the previous day.

"You trust these bank guys not to turn us in to the new regime?" Nick asked the general.

"Not a problem. Banking people love the Shah. He has made them rich," the general replied.

"Right," I said. The bankers were the weak link. Unless they were planning their own escape, what better way to ingratiate themselves with the new regime than to turn in Americans who were looting Iranian assets?

A little after 3:00 P.M., the first van arrived back at the building, followed shortly by the last two vans. They were all jammed to the doors with duffel bags stuffed with the money.

The general sensed our nervousness.

"Nothing to be concerned about; everthing's going smoothly."

Yeah, easy for him to say.

The three vehicles lined up, with me and my driver in the lead van because I knew where the plane was waiting, Nick was in the second van, and a young lieutenant whom the general had ordered to accompany us was in the last one. I surmised that if we were caught, the general didn't want his name associated with the scam and had decided to sit this one out. Couldn't blame him.

We pulled out onto a mostly deserted highway for the short trip to the airport.

Five minutes into the trip, things looked like they were going to work and I began to deflate. "We're gonna make it," I said into my radio.

Nick replied, "I'm counting my money already."

No sooner had he uttered those words than a dozen military half-tracks rolled past us, heading in the same direction as the airport.

"Who're those guys?" I asked into the radio.

There was a pause. "The Ayatollah's troops," the lieutenant said ominously.

The first thing you do when you're taking over a country is to seize the airports and the radio and TV stations. The revolution had begun and we were right in the middle of it.

I was sweating despite the brisk weather. We had a problem.

We were being careful to keep just under the speed limit when the half-tracks had rolled right past us. The half-tracks had wheels in the front and tanklike treads in the back. As such, they couldn't go that fast; they were doing maybe five-five miles per hour. Our only chance was to pass them and get to the airport before they did. I had no desire to spend the rest of my life in an Iranian prison, getting tortured on a daily basis.

"Step on it," I told my driver, "Pass the half-tracks. We've gotta beat these guys to the airport." I radioed what we were doing.

We accelerated to ninety miles per hour, passing the half-tracks like they were standing still. Captain Ferrara had previously received instructions to be prepared to have wheels off the ground at 4:00 P.M. sharp. We were going to be ahead of schedule. For obvious reasons, no flight plan had been filed, and the plane was sitting next to a hangar at the far end of a runway. It was going to be a mad dash to unload the loot and get the hell out of Dodge.

The strategy was to roll up to a locked gate where the security guards had been paid off. They'd open the gate, we'd drive up to the plane, transfer the cash, and take off.

As we approached the gate, my heart dropped to my testicles. Our bribed guards had been replaced by military personnel, and we had no idea whose side they were on. They wore the uniforms of the Iranian army, but I was pretty sure that by this time they had been compromised and were now under the Ayatollah's control.

The lieutenant's voice was loud and clear over my radio. "Do not stop at the gate!"

No shit.

We drove past the gate at a sensible speed, not knowing where the hell we were going. In less than two minutes, we were at the end of the airport, and in the distance—beyond a double-anchor fence topped with barbed wire—sat our plane, glistening in the late-afternoon sun.

So near and yet so far away. Now what?

The lieutenant yelled over the radio, "Go through the fence!"

No one moved.

I was in the lead vehicle, so I figured it was my job to say something. "Where? There's another gate?"

The lieutenant's van pulled up alongside mine, and he poked his head out the passenger window. "We make our own gate. Follow me!"

The lieutenant's van plowed through the double fence, with me right behind him. His van began dragging a significant portion of the fence, which was now wrapped around his vehicle. My driver floored the van and sped through the gap in the fence.

I was already getting out of the vehicle before it came to a complete stop; everyone began scrambling to unload the cash.

Three men, including Captain Ferrara, ran from the plane to lend a hand. Everyone created a line and began tossing the bags forward into the aircraft. The lieutenant lent a hand. He was sweating.

"Hurry," he said, "we don't have much time. Someone had to see us crash the fence."

The bags were loaded in less than five minutes, and our Sicilian baggage handlers tripped over one another scrambling to board the plane. I was listening for approaching sirens but heard none, although the Ayatollah's men could have been on their way, because I couldn't hear anything other than our plane's jet engines warming up.

The lieutenant stood by his vehicle as Nick and I approached and shook his hand. I was wrong to suspect the general or his men of collusion with the opposition forces; he had been a man of his word.

"There's plenty of room on the plane, Lieutenant. We can put you in first class," I said with a weary smile.

He shook his head. "I'll be fine. In a few days, I'll have a new boss, and life goes on," he said stoically.

Nick and I ran for the plane, fully expecting to be chased down the runway by a platoon on half-tracks firing machine guns. It didn't happen.

The flight to Sicily was without incident. I tried to sleep during the trip, but I was too ramped up to even close my eyes. Only when we landed safely did I relax, and the events of the last few days caught up to me. I was so whacked, I could barely speak. Nick, normally an animated mile-a-minute talker, could only grunt when I tried asking him how he was holding up.

We were met by ten mafiosi with rifles when we landed. While we paid off the crew who had accompanied us to Tehran, the riflemen ringed the aircraft and stood guard. No one from Sicilian customs even approached us. There were a lot of others, it seemed, getting a piece of the action.

It took an hour to refuel the plane and do whatever safety checks had to be done. We got the thumbs-up from the good captain, and we were off to Rome, less than a two-hour flight.

We transferred the cash to a waiting truck at Leonardo da Vinci International Airport, once again without interference from customs. Afterward, Nick and I cabbed it to the Ambassadori Hotel. I never thought I would be as pleased as I was to get rid of money, and was happy to hand it over to the Vatican Laundromat.

As we staggered down the hallway to our respective rooms, Nick said, "We're rich, buddy."

To which I replied, "Fuck the money; sleep is more important."

I felt differently the next day. My payment for the Iranian job was enough to keep me solvent for the rest of my life, but of course I wasn't about to retire at thirty-five years old. My Las Vegas hotel project was in the works, and I had more ideas churning in my brain, enough to keep me busy for years to come. I wasn't really concerned about how much money I made; I needed the action—the thrill of risk and reward—to keep my fires burning. Almost forty years later, I still have the same mind-set.

On January 16, 1979, the day we landed in Rome, the Shah fled Iran. He would eventually wind up in New York, where he sought medical treatment for cancer, and would die of the disease on July 27, 1980.

A week after Nick and I arrived back in the States, the Ayatollah, now firmly entrenched as Iran's new leader, declared that the Shah fled the county penniless, and the Iranian people were now free of his despotic rule.

I had to laugh. Technically, the Ayatollah was correct: The Shah did flee Iran penniless, because his fortune was safely in the vaults of the Vatican Bank, courtesy of two Americans.

I spent the rest of the year working on the myriad details that needed to be completed before we could begin construction of my baby, the Renaissance Hotel and Casino.

As the new year approached, plans for the groundbreaking ceremony were in full swing.

A huge party tent had been erected on the land where the Renaissance was eventually going to be. On April 1, 1980, every major celebrity who was in Las Vegas attended the celebration, including Wayne Newton, hotel magnate Steve Wynn, Liberace, Lola Falana, Bobby Vinton, illusionists Siegfried & Roy, plus the governor of Nevada and the mayor of Las Vegas.

The theme of the party was "Can You Dig It?" and a band was present to lend musical accompaniment to the festivities.

At the stroke of midnight, I pulled up to the tent in a bulldozer, cradling a magnum of champagne. Simultaneously, fireworks lit up the Vegas sky. One of the pyrotechnics blazed the name Renaissance Hotel overhead just as I dug the first shovel of earth from the desert floor.

The party went until dawn. The culmination of every dream I'd ever had of becoming a success was coming to fruition. I was putting mob life on the back burner and adding to my résumé the title of legitimate businessman. After the last guest had left, I surveyed the empty lot on which would stand Las Vegas's newest luxury hotel. My sense of satisfaction was indescribable; I felt like the king of the world.

Within a month, I would be dethroned, and everything would go to hell.

The country was in the throes of a financial crisis, mostly powered by the spike in the price of foreign oil imports. Jimmy Carter was in his first—and last—term as president, and I thought he was doing a less than stellar job of getting us out of the financial mess we were in.

About a month into the construction of the Renaissance, interest rates skyrocketed to 19 percent. I wouldn't have given a damn if my only concern were my mob endeavors, because inflation doesn't have an effect on the Mafia's income. The mob even thrived during the Great Depression. But now I was concerned because construction loan interest charges mirrored the inflation rate, plus a few points.

I used very little of my own money to start construction of the hotel. The first rule of business: Use other people's money. It wasn't a problem floating a loan at a reasonable rate. My interest rate, however, ballooned from reasonable to outlandish almost as soon as I shoveled the first scoop of dirt to begin construction.

While I was trying to come to terms with the high interest rates, I was hit with another problem, one that could result in jail time.

The FBI had a wiretap on the Kansas City faction of the mob. The feds had wiseguys Nicky Civella, Joe Agosto, and Carl DeLuna on tape discussing a possible investment of thirty million dollars in my hotel.

There are strict rules governing who can invest in the Las Vegas casino business. Not surprisingly, the mob isn't on the list of approved investors. The Las Vegas Gaming Commission kept a close eye on all aspects of gaming. After years of trying to get the mob out of Las Vegas, the FBI now had solid information that wiseguys were considering an investment in the Renaissance. It was my responsibility to keep the Gaming Commission informed every step of the way as to what business decisions were transpiring with my hotel. I couldn't say "Oops, I forgot to mention those guys as possible investors." The onus was on me to keep the Gaming Commission in the loop at all times, and failure to do that was a felony.

I was also concerned about whether I had been recorded while making calls to my friends in Kansas City. I spoke to those guys often, Nicky Civella being a good friend. I began the impossible and unnerving task of trying to remember everything we had discussed since the idea of building a hotel entered my mind.

I now had two things to worry about, and neither was going away.

I discussed the problems with my attorneys, who reminded me that I had another problem: the lease. I'd taken a ninety-nine-year lease on the property where the hotel was being built, and my lawyers told me that I'd be stuck paying it off even if the hotel went belly-up.

I could do nothing about the interest rate except use my own money for expenses, and that was foolish. As far as the federal wiretaps were concerned, the only way I could wiggle out of that mess was to pull the plug on the hotel; that way, I wouldn't be breaking any laws, because I couldn't involve the mob in a business venture that didn't exist.

I had a few sleepless nights deciding what to do. Eventually, logic made my decision for me. There was no way I'd pay 19 percent interest on a loan, so the decision was evident. I had to walk away from my dream, but I still had the lease hanging over my head.

I called the landlord and told him I might have to suspend construction on the hotel temporarily, and I asked if I could halt lease payments until construction started up again. He told me that wasn't a problem—what's a few months when the lease went for ninety-nine years? I had the lease contract rewritten to reflect the new verbiage, which read, in part, that as soon as the construction resumed, I'd resume paying the lease. The landlord didn't think the agreement through, because there was no restart planned—ever—so I got away with reneging on the lease payments. Unethical? You bet, but I wasn't about to eat millions of dollars in lease payments for a hotel that was never going to be built.

Then, as luck would have it, there was an unfortunate fire in the office trailer on the construction site, and all the records pertaining to the construction of the hotel were destroyed. What can you do? Stuff happens.

Years later, I'm reminded of the movie *Godfather III,* when the now elderly and sick Michael Corleone bitches about how every time he tries to leave the mob, he gets pulled back in.

I was going back to what I knew best.

One of the most sought-after invitations in Hollywood was to President Ronald Reagan's seventieth birthday party in February 1981. The bash was being held on the back lot of the NBC studios in Burbank, California, with two hundred of Hollywood's elite, in addition to politicians and world leaders, attending. And me.

Frank Sinatra, who had long since forgotten about my stunt at his daughter Nancy's party in Las Vegas, had gotten me an invitation to the black-tie event.

I knew Reagan, having been introduced to him by the president of the Music Corporation of America (MCA), Lew Wasserman, in Matteo's Restaurant, a Hollywood hot spot where I had a standing reservation every Sunday night whether I was in town or not. Reagan had been the president of the Screen Actors Guild before becoming governor of California, and he was at Matteo's almost as often as I was. I'd often run into him at the Polo Lounge in the Beverly Hills Hotel, too.

Ronald Reagan was a personable and very approachable individual, insisting that everyone call him "Dutch" the night of the party. He never failed to recognize me over the years, and often took time out to chat. Without Sinatra's pull, however, I'd never have wangled an invite to what was surely the Hollywood event of the year.

Old Hollywood had a strong presence at the party, and while nothing much impressed me anymore, I was in awe of the iconic star power that was present. The Hollywood of today is in sharp contrast to what it was when most of the invitees were growing up. Movie stars kept their private lives private when they could, and scandals were rare. A sex or drug scandal could derail a career; now such a scandal enhances it. Whether these lionized actors were as pure as we were led to believe made little difference; old Hollywood knew decorum and how to create an aura of respectability.

Many motion picture icons were there, including Jimmy Stewart, Fred Astaire, James Cagney, Lauren Bacall, Cary Grant, Katharine Hepburn, William Holden, and numerous others whose names I've forgotten. I was reminded of where I came from, and was humbled by where I was standing; it was a far cry from selling pens on the street in midtown Manhattan. Mingling with these people was an experience, and I was polite, but I kept my usually verbose personality in check. I stuck with Sinatra, Dean Martin, Sammy Davis, Jr., and the rest of the crew with whom I was most comfortable.

It was a whirlwind night of speeches, laughs, and memories, and an event I'll never forget.

But after the hoopla died down, it was time to return to reality.

While deciding what to do next, I figured I would do what I do best—spend money. I bought another Bentley. Not that I needed one—I still owned a serviceable Bentley—but I figured, What if one is in the shop?

A few weeks later, after a particularly heavy partying night, I wound up in bed with some woman I barely knew, and woke up to a ringing phone.

"Yeah," I said when I answered, my head pounding. "What time is it?"

After a brief moment of silence, the caller said, "Uh, a little after eleven A.M. Is this Mr. Russo?"

"Uh-huh," I said. I did my best to sound lucid. "Who is this?"

"Ralph, from Towbin Rolls-Royce. We parked your new Rolls in your driveway, sir. Just thought we'd let you know. Keys are in the mailbox. Enjoy the car, Mr. Russo."

I had no idea who this guy was or what he was talking about, and told him so.

"I'm Ralph Friedman, from Towbin Rolls-Royce," he repeated. "The Silver Cloud you bought last night, Mr. Russo, we just delivered it to you. It's in your driveway. This is Gianni Russo, yes?" he asked.

I assured him it was, swung myself out of bed, and looked in the driveway. Sure enough, there was a brand-new, gleaming eggshell blue Rolls-Royce parked regally in my driveway.

I had bought a friggin' $300,000 car and had no recollection of doing it.

Not wishing to look like an asshole, I covered and said, "Oh, yeah, sure. Thank you."

I cut back on my drinking after that.

I had pursued my acting career since appearing in *The Godfather*. I had been offered a variety of movie and television roles, and had taken the parts I liked. I'd done two, both in 1975. The first one was *Lepke*, a biopic of gangster Louis Buchalter's life, with Tony Curtis, and *4 Deuces*, another gangster picture, this one with Jack Palance. I also made a picture in Italy. I'd recently been offered a daytime television quiz show on NBC called *Celebrity Sweepstakes,* taped in Los Angeles, and decided to give it a shot because it offered a chance to broaden my résumé.

I was on a panel with two other celebrities, George Hamilton and Dionne Warwick. Contestants bet money on which of us could successfully answer questions a brain-damaged donkey wouldn't have trouble with. *Jeopardy!* it wasn't. We shot five episodes every Sunday, changing clothes between episodes to make it appear that we had taped the show on different days.

I was talking to Dionne Warwick one day between episodes, and I asked her, "What ever happened to your career?" I'm not normally so blunt, but Dionne was a caustic, abrasive person, and I decided to take her down a peg. In truth, she hadn't had a hit song in quite a while, and it was no secret that she was broke and her house was in foreclosure.

She was caught off guard and was momentarily speechless; then she came at me.

"You've got some nerve saying that to me."

"Legit comment," I said, then added, "Before you go off on me, just let me say if you let me manage your career, I'll make you a ton of money. You're not realizing your full potential." I knew nothing about managing talent, and threw this out on the spur of the moment. Realistically, however, I'd always wondered how talent managers had the balls to take 15 percent of an entertainer's money for what I thought was a commonsense business that anyone who was glib could pull off. I was nothing if not glib.

I could tell she was intrigued . . . or maybe desperate.

"Oh, really?" she said. "And you say that because . . ."

"You sing classics; you've got to branch out to pop tunes. Someone with your great talent can handle any type of song." Stroking her ego can't be a bad idea, I thought.

She smiled. "Let me think about it."

It didn't take her long to agree to let me manage her. She had little to lose, as her career was already circling the drain. And the rest, as they say, is history.

We called the company we formed December 12 (Dionne and I shared the same birth date, as did Sinatra), and I moved into her house at 207 North Elm Street in Beverly Hills when she was on the road, which was usually from three to four months at a time. The house was across the street from the Menendez family home, which was later made infamous as the location where the two kids, Lyle and Erik, shotgunned their parents to death. Dionne's kids, Damon and David, were the same age as the Menendez brothers and would play with them in their respective yards when they were growing up.

While I was in the process of rejuvenating Dionne's career, I wrote and produced a movie called *P.C.H.*, starring Sally Kellerman, Elliott Gould, Jack Scalia, and Robert Mitchum's grandson, Casper Van Dien. The then unknown Denise Richards was also in the picture. I also produced and wrote another movie, *For Which He Stands,* with Robert Davi and William Forsythe. I was on the creative end now, and I was loving it.

I was able to acquire the song "I'll Never Love This Way Again" for Dionne, which she recorded with Barry Manilow, who had arranged it. It would be her biggest hit to date, and it helped propel her to superstardom. Almost immediately after the song became a hit, I was approached by other singers and actors—most of whom I had never heard of—who asked me to manage them. I decided to stick with Dionne exclusively, at least for now. I would wind up being her manager for fourteen years, never taking on another client. I had too many other irons in the fire to be saddled with babysitting a bunch of spoiled Hollywood brats. I would get enough attitude from Dionne, who began to go full diva on me and got to be a real pain in the ass. I booked her for three straight years on the road so that I wouldn't have to deal with her whining in person every day.

Wherever Dionne appeared, she *demanded* that everything on the stage be white. Besides her outfits, she wanted white drapes and flooring, a white piano player dressed all in white, *and* a white piano.

She called me right before a concert in Japan, bitching that her piano wasn't white and she wasn't going to perform.

"I'm not going on," she told me. "My piano isn't white. It's supposed to be white."

The show was scheduled to begin in an hour. I was pissed. "You're going on," I said. "We have a goddamn contract. There're thousands of people who paid to see you."

"No, I'm not!" I could almost hear her stamping her foot.

I'd had it with this broad. "Listen to me, bitch. You already spent the money." She had gotten $500,000 for that concert. "What do you want me to do, fly out there and paint the fucking thing? A bit of a commute, don't you think?"

We went back and forth for ten minutes; finally she relented and did the concert.

I'd rather have drunk toxic waste than have had to deal with any more "talent," and was glad I'd decided to limit my clientele exclusively to Dionne Warwick.

My efforts didn't stop at just booking concert venues for her. I cut a deal with Paul Mitchell, the beauty products manufacturer, to come up with a fragrance and name it Dionne. It was a spectacular success.

In an effort to get her publicity, I managed to get Dionne named President Ronald Reagan's ambassador for health, largely a ceremonial position, but she did speak occasionally, promoting a healthy lifestyle. This from a woman who smoked three packs of cigarettes a day. She held up the swearing-in ceremony the day she got the appointment from the president because she had to have a smoke, and never sang without a cough drop in her mouth to lubricate her vocal cords.

The culmination of my time with Dionne was when she won a Grammy for her song "That's What Friends Are For." The ceremony was held in Santa Monica. I was standing on the stage with Carol Bayer Sager, who wrote the song, and two other honorees, Stevie Wonder, who was seated at a piano, and Gladys Knight. Once again, I had to marvel at what I'd become, and was thankful to God for giving me the opportunity to be a success.

Things were going very well for me. My show-business career was booming and I was content with my life. Then I received a call that would make me break out in a sweat.

New York City police detective Sgt. Joe Coffey called me one day out of nowhere and reminded me of a time in my life I hadn't thought about in years.

"This Gianni Russo?" Coffey asked after introducing himself.

"Yeah," I said, an icy finger of dread running down my back. In my circles, any contact with a cop can only mean bad news. It's tantamount to a CEO of a company answering his front door at home and finding a crew from *60 Minutes* standing there.

"We're investigating a cold case you might be able to help us with. Can you talk now? I'll only need a few minutes of your time."

Coffey seemed friendly enough, but all cops do when they're trying to get information out of you.

"Sure, Sergeant," I said, a quiver in my voice I hoped he wouldn't detect. "If I can help . . ."

"We're looking into the homicide of an orderly at Bellevue Hospital named Harold Stanton in 1954. He was assigned to the polio ward and was stabbed to death when you were a patient there. Do you recall this Stanton guy?"

I had to sit down. Why after all these years would the cops reopen this case? My head was swimming.

I hesitated for a moment, as if I were thinking. "Stanton? No, I don't think so. That was a long time ago, Sergeant. I was a kid."

"You're sure?"

I let out a small chuckle, as if the ridiculousness of the question was amusing. "Oh yeah, I'm sure. I can't recall the name at all and don't recall—what, a murder? Definitely not."

I could tell he didn't believe a word I was saying, but he ended the conversation by saying that he would be in touch.

I sat holding the phone in a tight grip for a few minutes, deciding what to do. Frank Costello had told me shortly after I began working for him that he had taken care of the "problem at the hospital" and not to worry about the incident anymore. I'd never told him what happened, never even mentioned the incident; he had just taken it upon himself to check my background before taking me under his protective wing. After that brief conversation, I had pushed the incident out of my mind. I had found out a few years later that the sharpened stick I'd used to defend myself against Harold had vanished from the NYPD's property facility in Queens, and the case was dropped by whatever detective was handling it.

Now, almost thirty years later, the nightmare had resurfaced. Mr. C. was gone and my only connection to those days was Aniello "Neil" Dellacroce, the highly respected capo and elder statesman with the Gambinos.

It took me a few days to set up a secure phone call to Dellacroce. He was old-school and didn't talk on a phone unless urgent necessity dictated it. We got along very well, and he respected me because I was a good earner and could be trusted. I wouldn't ordinarily have reached out to him to talk business, but Coffey's phone call had gotten to me.

Despite the security measures, we both knew the fewer words exchanged the better, with no names mentioned.

"You are well?" I asked.

"As well as can be. And you?" he replied, and muffled a cough.

"Concerned. I'm calling about—"

"I know what you're calling about," he said, interrupting me. "That problem was taken care of years ago when you were told it was taken care of. You have nothing to worry about."

"So, why'd this guy call me and bring it up?"

"Because someone wants to knock you down a few pegs."

"Who?" I asked. I didn't want to press the old man, but I needed information, a way to fight back.

There were a few moments of dead air. "Maybe someone in Queens is jealous of your success. You have a good day, Gianni." He coughed once more and was gone. I would never talk to him again; in two years, Dellacroce would die of brain cancer.

I'd been having problems with John Gotti for years. They were nothing major, just annoying bullshit, like insect bites. It seemed the more success I had achieved, the pettier the demands and rumors of backstabbing gossip I'd hear about me, all emanating from Gotti. He wasn't only petty with me; he would gossip like an old lady about anyone he deemed was smart and making money. Gotti, despite his notoriety and the confident bravado he showed the press, was paranoid, reckless, and a degenerate gambler with low self-esteem. He thought everyone was out to get him and he trusted no one.

I would get calls from Gotti periodically, asking me for favors, or proposals for business deals, all crooked. Not that I was above a good scam occasionally, but I didn't want to deal with Gotti, who had a big mouth, and most of his ideas involved my connections in Las Vegas with people whom I guarded and protected. I didn't want the East Coast taint of Gotti and his irresponsible schemes as part of my life.

He had called me recently regarding placing slot machines in casinos.

"I could have dozens of machines to you by the end of the week," he had told me.

I had explained to him numerous times that any business involving gambling in Vegas had to pass through the Gaming Commission, which would examine any proposed deal under a microscope. If there was even a hint of illegality or mob involvement, the FBI would be called in. The last thing I needed was to be banned from Las Vegas. On the other hand, I needed to turn Gotti down without pissing him off, because he could make my life miserable.

"Sounds like a good idea, John, but we have to be legit," I said, and ran through the myriad list of rules and regulations required to do business in Sin City, then added, "The first thing you need to do is form a corporation, make sure your taxes are in order, then—"

"I'm not doing that bullshit, Gianni," Gotti said, interrupting. "We'll just put the fucking machines in the casinos. You can say you own them."

I knew I'd lost him when I mentioned the word *corporation*, which I'd done on purpose. Gotti was averse to doing anything that was legitimate. For ten minutes, I explained to him why passing the slot machines off as mine wouldn't work, mainly because they couldn't be traced back to me. After ten minutes of getting his plan knocked down, he gave up in frustration.

"Aw, fuck it," he grumbled, and hung up.

He probably had fumed about yet another rebuff from me and had had some friendly cop boss at headquarters make a call to Coffey about the Bellevue thing. Coffey was an honest cop, but when you get a call from a mob boss to follow something up, you do it. It was no secret in our circles what had occurred in the polio ward back in the day, and that I needed to be reminded of it. Gotti was also a control freak who liked to micromanage. Well, I couldn't be controlled by him, and that might have pissed him off.

What I had going for me was that at the time Gotti was a crew captain—a capo—and not the boss of the Gambino family, which he'd become in a few years, when he would murder the boss, Paul Castellano, and take over the reins of the family. Presently, he was under the control of Dellacroce, who had Castellano's ear, and I'm sure after Dellacroce and I completed our call, he was on the phone to Gotti, telling him that whoever had resurrected the Bellevue incident better make sure nothing else was said about it.

I never heard from Sergeant Coffey again.

Despite my increasing show-business success, I had plenty of downtime and was looking to get involved in another business.

An idea was germinating in Las Vegas. Despite its reputation as a twenty-four-hour town, it was next to impossible to get a good meal after midnight almost anywhere. Most of the coffee shops were open 24/7, but they all offered the standard fare—eggs, hamburgers, and any Greek dish you could think of—but nothing was exactly gourmet fare.

I had an idea of opening up an elegant supper club with entertainment, where I'd offer epicurean dining from 6:00 P.M. to 6:00 A.M. All I needed was a location; I planned on using my own money, because not much would be required. After the Renaissance Hotel debacle, I wouldn't even listen to people who might want to invest, let alone discuss business on the phone.

I hunted for a suitable location, excluding Strip locations as too expensive. Real estate prices even one block off the Strip were reasonable and easily accessible by anyone, and I liked the idea of an exclusive club off the beaten path—the hidden gem in a sea of gaudy neon light.

I contacted my friend Moe Dalitz, who owned significant real estate all over Vegas and beyond. He had a seven-thousand-square-foot vacant building located on State Street, which was perfect. It needed a little renovation, and I could remodel it to my liking. I bought it.

Hotel magnate Steve Wynn had heard that I was opening up a club and called me. "I'm remodeling the Golden Nugget and getting rid of the bar. You can have it, no charge."

The Golden Nugget was located in old Las Vegas and had been one of the first hotels built, even prior to the big boom. Wynn had bought it recently and was gutting the entire building.

"What's it look like?" I asked.

"It's round."

Great, I thought, that tells me a lot. "What else? How big? What's it made of?"

"Tell you what," Steve said. "You can come to the Nugget and look at it right now, or look at it later on the sidewalk, because that's where it's going if you don't take it."

I was at the Nugget within the hour.

The bar was beautiful; about seventy feet in circumference, with a black onyx overlay. I couldn't believe he was giving the bar away, but that's the way he did business. One of the most successful hotel owners on the Strip since Vegas emerged from the desert, Steve Wynn did things his way.

The bar would go right in the center of the main room, in the middle of the dance floor, so drinkers would be close to some of the most beautiful people in Vegas gyrating to the tunes of live music or that played by DJs. No one would be without a view of what was happening in my new club, which I named Gianni Russo's State Street.

Advertising is always a significant portion of any club's budget. There are numerous ways people can spend their money in Vegas, and club owners were always trying to outdo one another with glitzy advertising to attract them. Tourist brochures, magazines, and pamphlets advertising nightclubs were everywhere, and it was difficult to become noticed, especially if you were the new kid on the block, like I was. The conventional way of thinking was the larger the ad, the bigger the return. I'd decided to buck the "bigger is better" trend.

What I had going for me was my ability to attract celebrities. After being in Las Vegas for a few years, I'd gotten to know every major star and those who thought they were major stars. Attracting celebrities is an exercise in self-perpetuation. I needed only a few A-listers at the beginning; as soon as the word got around that Frank Sinatra and Dean Martin were regulars, all the celebrities who wanted to breathe the rarified air of Frank and Dean would flock to the club. Soon Gianni Russo's State Street was the place to be.

The list of entertainers who became regulars was endless: Paul Anka, Julio Iglesias, Muhammad Ali, Wayne Newton, Don Rickles, Engelbert Humperdinck, Diahann Carroll and her husband, singer Vic Damone (a degenerate gambler who never got paid for his appearances in Vegas; he was always working off a gambling debt). While Sinatra was a big draw for tourists, he wasn't a regular. Past presidents Jimmy Carter and Gerald Ford, and current president Ronald Reagan stopped by many times. Paul Newman was at the club so often, he had his own private dining room, where he would bring his women, and there were many. Bill Cosby was a regular and wasn't liked by the staff. I wasn't crazy about him, either. He was very cheap, always stiffed the waitstaff, and *never* paid his own check. Someone in his party, or a starstruck fan, would do the honors. He'd just sit at the table with the check—the white elephant on the table—until someone grabbed it, more out of embarrassment than generosity.

The club was a mecca for beautiful women, including my waitresses. Beauty and class were prerequisites for getting a job at the club. In an effort to attract hot women entertainers, I made three phone calls one night, inviting Diana Ross, Dionne Warwick, and singer/dancer Lola Falana for dinner the following night. I'd given each the impression that she was my sole guest, and when they arrived and found out that they'd all gotten invitations, they were a bit miffed. But I charmed them with roses and a good evening and was forgiven my crudeness. I particularly liked Lola Falana, a tireless entertainer liked by everyone. She was just getting started in show business when she was discovered by Sammy Davis, Jr., who then gave her a role in *Golden Boy*. They started an affair, which lasted through his marriage to his third wife, Altovise.

A number of celebrities would give impromptu shows, some lasting an hour. Don Rickles did his insult stand-up routine often. Paul Anka would do his thing, as would most other stars, some of who were testing new material.

But I wasn't satisfied; I needed to get the word out to those first-time tourists who were just getting off airplanes. I knew that once they had been to the club, they would come back on their return trips.

I worked a deal with cabdrivers. I'd give two dollars a head to every driver who steered customers to the club. I had a lot of volunteers. A cabbie could make an extra fifty or one hundred dollars a night just by recommending my place to tourists who had no idea where to go for a good time. When Frank or Dean or someone of equal celebrity showed up, calls would be made to the taxi dispatchers—who were also on my payroll—to alert their cabdrivers. The cabbies did their part, and business kept improving. After a while, the other club owners in town got wind of my deal with the cabbies and started bitching about my unfair business practices. I told them to think up something original like I had done and they could trash their full-page ads, which cost thousands of dollars. You've got to think outside the box.

Everyone got a check, with some rare exceptions; cops ate for free, as did my closest friends—Frank, Dean, Sammy, and a few others—but the list wasn't extensive. Eddie Murphy was a regular. One night, he stopped by with a few people and did a stand-up routine for thirty minutes. The crowd went nuts; he was great. At the end of the night, after he and his crew ran up a three-thousand-dollar tab, he got up to leave, ignoring the check.

I caught him at the door.

"Eddie, you forget something?" I displayed the check.

He seemed confused. "Uh . . . I did a half hour of stand-up, man. I don't get a break?"

"Nope. Everyone pays," I said, and handed him the check. He paid it, and left a generous tip, too. Was he insulted? Not in the least; he was back the following week and many more after that. My "no favors" policy gave the club a reputation for exclusivity. Some celebrities like to be treated like everyone else; besides, if I comped every big name that came to the club, I'd go broke. The place was lousy with superstars.

I also dispatched emissaries to all the convention centers in town and got their booking schedules for the next three years, then sent the conventioneers menus, advertising dinners for $37.50. Booze was extra, of course, and my liquor prices weren't exactly customer-friendly.

The specialty drink of the house was the Rolls-Royce, which consisted of warm Rémy Louis XIII, which you would let roll around your tongue, chased by cold Cristal champagne, presented in a flute glass made of Waterford crystal, for the reasonable price of $125. Want a cigar with that? For twenty dollars, you got one of my gorgeous, barely dressed waitresses to deliver it tableside, clip it, and suck on it to make the end moist. If you were still able to smoke after that, you got it lit by a gold Dupont cigar lighter.

My chefs were paid top dollar to turn out extraordinary cuisine. Customers watched their food being prepared tableside—what's known as Russian service—and the dining room served from 6:00 P.M. until 6:00 A.M. The food became my biggest moneymaker, not necessarily because of the quality, which was superb, but because of the Russo billing system.

Major restaurants stopped serving at midnight. While I went until six in the morning, my credit card machines stopped submitting bills at midnight, which gave the impression that I didn't serve food after that. It was assumed by the IRS that my club was like all the other clubs in town. In reality, my biggest-spending customers were just walking in the door when the other Vegas hot spots closed their kitchens, and they were looking for a good meal.

I switched credit card machines at midnight. The replacement machines were connected to offshore banks, and all the profits went to me; Uncle Sam was not involved.

New Year's Eve was also a big deal; reservations went for three hundred dollars a head, which included food and minimal booze. I generally had the same customers every year; they'd reserve for the following year as they were leaving the club early on New Year's Day, after partying all night.

Sinatra attracted a huge crowd when he was at the club, and he was there the night I took the stage to sing, as I'd done from time to time when I could squeeze it in. Frank had taught me how to sing, a little at a time over the years. While I had gotten the basics down pretty quickly, I knew nothing about breathing, timing, and stage presence. He taught me everything I knew about singing and performing before a live audience, often tutoring me after he had completed one of his own shows and we had the room all to ourselves. The band would stay to accompany me. He was a perfectionist, and wouldn't be satisfied until I sounded good. Nearly forty years later, I still have steady singing gigs, and I can thank Frank Sinatra for launching that part of my career.

Don Rickles was with Frank that night, and he must've liked what he heard, because he signed me to be his opening act. I opened for Don for the next two years.

Donald and Ivana Trump stopped by my dressing room after one of my shows opening for Don, at Resorts International in Atlantic City. Donald asked if I'd be the opening act for their new Trump Marina Hotel there in Atlantic City. It was a one-night gig, but they treated me well—fifteen thousand dollars for the show, plus their best suite. I also managed to get them to agree to hire Don Rickles's twenty-three-piece band to back me up.

Actor Tom Selleck was riding high on his success in the television series *Magnum, P.I.*, and when he was in town, he would come to the club, often with Larry Manetti, who played his sidekick on the show.

On one memorable night, Tom, Larry, and Al Sachs, the president of the Stardust Hotel, were enjoying dinner when I sat down with them. Tom told me that the Ferrari motor company had given him a new Ferrari like the one his character, Thomas Magnum, drove in the series.

"A nice gesture," Tom said, "but it's black." The one in the series was red.

"What," I asked, "you don't like black?"

"Hate it," he said. He shrugged. "What can I say? I'm superstitious."

"You gonna sell it?" I asked. I didn't own a Ferrari, and having one in my ever-growing collection of hot cars seemed like a good idea.

He shook his head. "That gets back to Ferrari, I'll look like an asshole."

"Give it to me, you don't want it," Larry chimed in. Manetti was a great guy and everyone liked him, Tom included.

Tom reached into his pocket and dangled the keys, sliding them across the table "You want the car? Here you go."

Larry looked at him, dumbstruck. "For real?"

"For real," Tom said, rewarding those within eyeball distance the

Selleck grin and eyebrow jiggle. He looked at his watch. "I'll make a call and have the car delivered to your house right now. I don't even want to look at it. The registration'll be in the car."

Larry did everything but genuflect, but Tom played down his generosity. "Nancy'll love it. Enjoy." Nancy was Larry's wife, and the Manettis lived down the road from my L.A. home. Both were great folks. I could visualize Nancy flipping over the car.

After an hour or so, Tom and Al Sachs had to leave, which left Larry and me at the table drinking. Larry was getting a bit shit-faced, and I was holding my own . . . barely.

Larry had been unusually quiet after Tom had left; then out of nowhere, he said, "I hate that fucking car."

I was speechless. "What's to hate about a brand-new Ferrari you just got for free?"

"I dunno, it just isn't me. Too fucking noisy, and the insurance on the thing has gotta run twenty grand a year. If someone was to give me fifty grand right now, they could have it."

I wasn't sure I'd heard him right. He repeated it, and added. "You want it? Gimme the fifty grand and it's yours."

I didn't want to take advantage of a drunk, so I made sure he meant what he'd said. The car was worth at least $250,000, probably more because Tom Selleck had once owned it, however briefly. Larry was serious. I went to my safe in the office, got the money, and drew up a bill of sale on a table napkin, all nice and legal.

The car was in L.A., and I sent a busboy and valet parker to retrieve it. They were on a plane to Los Angeles within hours. I didn't want Larry to change his mind. They actually had to push the Ferrari out of the garage, for fear of waking up Nancy with the loud engine noise. Nancy, as expected, had fallen in love with the car as soon as she'd seen it. Easy come, easy go.

After the Ferrari was safely back in Vegas, I got a call from Larry's manager, who balked at the car deal.

"You took advantage of him; he was drunk," the manager said. "You should do the right thing and return the car."

"Is that what Larry said?" I asked. I knew Larry wouldn't try to back out of the deal. He had a few days after he got home to bitch about it, but he didn't. His only regret should've been passing up the opportunity of selling the car on the open market; he could've gotten at least $250,000 for it. But a deal's a deal, and Larry was always a man of his word. I have no idea how he dealt with his wife, but they're still married, and that says a lot.

Momentary silence on the part of Larry's manager. "Uh, well, no, but . . ."

"'But,' my ass. I gave him every chance to back out of the deal and he didn't. And I've got a signed bill of sale for it."

More dead air. "You do?"

"I do."

I loved that car, had it for a year, then sold it. A Tom Selleck fan made me an offer I couldn't refuse.

To say my life was going in the right direction was an understatement. While I still had low friends in high places, I felt I was distancing myself from a lifestyle that had given me more opportunities than most people get in a lifetime.

Things were about to change; I'd be forced to take a man's life in my club, and I'd risk my own trying to protect my family from death at the hands of the Medellín cartel and the wrath of Pablo Escobar.

10

PABLO ESCOBAR CHANNELS MICHAEL CORLEONE

The flight to Bogotá, Colombia, took ten of the most nerve-racking hours of my life. It made the trip to Tehran seem like a cruise down the Las Vegas Strip in my Bentley.

It had been less than a month since I'd killed Pablo Escobar's emissary in my club in Vegas, and while my idea of confronting Escobar was my only option to get him to back off from doing harm to my family, I was now realizing what I had gotten myself into. This better work or I'm screwed, I thought.

To say I wasn't concerned about my safety would be less than truthful, but my overriding fear was that Pablo Escobar would kill my daughter, Carmen, as the first step in revenge against me for killing his emissary in my club. The cartels were famous for exacting the most gruesome revenge tactics against those who wronged them. In this case, I was the target, but before they got to me, they would torture and kill everyone I held dear. After I lived through those losses, it would be my turn, and I'd be made to suffer the most hideous of deaths. I needed to smooth things over with Escobar before he unleashed hell on earth against my family.

I had no idea what to expect. John Gotti had made my meeting with Escobar possible, but John was no fan of mine, and I wouldn't have put it past him to set me up for murder.

Hey, Pablo! It's me, John Gotti. How you doin'? You know that asshole Gianni Russo who whacked your buddy? Well, I could have him down to you in a week. Do what you want with him; he's a fucking jerk.

And that would be that. Gotti would get rid of me and further cement his relationship with the boss of the most powerful cocaine cartel in the world. Maybe he would even get a price break on a few hundred kilos.

The flight was uneventful, but it was with great trepidation that I set foot on Colombian soil.

I had the address of a church about a ten-minute cab ride outside Bogotá, where the meeting was to take place. I was sweating like a fat man running a marathon when the taxi dropped me off in a small town and left me standing outside a quaint white wooden building with a crucifix extending from its steeple. It was a little after noon, and I knew enough about Colombian customs to know that the hours between noon and two in the afternoon were reserved for lunch and relaxing. The streets were nearly deserted, and I wondered if I was witnessing some siesta downtime, or if Escobar's men had ordered everyone to make themselves scarce.

It was hot, but I was in a lightweight suit, white linen shirt, with no tie, and loafers. I didn't want to disrespect my host by showing up in shorts and flip-flops, which would've been a helluva lot more comfortable than what I was wearing.

The church appeared empty except for one lone man who had his back to me and was kneeling before a bank of candles to the left of the altar. As I began to walk past the pews, men with short-barreled rifles rose from concealment on the benches. There were three of them on either side of the aisle.

I froze in place, but one of the men urged me forward with a gesture of his gun.

Proceeding slowly, so as not to spook the gunmen, I began to smell what appeared to be the overpowering odor of burning flesh. The closer I got to the kneeling man, the stronger the smell. When I got to within ten feet of the man, he rose and turned slowly to face me.

It was Pablo Escobar—no mistaking him; I'd seen pictures of the drug kingpin on television numerous times. He was wearing black pants and a billowing short-sleeved white shirt. He was shorter than I had expected, and not as heavy as he appeared in his pictures. His hands were by his sides.

I glanced at the fingers of his right hand, which were charred black. It was his flesh I'd smelled burning, and for a brief moment my stomach tightened in revulsion. He had been burning his own fingers. Was this his penance for being a brutal, coldhearted murderer, or just a way to start the day for him, like a coffee substitute?

In accented English, he said, "Welcome to Colombia, Mr. Russo."

Bursts of light suddenly appeared in my vision, and I felt as if I were falling into a pit, with everything going dark around me.

I woke up sitting on a wooden chair, my hands tied behind me, my feet secured at the ankles to the legs of the chair. My jacket had been removed and I had a helluva headache. I had gotten whacked on the head by a pro; one second conscious in a church, the next . . . here. I was alone, but I heard men speaking Spanish in a nearby room.

I was in what appeared to be a windowless basement. The chair wasn't anchored to the cement floor, and I tried to move it by maneuvering my body. That's when I felt the pain. In addition to my bursting head, my lower back and testicles were on fire.

The room smelled like death; the decay of human remains permeated the dirt floor. Blood smeared the walls, and there was a pile of green rubber body bags in a corner.

Short memory bursts began. I'd taken a bad beating and must've passed out. I realized that the chair didn't have a seat; I was sitting in a hole where the seat should've been. The more my head cleared, the more pain I felt all over my body. It was excruciating.

Three men came in, one carrying what looked like a cop's nightstick.

The other two weren't armed with anything but a bad attitude. All three began screaming at me in Spanish, and the guy with the stick took a swing under my chair and connected with my balls. The room lit up in a searing flash of white pain. I threw up reflexively, the vomit spewing forth like it had been shot out of cannon. Some of it must have hit one of my tormentors, because one guy began screaming at me, and the guy with the stick gave me another whack. I passed out.

I don't know how long I was in that room. Based on my level of thirst—but, surprisingly, no hunger—I would say at least a day, probably two. I was in and out of consciousness. The men came and went. I think I was beaten some more, but I can't be sure.

The last time I came to, the only person in the room was Pablo Escobar. He was looking fresh in white linen pants and a yellow cotton shirt, which was untucked. The first thing I noticed was his stare; he was looking at me with the coldest, deadest eyes I had ever seen, and I've seen my share of psychopathic killers who appear like they're trying to look through a bottomless pit of tar.

Right then, I knew I was going to die; there was no talking my way out of anything. No explanations of what had happened in Vegas were going to be entertained. Escobar was there to finish me off. The beatings I'd received so far were just to soften me up. Pablo was going to personally finish the job, and enjoy doing it.

I knew now that John Gotti had made a deal with Escobar. Gotti had delivered me in exchange for financial consideration in future drug deals and to get rid of an annoying distraction in his life.

Escobar took a step closer to me and smiled. I didn't even try to talk my way out of what was to come. I was ready to die, and began to pray silently. I wasn't going to give Escobar the satisfaction of my groveling; it would've done no good anyway. I took a deep breath, raised my head, and looked him in the eye, regaining a modicum of self-respect as I stared him down.

That's when I noticed the book.

Escobar was carrying a hardcover copy of *The Making of the Godfather*, a behind-the-scenes look at how the iconic picture had been made, from Puzo's epic novel through the production of the picture. I'd seen copies of the book over the years, and signed a few for fans, but had never read it. Why should I? I had lived it.

Escobar held the book in two hands so that I could see the cover. "Why didn't you tell me you played Carlo in *The Godfather*? This is my favorite movie ever."

"Nobody really gave me much of a chance to say anything." I was barely able to squeak this out.

He barked a command, and two of the gorillas who had been beating me rapidly entered the room and cut my bonds.

"You'll be taken to another location, cleaned up, fed, and given something for your pain," Escobar said. "Then we talk."

A cloth hood was placed over my head, and once again the room went dark, only this time I was conscious.

We drove for at least an hour, the smells of the village evaporating and replaced by the fresh aroma of vegetation and fresh mountain air. The humidity seemed to have lifted once we arrived at our destination. I was walked up a gravel driveway, led into an air-conditioned house, taken to a room, and pushed gently onto a bed. The hood was removed.

In limited English, one of my captors said, "Your room, clothes there." He pointed to a chair where pants, a shirt, and shoes were lying. "Clean up," he said. He tossed me a plastic pharmacy vial. "For pain," he said, and left. I examined the container, which had no label on it. The pills were a light blue. I had no idea what they were and decided not to take them until I absolutely needed them.

I stood up and walked to a window. Sitting down for any period of time was painful. The view from the room was spectacular. The house was surrounded by mountains and a low-hanging, light fog.

I made my way to the shower-equipped bathroom, slowly removed my clothes, and examined myself. My face was untouched—something I couldn't say about my balls, which were hideously bruised and swollen. I was in terrible pain. After a brief self-consult, I decided now was the time for the pain meds. I popped one and awaited the results. After the shower, I wrapped myself up in a terry-cloth robe, eased myself onto the bed, and was in dreamland within minutes.

I was awakened by a gentle shake from the guy who had brought me to the room.

"*El jefe* wants you downstairs."

I wanted to say "Fuck the boss," roll over, and go back to sleep, but thought better of it. Whatever was in those meds had done the trick. My jewels ached, but nowhere near the level of pain I'd endured just a few hours ago.

I was met outside my room by another goon, who had me follow him to a massive dining room on the ground level. I was walking as if there were a basketball between my legs.

Pablo Escobar was waiting for me, all smiles. I eased myself onto a chair and said, "Thank you for your hospitality." What I was thinking was, Thank you for not cutting off my head and sticking it on top of the church steeple.

"My apologies for the treatment you have received. We have dinner first; then we talk. Good?"

I nodded. I was literally starving, my last meal having been at least a day or two ago. I went easy on the food, however, for fear my empty stomach would rebel. The Colombian cuisine was excellent—lots of fish, rice, and veggies—served by a woman I thought must've been a former Ms. Colombia. There was very little conversation, mostly small talk about the weather and sports. I know nothing about sports, but I faked my way through it. I hate small talk, but I gladly joined in. This was the last guy I wanted to piss off.

Over the strongest, thickest coffee I've ever had in my life—I tried standing the spoon upright in the cup; it tipped over, but just barely—Escobar said, "So, what do we do here?"

I told him the story behind the shooting of his representative in my club with no embellishments, no bullshit. The last thing I needed was to be caught in a lie, trying to make myself look better. I thought that the facts spoke for themselves. I also was straight up with him regarding my thoughts about John Gotti's motives for setting up this meeting. I didn't ask him what Gotti had told him about me; I wanted him to reason it out for himself.

After my stroll down memory lane, I said, "That's it. I came down here to have you hear my side of the story—what actually happened."

Escobar looked at me, his head resting on closed fists. His eyes gave away nothing. For all I knew, he was plotting a particularly gruesome way to kill me.

After what seemed like a minute, Escobar took a deep breath and exhaled. "I believe you, my friend, and what you say regarding Mr. Gotti's motives also rings true. That disappoints me. My man was out of line and deserved what was coming to him. I wish to apologize again for your treatment, but understand that my knowledge of the incident comes from Mr. Gotti, whom I look upon now in a different light." He shook my hand.

"This matter has been cleared up, but I wish to ask a favor of you before I have my men take you to the airport for your journey home."

I'd had no idea I was to leave after this meeting, but that was good to hear. I was also so relieved with his assessment of the incident, I would've granted any favor within my power.

"Certainly, anything I can do," I said, trying to sound sincere.

What he wanted was for the two of us to act out a scene from *The Godfather*, the one where Michael Corleone confronts Carlo Rizzi about his duplicity and being instrumental in getting Michael's brother, Sonny, whacked.

It was like I'd gotten bitch-slapped with a tire iron. I couldn't believe this guy. I had met rabid fans of the picture over the years, but nothing like Escobar. I made sure I maintained a poker face. Escobar, I was to find out, fancied himself a bit of an actor. Who was I to disagree? Besides, it turned out he wasn't bad.

"Sure, it would be an honor," I said, trying to keep my voice steady, acting as though his request seemed perfectly reasonable.

I arranged the chairs to closely mimic the scene in the movie. Escobar, who by this time was insisting I call him Pablo, would play the Michael role, while I was in familiar territory being Carlo Rizzi.

I set it up verbally, and offered to write Michael Corleone's lines for him.

"No need, Gianni, I have them up here." He tapped his head.

We ran through the scene several times without acting, just to make sure we had everything right. Escobar was correct: He knew the Michael part.

The last time we went through the scene, Escobar actually handed me an envelope with a plane ticket in it, just like in the picture. At that moment, I got the nagging feeling that the end result of the scene would be the same as in the picture—Carlo was going to die, only this time for real.

I looked in the envelope, just as Brando had instructed me to do when we shot the scene. There were two real plane tickets in there—one for me to Miami, the second one to get me to Las Vegas.

It took all my acting chops to get through the scene. I was scared, and, I felt, justifiably so. Why wasn't Escobar having the scene videotaped? This was a *Godfather* movie buff's opportunity of a lifetime. I was sure that one of the richest men in the world must own a video camera. The only answer could be that I was going to die for real, strangled in the car that was supposed to take me to the airport, just like in the movie, and he didn't want it recorded for posterity because the tape would be damning evidence should it ever be leaked. No one but John Gotti and Escobar knew about this meeting. I would simply vanish. My legacy would have me being featured on an episode of *48 Hours* titled "Whatever Happened to Gianni Russo?"

Between my aching gonads and rubbery legs, I had a difficult time walking to the car in the circular driveway that was to take me to the airport.

A new Cadillac sedan was waiting for me. I went for the back door, but Escobar held the front door open for me.

"You ride in the front, Gianni. Better to see the beautiful scenery."

I slid onto the front seat. In the backseat were the two muscle guys who had beaten my balls to mush. One of them said, "Hello, Carlo." Carlo? We were still in *Godfather* mode. Those were the last words my Carlo character heard before Clemenza choked the life out of him.

A vision of my daughter, Carmen, flashed through my mind. I took a deep breath, knowing it would be my last. I didn't want to suffer, but I didn't fear death as much as the thought of how Carmen would wonder for the rest of her life what had happened to her father.

Instead of a Colombian necktie, I got a slap on the back and roars of laughter. My new best friend, Pablo, had stepped a few feet away from the car and was laughing along with the two killers in the backseat.

"Have a safe trip, Gianni," Pablo said, and waved as the car inched out of the driveway. I had just been the victim of the Colombian cartel's version of a practical joke.

I offered up a wan smile and returned the wave with little sincerity.

I tried, to no avail, to get some sleep on the plane, despite another one of Escobar's magic blue pills. Every time we hit even the mildest turbulence, I felt like my nut sack was going to explode.

The plane arrived on time at Miami International Airport, also known as MIA, which was what I would've been labeled had I not returned from Colombia. But I was halfway home and happy to be in the United States.

As I was standing in the aisle, waiting to disembark, the captain's voice came over the intercom: "Please return to your seats until further notice." A mere inconvenience compared to what I had been through in Bogotá. I returned to my seat.

Two men in suits boarded the plane and one took the mike from a flight attendant. "Will Mr. Gianni Russo please raise his hand."

Oh shit, what now? I raised my hand, and the two guys came over to where I was sitting.

"Russo?"

These guys looked like cops—their cheap suits with wrinkled lapels and their thick-soled black shoes always gave them away. I sighed. "Yep, that's me."

"Stand up, please," the taller of the two said. "We're DEA agents." He flashed some ID.

I rose and was roughly pulled into the aisle and handcuffed behind my back. "What the fuck!" I exclaimed rhetorically. I knew enough not to ask questions that I expected answers to, because I knew they weren't going to be answered. Instead, I complied docilely as an agent grabbed me by the elbows and ushered me out of the plane, down a flight of stairs, and out onto the tarmac. I had to ask them twice to slow down; these were young guys in a hurry.

"Why?" one of them asked.

"I hurt my back, spasms when I walk fast." Telling them I'd been tortured by the most notorious cocaine kingpin in the world didn't seem appropriate. They just grunted, but they reduced their pace.

In the distance was a small white commuter jet. Now I had a question that deserved an answer. "Where the hell're we going?"

Without turning toward me, they both said in unison, "D.C."

I stopped dead in my tracks. "Washington? Am I under arrest?"

They stopped and turned. The shorter of the two shook his head. "No. At this point you're a material witness, but things may change. You never know," he said with a shit-eating grin.

I didn't like any of this. I'd committed no crime, but I assumed my meeting with Escobar had been on someone's radar. I was to find out later that my arrival at the Ravenite Social Club for my sit-down with John Gotti had been noticed by one of the myriad federal agencies watching the place. I'd been followed to the airport for my trip to Colombia, and my arrival had been picked up on by DEA agents assigned to the Bogotá field office.

I shrugged. All I wanted to do was get home to Las Vegas and sit in a hot bath for a while. It appeared I wouldn't be doing that until after a stopover in Washington.

I sighed. "Let's do it your way."

We boarded the small jet and found our seats. My hands were still cuffed and I had my seat belt fastened by one of the agents. There was a third agent on the plane, plus two pilots.

Twenty minutes into the flight, I asked to use the bathroom.

"Sure," an agent told me, "go ahead." He swung his legs out of the way so I could pass.

I stood up but didn't move. "How do you expect me to navigate in there? Can you take the cuffs off? Or do you want to shake it off for me?"

The two agents looked at each other.

I rolled my eyes. "What am I gonna do, escape? We're thirty thousand feet in the air, for crissakes."

The cuffs came off. The bathroom was the size of a shoe box, and I took my time. I looked in the mirror and didn't like what I saw. I needed a shave, and had bags under my eyes that could've been searched by Customs. My Brioni suit looked like I'd been in it for a week, which was about right. After splashing some cold water on my face, I cursed the DEA and started back toward my seat.

The three agents were standing in the aisle, staring at me.

I stopped dead in my tracks. "What now?"

The agent who had been on the plane when we boarded said, "You were in *The Godfather*, right?"

"Yeah," I said, "so what?" I was getting a little peeved.

The agent turned to my keepers. "See, I told you. He was Carlo. I knew it!" He seemed very proud of himself, like he had provided a correct answer on *Jeopardy!*.

"Who gives a fuck?" I muttered under my breath, and turned my back to them, waiting to have the cuffs reapplied.

"No, no, have a seat. No cuffs," the agent who had recognized me said.

For the rest of the flight, I was treated with respect. I've gotten more mileage out of that picture than anything I've done, and my movie résumé is pretty extensive. To this day, I get recognized on the street almost daily as that "Carlo guy" from *The Godfather.*

I endured hundreds of questions about the picture and answered them politely, without broaching the subject of my detention. Whatever they thought they had on me was bullshit; I hadn't done anything wrong and didn't know what the hell they were looking for.

A car was waiting for us when we touched down in D.C., and we drove the short distance to the DEA headquarters on K Street. Once there, I was introduced to a platoon of agents, who had turned out to meet that "Carlo guy." They were more interested in my Hollywood career than they were in my alleged criminal activities.

I explained my reason for going to Colombia, reliving the shooting in my club in minute detail. I found it difficult to fathom why they hadn't known about the shooting; surely they had informants in the coke trade. Had they done their homework, I wouldn't have been in D.C.

I was shown a huge whiteboard with pictures fastened to it by magnets. There were numerous shots of me entering the Ravenite Social Club, at JFK, and arriving in Bogotá. If they had any pictures of me after that, they weren't sharing them with me. The DEA had thought I was Gotti's new cocaine connection.

The good news was that someone made a few calls, presumably to Vegas to confirm my story, and I was told I could go.

"Go where?" I asked. "I'm in Washington. I'm supposed to be in Vegas."

"Well, you have our apologies, but we don't provide transportation," an agent told me.

"How about a ride to the airport, then?"

I got the lift.

I began concentrating on my show-business career. Over the next few years, I would make three pictures. One was *Chances Are,* with Cybill Shepherd and Ryan O'Neal. I played—what else—a gangster. I also played a drug lord in *Striptease,* with Demi Moore.

I would bounce back and forth between Las Vegas and New York. Brando was in New York often and we would meet up whenever our visits coincided. I traveled to New York one time because I had been contacted by Marty Bregman, who had produced *Chances Are* and *Striptease.* He offered me a part in his new movie, *The Freshman,* which would feature Matthew Broderick.

"You think you could interest Brando in the lead?" Marty asked.

"I dunno," I said. "What's the picture about?"

"It's a spoof on *The Godfather.* He'll love the script."

Marlon Brando hated doing *The Godfather* and everything about the picture. Mentioning the movie to him brought out venom. He was only paid one million dollars for his starring role in the movie, which turned out to be one of the best-reviewed movies in history, and certainly one of the biggest moneymakers. Brando was pissed when he tried to renegotiate his contract after the fact and was told he was locked into the original deal.

"The last thing Brando would want is a part in a movie that reminds him of *The Godfather.* I wouldn't even bring it up to him."

"He'll be paid ten million dollars," Marty said.

"Forget what I just said. I'll reach out to him," I replied. Brando was always crying poverty, which I didn't believe, and I knew that despite his dislike for everything *Godfather,* ten million dollars would be the biggest payday of his career and he wouldn't pass it up. Brando would do practically anything for a quick buck.

A few years back, media billionaire John Kluge, who was once labeled by *Forbes* magazine as the richest man in America, called me with a request.

"You still have contact with Marlon Brando?"

I'd known Kluge for years—call us good acquaintances—and had been to his penthouse in the Waldorf Towers a few times.

"Yeah, I see him whenever he's in New York. Why?"

"This may sound like an odd request," Kluge said, "but I'm having a dinner party for about twelve close friends and I'd like Brando to attend. He'll be a surprise for my guests."

"I don't think so, John. Brando's a private person. I can't see him going to a dinner party where he doesn't know anyone."

"Can I sweeten it up for him? Say twenty-five thousand dollars' worth of sweetener?"

I hesitated. "You mean you'd pay him twenty-five grand to attend?'

"I would. I'm a huge fan, and I don't know anyone else who isn't. Do you think he'd do it for the money?"

I really didn't know, and I told Kluge that. "I can ask him. How long would he have to be there and when's the party?"

"Two hours max, and the party is when he's in town and available. And you're invited also."

I thought he might do it. Twenty-five large to break bread with a bunch of Brando sycophants for a few hours seemed like something he might go for.

Brando was scheduled to be in New York the following week. I called him with Kluge's request.

"Twenty-five thousand dollars? This guy serious?" Brando asked.

"Very. I'll be there, too, if that means anything. Think about it."

"Hey, who has to think?" Brando said, "For twenty-five grand, I'd have dinner with Hitler. I'm in."

I called Kluge and told him the good news. He was ecstatic. "I won't forget this, Gianni."

Sure, I thought. As soon as the party was history, I would be, too, until the time came for me to do Kluge another favor. But this is how the world worked, and if I could have media giant John Kluge owe me a favor, it would be a good thing. We settled on a date to coincide with Brando's New York visit and we were in business. He also had a messenger deliver half of Brando's fee to me the following day. The other half would be payable when Brando showed up at the party.

I arrived at the Monkey Bar in the Hotel Elysée, Brando's favorite haunt, the following Friday night, as per our agreement. Brando was there, looking like he'd just rolled out of bed, but that was his standard uniform. He was sitting at a table in the back of the bar. He wasn't alone.

With him was the biggest German shepherd I'd ever seen. He was lying down at Brando's feet and seemed content to survey the room. Brando spotted me and waved me over.

"What's with the fucking dog, Marlon?" I asked after a quick handshake. The dog just glared at me.

Brando told me the dog's name, which I've since forgotten. "He travels with me wherever I go. Good protection; anyone fucks with me, the dog'll eat his arm. And he's a better friend than most of the assholes I know." He hesitated. "Present company excepted, of course."

I rolled my eyes. "What're you gonna do with him?" I looked at my watch. "We've got to be at the Towers in twenty minutes."

Brando downed the rest of his drink. "He's coming with us."

"You're fucking with me, right?"

He smiled. "Not in the least. For the money, Kluge gets the dog, too."

There was no talking him out of it. I had a limo outside, and the three of us were off to the party. I was wondering how Kluge would take the uninvited "guest." The last thing I needed was for him to stiff Brando for the balance of the money, or, worst-case scenario, throw us out.

Neither happened. Kluge welcomed us with grace and class, petting the pooch and introducing us—including the hound from hell—to his dozen well-heeled guests.

A place for the dog was added to the fifteen-foot dining room table. He had his own chair, which he sat on like a well-mannered guest. The friggin' dog ate off the best china, like the rest of us; the only difference was that his doggy beverage wasn't the wine we were having, but water served in a crystal bowl.

Brando was charming and talkative—in other words, he was acting. He spoke about his career, answered questions—most pertaining to *The Godfather*, which he called his "favorite movie." He said it with a straight face and seemed sincere. And the Oscar goes to . . .

Brando glanced at his watch only once, precisely two hours after our arrival. He leaned into me and said, "Time to get the fuck out of here."

After fawning goodbyes and promises to stay in touch with everyone in the room, Brando was slipped a cash-stuffed envelope by our host, and we were gone.

We went back to the Monkey Bar and got drunk. A few years after the Kluge party, I was in L.A. and met Merv Griffin and Brando for dinner at Trader Vic's. Brando brought the dog, who by this time was beginning to look a lot like his owner, which wasn't a good thing. More on that later.

Brando took the role of the aging Mafia don, Carmine Sabatini, in *The Freshman* without any negotiations and got paid the ten million dollars up front. I advised him to have the money wired to Tahiti, where he could avoid the big U.S. tax bite. Brando was a resident of Tahiti. He owned an island in the chain of Society Islands and would make it his permanent residence. Sinatra often lent his private jet to Brando so he could travel back and forth and avoid flying on a commercial airline.

The Freshman was shot mostly in Toronto, where it was cheaper to make pictures, but we spent about three weeks shooting exterior locations in New York's Little Italy. I played a no-name maître d' in the picture, and in one scene, Brando's character was watching me argue with a patron, and the actor went off-script, saying, "Carlo, you still arguing?" as an homage to my role in *The Godfather.*

Brando and I would spend a lot of time in the Monkey Bar when we were shooting in New York. Whatever we were talking about would invariably morph into a conversation about John Gotti. Brando had a burning desire to meet Gotti, a real, live Mafia boss. By this time, Gotti had had *his* boss, Paul Castellano, murdered, along with his underboss, and my friend, Tommy Bilotti, in December 1985. Gotti then assumed the throne as boss of the Gambino crime family, where he had remained.

"Come, on," Brando said, "you know Gotti. Make arrangements for us to meet. We're, like, three blocks from the Ravenite. Make it happen." He added, "Please," as an afterthought.

When we were shooting in Little Italy, we were only a few blocks from Gotti's headquarters, true enough, but I didn't want to make it seem like it would be an easy meeting to arrange. To have Marlon Brando owe me a favor could pay off in the future.

"I don't know," I replied. "He may not want to meet you. I'll call in some favors and see what I can do."

The less I was seen entering the Ravenite, the better, and I still wasn't a big fan of Gotti's, particularly after I suspected he had me set up to be whacked in Colombia. I called his right-hand man, Joe Watts, with whom I'd always maintained a good relationship.

I didn't mention anything about Brando to Watts initially, just made like I was calling to say hello. I knew he'd get around to the fact that the picture was being shot in the neighborhood, because it was big local news. I was sure Gotti, the megalomaniac that he was, would want to meet Marlon Brando.

"Hey, Gianni," Watts said, "can I ask you a favor?"

Here it comes. . . .

"Sure, Joe, anything."

"John's always been a big Brando fan; you know, *The Godfather* thing. You think you might be able to arrange a meeting?" Watts hesitated. "He'd have to come to the club. John's keeping a low profile since the thing . . . you know."

"'The thing' Watts was referring to was an attempt on his boss's life three years earlier, when a car bomb meant to take out Gotti killed his capo, Frank DeCicco, instead. The hapless DeCicco had gone to retrieve Gotti's car, which had been rigged with a command-detonated bomb, while Gotti attended a meeting in Brooklyn. The dummy sitting on the switch across the street from the car mistook DeCicco for Gotti and blew the bomb. The attempt on Gotti's life was in retaliation for the unsanctioned assassination of Castellano a year earlier, and had been ordered by Anthony "Gaspipe" Casso, a Lucchese crime family capo, who was pissed off that Gotti had taken out the boss of a family without Commission approval. While Gotti had survived, he knew enough to keep a low profile.

I didn't answer right away, giving the impression that his request required some thought. "I'll see what I can do, Joe. Brando likes to keep to himself; I'll see if he wants to meet with John."

Now both Brando *and* Gotti would owe me. Brando might be influential in getting me a good movie role, while Gotti might take a breather from trying to have me killed.

Watts was very grateful, and would've genuflected had we met in person. Watts was very loyal to Gotti, and would've done damn near anything to please him.

I went back to Brando and told him it hadn't been easy but that I had arranged the meeting.

"That's really great, man," Brando said. "I owe you one."

There you go.

The meeting was to be held in the Ravenite on a Monday night, during a crucial football game, which would be televised, the theory being that the feds wouldn't have a great presence if they had a presence at all, because, one, FBI agents disliked working at night or on weekends, and, two, most Americans would be glued to their TV sets to watch the game, federal agents included.

We were scheduled to film some street scenes that night, and I was given an hour window to get Brando back to the set. An assistant director handed me a radio.

"Stay in touch. If I have to contact you, I'll refer to Brando as 'the Principal,' in case the paparazzi are listening in." He looked at his watch. "You have one hour."

I rolled my eyes, the D-day invasion hadn't been planned this well.

Brando emerged from his trailer dressed like Don Corleone, wearing a dark vested suit and porkpie hat. All that was missing were his stuffed cheeks.

"I look like a gangster?" Brando asked.

"You look like Don Corleone before he got shot," I said.

He nodded. "That's the look I was after. Let's go."

It was a short walk to the Ravenite, but we took a limo.

The Ravenite was unusually barren of wiseguys, with the exception of Joe Watts, who rarely left Gotti's side. I guess Gotti had gotten out the word to stay away from the club while he entertained Brando.

Gotti greeted Brando warmly, but no hugs and cheek kisses, which was his style. I'd told Watts that Brando didn't like to get up close and personal with anyone unless it was a female.

Gotti barely gave me a nod. I figured he was pissed off that I was still breathing. He and Brando sat at a battered Formica-topped table and talked. I backed off, along with Joe, letting the real gangster boss converse with the thespian gangster boss.

An hour passed. Brando didn't appear as if he was ready to leave, although he was aware that he'd turn into a pumpkin if he wasn't back on the set.

Sure enough, the radio burped. It was the AD who had given me my orders for the night.

"Where's the Principal?"

"Still talking with his new best friend." I glanced at the table when I heard a roar of laughter. It was Gotti responding to a magic trick that Brando had just performed for him. I couldn't believe it. Brando was doing magic for John Gotti. It was times like these I wished I'd had a camera. They had both forgotten about the football game, which was playing on the stolen TV on the bar.

"Well, get him moving, for crissakes! Time is money. He's due on the set."

I sighed. "Give him a few more minutes; they're winding up their powwow." Truthfully, it appeared that Gotti and Brando were just warming up. I fully expected them either to reenact a scene from *The Godfather* or break into a duet.

Another hour passed. Brando apparently knew more magic tricks than Houdini, because he was still at it. The AD was calling me every five minutes, getting more and more exasperated. I kept on putting him off. "Any minute now, we'll be on our way back."

Then the radio went strangely silent. I had to make sure it was still working.

Joe Watts came up behind me. "You've got a visitor."

"Huh? Where?"

Watts jerked a thumb over his shoulder. "Outside."

The AD was outside on the sidewalk, pacing like an expectant father. He whirled as I exited the club.

"What the fuck, Gianni? Where's Brando?"

The Principal was back to being Brando; I figured a code name wasn't necessary now that the AD wasn't using a radio.

"You mean the Principal?" I asked. This little twerp deserved to get his balls broken.

"Listen to me," he said. "We're losing hundreds of thousands of dollars an hour here. Go back in there and get Brando out here *now*!"

"Why don't you go in there and get him? The Principal is kind of busy with the other Principal. You want to go in there and tell John Gotti his playdate is over?" I stepped aside.

It was like the AD had his shoes nailed to the ground. "How much longer?" he asked, resignation in his voice.

I smiled. "Should be any minute now."

An hour later, Brando and Gotti emerged from the Ravenite. As the AD led Brando to his waiting limo, I began to walk toward the limo I'd arrived in.

From behind me I heard, "Hey, Gianni." I turned to face a smiling John Gotti.

"Thank you for doing this," Gotti said, then turned and went back into the club.

11

SUNDAY SAUCE WAS NEVER LIKE THIS

Anthony "the Ant" Spilotro was a psychopathic mob enforcer based in Chicago. For reasons no one has been able to discern, the Outfit decided to send him to Las Vegas on New Year's Eve, 1976, to be the "eyes and ears" of the Outfit and to keep things "running smoothly."

First of all, things *were* running smoothly in Las Vegas. Everyone was making money, the flow of skim to Chicago continued unabated, violence was kept to a minimum, and the cops and politicians were our best friends. The last thing we needed was a babysitter, particularly a guy like Spilotro, whose idea of keeping things running smoothly was to murder people to keep them in line. Spilotro was portrayed in the movie *Casino* by Joe Pesci, who couldn't have done a better job if he'd been the Ant's twin.

Nicknamed the Ant because of his diminutive size, Spilotro decided he was going to make Vegas "his town" and make everyone's life miserable in the process, mine included.

Shortly after he arrived, Spilotro formed a burglary ring, which was called "the Hole in the Wall Gang" by the press because Spilotro and his crew would break into their targets by drilling through outer walls to get to the loot. Their marks were usually jewelry stores. Not satisfied with the mountain of money he was making doing burglaries,

Spilotro branched out to shaking down anyone who would stand still long enough to get approached. He didn't care who you were; if he told you to pay him, you'd better do it. To make his point, he once inserted a guy's head in a vise and squeezed until the poor bastard's eyes popped out.

The Ant's only friend in Vegas was Frank "Lefty" Rosenthal, a Jewish gambler who made a name for himself by becoming a money-making machine for the Outfit. He was portrayed in *Casino* by Robert De Niro. Rosenthal was a genius at odds making, and the Outfit left him pretty much alone to do what he wanted, just as long as the cash kept flowing east. Spilotro rewarded Rosenthal's friendship with him by turning his wife, Geri—played by Sharon Stone in the movie—into a falling-down alcoholic cokehead, and, in October 1982, by trying to kill Lefty with a car bomb. Lefty survived; Geri didn't. She OD'd on coke and booze in an L.A. motel in 1982 and died.

Moe Dalitz, who owned half the town, and was in negotiations to buy the other half, actually gave Spilotro a house when the Ant got married, in order to keep him off the Strip. As twisted as Spilotro was, the head case was an excellent dad to his only child. No matter where he was, he would drop what he was doing—or whom he was doing—and go home to cook breakfast for his son before the kid went to school.

I tried staying clear of the Ant, but Vegas is a small town and I'd run into him occasionally; couldn't be helped. The first time I met him, I was in the lounge at the Riviera, watching a show with a group of friends. He came over to my table, introduced himself, and shook my hand—a dead-fish, limp handshake, always a bad sign.

He was very polite and unassuming, but that was his act. If you went along with whatever request he had, there wouldn't be a problem. Turn him down, and the real Spilotro would emerge, which wasn't pleasant.

After the niceties, Spilotro got down to business.

"Hey, Gianni, I'm looking to open up a gift shop in a hotel. I was thinking you could rent me some space in the place you're building."

I had just begun the construction phase on my new Renaissance Hotel, and while I *was* looking for vendors to lease space, I'd sooner have done business with a bunch of zombies looking to open up a fast-food restaurant. The last thing I needed was a lunatic wiseguy as a tenant. Even if he'd been sane, the hint of any mob influence in any Vegas gambling business was enough to bring the wrath of the feds down on me. I was soon to find that out the hard way because of my Kansas City connections.

I feigned interest, like I'd done with John Gotti when he tried to push his hot slot machines on me, and went through the same spiel—form a corporation, make past income taxes available, jump through a dozen more hoops, and so on. That would have dissuaded almost anyone, but not the Ant.

He went from Mr. Nice Guy to spewing veiled threats.

"You know, people who don't do business with me sometimes have problems. You know what I'm saying, Gianni?"

I played the naïve citizen. "Oh yeah, I hear you, Tony, but my hands are tied here. I'm getting a gaming license. Everyone who does business with me goes through the same background check I'm gonna go through myself. Believe me, I'd like you at the Renaissance; you'd add class to the place. Follow the rules, like I'm doing, and I'll have the lease papers drawn up, no problem."

I saw that Spilotro was getting pissed, but I maintained my composure and nodded a lot. In the end, he pulled a Gotti and said, "Aw, fuck it, I don't need this shit," and left. In fact, he reminded me very much of Gotti—a degenerate gambler with a Caesar complex, who thought everyone worshipped him.

He was gone, but that encounter was just the beginning. Over the years, I'd get word that he was complaining about me all over town. His anger was building, not so much because of what I'd done to him—which was nothing—but because, like John Gotti, he resented someone connected with the life who was successful in the legitimate world. Like most tough guys, particularly short tough guys, he was a bully with an inferiority complex, knowing that without his reputation as a loose cannon, he couldn't make a success of himself outside the criminal world.

By the time the Renaissance project went belly-up, Spilotro's name had been entered into the infamous "Black Book," which barred him from entering *any* licensed premise in Vegas, not just casinos. Any business that held any kind of license, including a liquor license, was off-limits to the select few who were in the Black Book. There were only about ten to twelve people in the book, which meant you had to be a really notorious character to find yourself in it. Spilotro's claim to fame was his connection to the Outfit, and the rumors that he was committing numerous crimes in Vegas just added to it. Anyone who owned a licensed business in Las Vegas even seen talking to someone in the Black Book had a problem.

I had opened State Street, and was enjoying the benefits that came with running a successful business, when Spilotro showed up at the door with seven of his buddies, undoubtedly members of his burglary crew.

My doormen knew Spilotro by reputation and were aware that he was in the Black Book. I was summoned to the door when the Ant began to get belligerent when he was refused admission to the club.

He was cursing up a storm by the time I made it to the door, but he stopped when he saw me, figuring I'd let him and his entourage inside, since I owned the place, which was exactly why I *wouldn't* let him in. I was taking a chance even by talking to the psycho.

"Hey, Gianni," Spilotro said, "this mook"—he pointed to my doorman—"won't let us in your club. Set this asshole straight, will ya? We're buddies, right? We'll be good, I promise." He smiled as if making a joke, assuming that our "friendship" would allow him to come into the club. He started to make a move toward the door.

I stepped in front of him.

"Listen, Tony, you're in the Black Book; you know that. No way I can let you inside. I'll lose my license."

Spilotro went from smiling to turning dark in a flash. "Hey, it's four o'clock in the fucking morning. Who the fuck is gonna see me? We just wanna have some dinner, a few drinks."

"Can't do it, Tony," I said. By this time, my doorman had summoned four security guys from inside the club. The last thing I wanted was a brawl on my hands, but I'd accept that over potentially having someone spot him in the club. I'd be out of business in a day.

"No can do, Tony," I said, and waited for the first punch to be thrown. Spilotro backed down, but not without a veiled threat.

He leaned into me. "You'll be seeing me again, you fucking scumbag."

He left with his crew, but my problems with him were just beginning.

I would hold dinner parties at my house on La Paloma Drive every Sunday. In Italian families, Sunday dinner is a big deal—a social event where family and friends get together to enjoy one another's company, eat, drink, and have a good time.

At one time or another, every major celebrity in Vegas stopped by for "Sunday sauce," as it was known around town. I've been dropping names throughout this book, so I'll dispense with listing the stars who would show up on Sundays, but I will relate one celebrity story that became part of Las Vegas lore.

Siegfried & Roy had one of the most popular acts on the Strip. They were illusionists with a different slant on magic. They incorporated the most beautiful wildcats I'd ever seen in their act, which was an extravaganza of light and showmanship. They had rare white tigers, as well as lions and leopards, involved in their performances, which were always sold out. They would cuddle and play with the dangerous beasts as if they were stuffed animals.

They came to the Sunday sauce dinners many times. On one particular occasion, they brought a tiger with them. While it wasn't fully grown, it still weighed at least one hundred pounds, but they assured me that the cat was docile and the kids would enjoy it.

A few minutes after they had arrived, the cat took a liking to one of the women; I've forgotten who it was. At first, he was a little aggressive, straining at the leash, which Roy was handling. Then the feline terror began growling, broke free of Roy's grasp, and went charging across two rooms toward the woman.

I was between the woman and the cat, and whirled in time to see the furry beast flying through the air at the woman. I was lucky to be where I was, because I thought quickly and punched the cat on the side of his head as he was passing me. He dropped to the ground, unconscious. That cat was out for the count, and Roy thought I'd killed it, and he began throwing a hissy fit. Everyone was screaming, expecting the cat to get up and continue raising hell.

Ten minutes later, the cat was still out. The illusionists left with the beast still in dreamland and cradled gently in Siegfried's arms. They never came for Sunday sauce again. A few years later, Roy was cuddling a tiger onstage when the cat snapped and tried to eat his head. The word got around Vegas that it was the same tiger I'd KO'd, that it had been suffering from PTSD, had a flashback, and reached out and touched the nearest human, who just happened to be Roy. It was touch-and-go for a while with Roy, but he survived; however, Siegfried & Roy would never perform again.

There were no tigers after that at any Sunday dinner. I loved to cook and would begin to prepare the feast in the morning, a meal that would feed about twenty adults and their kids. The adults would gather in the dining room, while the kids had their own separate dining room.

The wine would flow, and the food, which usually consisted of four courses, would be served starting at 3:00 P.M.

One Sunday, my guests were seated at the dining room table and the kids were in their room when the shooting started. The kids' room, being behind the dining room, was surely the reason why none of them was hurt or killed.

Unbeknownst to my guests or me, two cars had come to a stop in front of my house and an estimated five to seven men armed with rifles and automatic weapons had gotten out. They began to spray the house with bullets from left to right. Fortunately, the dining room was located on the right side of the house, and those who weren't quick enough to understand that we were under attack were dragged to the floor by those who knew what was going on. In other words, the women were hauled to the floor by their husbands and boyfriends.

Glass, furniture, vases, artwork, and everything else that makes a house a home began exploding in a cacophony of earsplitting gunfire. Screams were drowned out by what sounded like one big roar of noise that seemed to go on forever. In reality, the shooting lasted for about fifteen seconds and then the shooters were gone.

A bunch of us raced through the debris to get to the children's dining room. The kids were still sitting on their chairs, frozen, with wide-eyed fear on their faces. Not one of them had a scratch.

My house, like most other houses in Vegas, was made of stucco, which wasn't strong enough to stop a bullet. I had fortified the house a few months earlier, right after a huge Thanksgiving dinner I had hosted. I had several of the guys who had come to that dinner come back the following day with sledgehammers, and we all took down the dining room wall and demolished the floor, replacing them with a new concrete, rebar-reinforced floor, and running the concrete and rebar up to the windowsills, which gave me a bulletproof wall (at least about four feet of it). Shortly after that, I had a state-of-the-art alarm system installed, which Pablo Escobar's men would breach after I killed Pablo's man in the club.

I can't say that I had anticipated the shooting at the house, but Spilotro was always on my mind and I knew he'd seek revenge against me for not cooperating with him. Besides the Ant, I dealt with a wide variety of violent people and I never knew who might come for a visit with guns blazing. For me, it was a matter of having a tactical advantage. Had it not been for that concrete wall, there might have been injuries, or worse. It certainly shielded the kids from harm, the room where they were eating being located directly behind the adult dining room. Carmen, my daughter, was back there with the kids, making sure they stayed out of trouble, and that may have saved her life.

I was livid, and I was positive the Ant was behind the shooting. He had pulled similar shootings at his enemies' homes, but usually in the middle of the night, to make a point. I don't believe he was intentionally looking to hurt anyone, just to remind me that the next time he asked for a favor, I'd better comply. I was sure he'd done his homework and knew that I hosted those Sunday dinners, and in what part of the house my dining room was located. He'd commenced firing on the opposite side of the house, walking the rounds to where the people were, giving us time to hit the floor. Most of the rounds went high, but some didn't. With a few hundred rounds fired, any one of which could've been stopped by one of my guests, it was beyond a reckless act. This first time was a warning; the next time might be for real.

Something had to be done.

I had to stick around Vegas for two days and work with the police, allegedly to help figure out who had done the shooting, but I didn't share my thoughts regarding Spilotro's involvement. I stuck to the "I have no idea" mantra because I was going to handle the problem my way.

Once again, I was concerned for my daughter, who was still living with me. While I'd gone through similar concerns when the Colombians came after me, there was a major difference: With the Colombians I knew exactly what to expect, not so with Spilotro. He was extremely unpredictable. He could target my entire family, just me, or blow up my club with or without customers inside. I wasn't about to go head-to-head with the wacko, because I'd lose. Not only am I not vicious but I'm not a tough guy, never have been.

I decided to talk to his boss, Outfit leader Tony Accardo, with whom I had a very good relationship. Accardo was a legendary Mafia boss, cut from the same cloth as Frank Costello. Both were gentlemen whom I'd never heard raise their voices or disrespect anyone, which doesn't mean Accardo was a pushover. If Accardo had a problem, he liked to talk about it rather than break out the weapons. I'd been with him a few times during the Vatican Bank days when we'd run into some logistical difficulties.

"C'mon, Gianni, let's take a walk around the golf course and talk," he would say, and we'd reason out the problem during a slow stroll, then go back to his house, where he'd cook a lavish dinner just for the two of us. The end result was a reasonable solution to the problem and a great meal. Violence was always a last resort with Accardo.

I called him requesting a sit-down regarding a matter of personal urgency.

"Of, course, Gianni, you're welcome in my home anytime."

Twenty-four hours later, I was sitting in his living room. After the traditional inquiries about our health and families, Accardo said, "It's about Spilotro, right?"

It's a boss's job to stay on top of goings-on with his troops, but Accardo didn't have to be a management genius to know that the Ant was bringing too much heat on the Outfit, even without the Wild West tactic at my house.

"What's he done now?" Accardo asked, exasperation in his tone.

I told Accardo about the shooting. "I've been dealing with his threats for ten years, and I never considered talking to you about any of it. I was handling the bullshit myself. But this? He's gone way beyond being an asshole. There were children in the house. I'm coming to you now to ask you, as his boss, to rein this guy in before he hurts one of us. I don't think he knows that we're all in this together."

Accardo's reaction was to sigh and shake his head.

"I've told Anthony numerous times to keep a low profile. The stick-ups, the burglaries, the rest of it . . . it's gotten to be too much. Now this? At your home? I've gotta reel him in."

He rose, signaling the end of the meeting. I shook his hand and he walked me to the door.

"Rest assured, I'll take care of the problem," Accardo said. "You and your family don't need to worry."

We hugged, and I was on a plane back to Vegas in two hours.

I assumed that Accardo would call Spilotro back from Vegas for good and give him an enforcer job, which was all he was good for.

For the next few days, I heard nothing from Spilotro, but that wasn't unusual. Months would go by sometimes when I didn't see him, but like a homing pigeon, he would find his way back to me with more intimidation and threats. To have him shoot up my house and not follow it up with some sort of an offer I had better not refuse was a waste of good bullets and manpower. In my mind, it was a race between that happening and Accardo summoning him back to Chicago.

Accardo got to him first. Spilotro was ordered to Chicago in mid-June 1986, a few weeks after he shot up my house. Whenever a mob soldier is summoned to "headquarters," it's usually for something that he's done wrong. Spilotro might have been a psychopath, but he wasn't an idiot. His behavior during his years in Vegas had been a direct slap in the face to Accardo and the rest of the Outfit bosses, and he probably figured he was going to get a dressing-down and possible reassignment.

Vegas was a pot of gold for the Ant, and he didn't want to be recalled. To that end, he decided to take his brother, Michael, with him to the meeting in Chicago. Michael was also a made guy, but unlike his nut brother, was well liked, a good earner, and sane. The Ant wanted Michael with him for moral support and to help him convince the bosses that if given another chance, he'd toe the line and make Las Vegas an even bigger moneymaker for the Outfit.

I'm sure he also felt that with Michael with him, he'd be relatively safe, because his brother wasn't on anyone's shit list, and the two of them would stay close for the trip east. He also knew that he would be among friends in Chicago, and that probably made him feel safer.

In the Mafia, if you're going to get whacked, it's undoubtedly going to be your friends who are going to do it; taking that one step further, it's usually your closest friend who pulls the trigger. You go to your death calm and not suspecting a thing, with no opportunity or inclination to fight back. Why would your best friend kill you? Because he was told to, simple as that. A soldier's first allegiance is to the "family," and when ordered to do something, you do it with blind devotion.

On or about June 10, 1986, the Spilotro brothers were lured to the twelve-thousand-acre Willow Slough preserve near the Illinois-Indiana state line. Michael—the brother everyone allegedly liked—was stripped to his underwear and severely beaten and tortured while his brother was forced to look on. Barely still alive, Michael was rolled into a previously dug grave.

Now it was the Ant's turn.

He was also stripped to his drawers, then beaten slowly and methodically, as only another psycho could do; in this case, there were at least three men administering the pummeling. When the Ant was in the same shape as his brother, he was rolled into the same grave.

Anthony and Michael Spilotro were then buried alive. Their bodies were discovered a few days later, which was part of the plan.

A point was made, Mafia-style. The Ant had blown off repeated warnings to toe the line, so he had to be made an example of, should others even consider becoming disobedient. Michael Spilotro, the poor bastard, was collateral damage. The bosses wanted the Ant's last memory in this life to be that of watching his brother getting tortured, and knowing he'd be next.

To this day, I wonder if my visit to Anthony Accardo was the proverbial straw that broke the camel's back, and he ordered the Ant's demise, or if the deed had been planned before I even got to Accardo, who was the only person who could order the death of a made man.

I guess I didn't know Accardo as well as I thought I did. I was certain that he would recall Spilotro and that would be that; Las Vegas would return to business as usual and everyone would be happy . . . except the brothers Spilotro. The manner of death foisted upon the brothers—being beaten by baseball bats—was said to be Accardo's favorite method of dispatching his enemies during his days with the

Capone mob back in the 1920s. Back then, he was known as "Joe Batters."

I'd spend a lot of time with Accardo over the years after the Spilotro brothers' deaths; he never once brought up their names.

Anthony Joseph Accardo died in 1992, at the age of eighty-six.

12

A DOOR CLOSES WHILE ANOTHER ONE OPENS AND BRANDO LIVES A NIGHTMARE

Amid much inner turmoil and many sleepless nights, I decided to close State Street.

In the immediate aftermath of the shooting at my house, and my killing of Lorenzo Morales at my club in October 1988, I was besieged with gangster groupies wanting to sit in the booth where Morales had met his end, or wanted to take pictures with "the guy who got his house shot up." The TV show *Entertainment Tonight* covered the shooting at my house, and didn't help by alluding to my role in *The Godfather*, comparing me to a real-life Carlo Rizzi, my character in the movie.

My purpose in opening up the club—in addition to making a ton of money—was to legitimize myself (or as close to that as I could get) and gradually separate myself from the mob. Now I found myself with a growing reputation, which was spun from media hype that I was some super bad guy.

It was time to move on.

The plan was to chain the door to the club and walk away. Selling State Street crossed my mind because it had been a huge success and buyers wouldn't be hard to find. Most of that success, however, was because of my celebrity connections due to my acting career, and appearing at my own club with a nightclub act. If I sold the club, all the goodwill that I brought to the place would go with me, and it would affect the asking price. People in my position would usually enter into an agreement with the new owners to stick around, as if I'd never sold it. I'd be drawing a salary, albeit a good one, but I wouldn't be able to escape what I was trying to flee from.

Additionally, no one knew about my unique credit card billing system, where I'd had two sets of credit card terminals, one for before midnight and one for after. I wasn't about to share that information with a new buyer, who could use the information as leverage should he have IRS problems.

On New Year's Eve, 1989, I got onstage at my club and announced to the jam-packed house of regulars that I was closing the club, effective immediately.

The instantaneous reaction was stunned and utter silence, which is saying something about a room packed with four hundred partying drunks. Within seconds, however, the house erupted into raucous laughter; everyone thought I was joking.

After I assured them I wasn't, I received a standing ovation and a lot of tearful farewells. There wasn't a dry eye in the house, mine included.

Chaining the front door that morning was one of the toughest things I've ever had to do. I'd been successful in a very difficult business and it was hard just to walk away. Clubs in Las Vegas have a short shelf life; mine had lasted seven years.

I'd been leading the single life for years; nothing or no one impressed me much anymore. There were more beautiful women in Las Vegas and L.A. than anywhere else in the world, and I'd dated my share. There was never a love connection, and I wasn't looking for one. I wanted to have a good time. So far, my well-thought-out plan was working.

Then Pamela came into my life and everything changed. She was gorgeous, classy, well-spoken, and smart. But aside from her obvious attributes, she reminded me somewhat of Jessica Wexler, the true love of my life from my Miami days. I'd been willing to do anything for that woman, and had started my conversion to the Jewish faith, when her family convinced her that I wasn't good enough for her, and spirited her out of Miami. She was pregnant with our child at the time, but her family pressured her into getting an abortion. That time in my life was extremely painful, and I didn't realize how much it had affected me until the day I met Pamela, and the resemblance brought me back to the euphoria and the pain that was my relationship with Jessica.

Pamela wasn't the typical Vegas beauty looking to snag a rich man. When she came into State Street one night with her mother, I was immediately smitten.

We began dating, but she was cautious around me because she had heard that I was a player and had mob connections. She had also heard about the drive-by shooting at my home.

I might've been with a lot of women, but when I began seeing Pamela, I stopped looking. I was that serious. Ever since Jessica, I'd been cautious about getting close to anyone, for fear of losing them as I had Jessica. With Pamela, I was willing to take a chance on the future.

I also downplayed the gangster rumors, explaining that owning a club in Vegas required that I come into contact with all sorts of people, and you couldn't swing a dead cat in Las Vegas without hitting a wiseguy. The Spilotro drive-by shooting I wrote off as an extortion attempt, which it was.

She must've seen that I was trying, because she gave me the benefit of the doubt, but I understood that I was on thin ice regarding any future mob interactions.

Then I'd killed Pablo Escobar's man in the club. That took a lot of explaining, but it was evident from the grand jury verdict that I had acted in self-defense. Still, I had to watch myself if Pamela was going to stick around. To her way of thinking, trouble followed me.

We had been seeing each other for a while when I took Pamela and her grandmother to dinner in a Beverly Hills restaurant. For the previous six months, I had been the target of a punk named Joe Denti, who fancied himself as a big-time gangster, and was leaning on me to get involved in his illegal schemes. I was having none of it because I was distancing myself from that lifestyle, but, most important, because Denti was an asshole. He made Tony Spilotro look like Frank Costello.

The three of us were in the restaurant, having a relaxing meal, when two of Denti's goons approached our table and asked me why I was ignoring their boss. Pamela and her grandmother were visibly upset; I wanted the two idiots away from the table.

"Can't you see I'm having dinner? Tell Joe I'll call him when I get a chance," I said.

"No," one of them said. "The boss wants to see you now."

I felt as if I were living in the middle of a Jimmy Cagney movie.

These guys weren't taking no for an answer, but in order to defuse the situation, I suggested we talk outside. While I had no intention of going past the lobby with these jerks, I'd at least get them away from the women.

I excused myself and followed the gorillas toward the door.

When we'd cleared the dining room and were out of sight of Pamela and her grandmother, I said, "Hey, hold up." They turned toward me. "Tell Joe I'll call him first thing in the morning," something I had no intention of doing.

The one closest to me said, "You're coming with us, fuck face," pulled back his coat, and went for the pistol that was in his waistband.

After the State Street shooting, I had upgraded to a .38-caliber Smith & Wesson Airweight revolver, which I had my hand wrapped around in my front right pocket.

I fired two rounds through the pocket, hitting the guy with the gun in the knee and the other in the shinbone. They both went down.

People began screaming behind me.

I walked backed to my table and announced to the ladies that we had to leave. They must've recognized my demeanor as stressed and upset, because neither questioned the order; they just got up and started to walk toward the door.

"Not that way," I said, "too many people." A stream of patrons was bottlenecked at the front door, trying to get out of the joint. "Follow me," I said. We went through the kitchen and out the rear exit.

I reported the shooting to the police, and it was deemed justified. I had assumed I was about to get kidnapped at gunpoint and had protected myself with my licensed weapon. Both goons were delivered to a hospital by ambulance, where one of them was arrested for carrying an unlicensed concealed weapon, which he still had with him when the EMTs carted him away.

I never heard from Joe Denti again.

It was tougher to convince Pamela that I was once again a victim and one of the good guys. This was the third shooting in which I'd been involved in a relatively short period of time, and I could understand her trepidation about staying with me.

Pamela was a decent, clean-living person. Her closest association with my world was watching reruns of *Crime Story* on television. It took a while, but over the next few months I was totally involved with my acting career, and that convinced her that I was concentrating on playing gangsters, not being one.

I asked Pamela to marry me, and she accepted. I was truly driven to start a family, to completely turn my back on anything remotely illegal or unethical, and to begin my life with a remarkable woman.

We began making plans for our wedding, which would take place in L.A. This time around, I was actively involved in making the arrangements and actually enjoyed the process. One of my considerations was what to do about my friends and associates in New York. Many of them wouldn't be able to attend the L.A. nuptials due to legal considerations (such as house arrest and parole travel limitations), but most wouldn't want to bring undue attention from the FBI to an otherwise joyous occasion.

While I was leaving the lifestyle, I didn't want to snub people I'd known literally all my adult life. I was honest with Pamela, explaining my ties to New York and how I thought it would be respectful for us to go there and have a prewedding celebration with my friends. Pamela, classy lady that she was, agreed.

Pamela and I flew to New York. Joe Watts, John Gotti's bodyguard and confidant, and a close friend of mine for many years, arranged a grand party at the Essex House, where Pamela and I stayed.

The party was packed with wiseguys from all five families, and wherever Joe Watts went, John Gotti was sure to follow. Gotti was well aware of Joe's loyalty and friendship, and he didn't want to disrespect that arrangement by being a loud asshole at the party. He behaved like a gentleman.

New York had been hit by an arctic cold spell that weekend, and Pamela hadn't brought appropriate winter clothing. In fact, a few of the New York women hadn't expected the subzero weather, either, and had not dressed accordingly.

As the party was nearing an end, some of the women were dreading leaving the warmth and comfort of the hotel, and Joe Watts came to the rescue.

"Everyone stay put; I've gotta make a call," he said.

Within the hour, a man from the fashion house Fendi showed up with a rack of fur coats . . . expensive fur coats. He wheeled them into the banquet room and received thunderous applause and a standing ovation from everyone.

Joe draped an ankle-length Blackglama mink coat around Pamela's shoulders and told her, "Your prewedding gift. Enjoy." The rest of the coats were on loan; Pamela's was hers to keep.

She was speechless, got teary-eyed, and tried to give the coat back to Joe. I had to whisper in her ear, explaining that giving back the coat would be an insult. She understood; she hugged and thanked Joe, who had a broad grin on his face.

Pamela fell in love with my guests; thankfully, she didn't see the lethal side of them.

We were married on Thanksgiving weekend in 1990 at the Church of the Good Shepherd on Santa Monica Boulevard, followed by a reception for three hundred people in the Crystal Room at the Beverly Hills Hotel, where I reserved twenty-four rooms for our out-of-town guests. I also arranged for a motorcycle escort for the entire day from the Beverly Hills Police Department.

I was spending most of my time in L.A. acting in movies and TV shows, so the natural progression would be to move there. We bought a three-story English Tudor off Mulholland Drive, in an area known as Westchester Estates. It had a four-car garage, a tennis court, a pool, and a huge koi pond, and I brought in twenty forty-foot-tall redwood trees to plant around the property. The house cost millions, and I shoveled in millions more after that, remodeling it to our specifications. I would have had to sell a lot of ballpoint pens in midtown Manhattan to afford that house.

By the time I was done, it was our dream house, and I swore I'd never sell it.

But in eleven years, events would unfold that would force me to sell the house and make myself scarce in Europe, but that's a part of the story to be told in another chapter.

I was close to Marlon Brando, who lived nearby; plus, my new neighbors were Jack Nicholson, Dr. Dre, Tom Selleck, and Heather Locklear. Miguel Ferrer, George Clooney's cousin, lived next door, and George would stop by often.

I still kept my apartment on Wilshire Boulevard, just in case my house got swallowed up in an earthquake. You never know.

May 16, 1990, is a day that's etched in my brain forever.

Marlon Brando called me at home at 1:30 A.M. in a panic.

I had been awake in front of a TV with a drink, but I was beginning to drift when the phone rang.

"Gianni, you've gotta help me," Brando said. He sounded terrible, his voice raspy, like his Don Corleone character with a bad cold.

"Yeah, what? What happened?" The drink found an end table, and I sat at the edge of my seat.

"It's Christian," he said, choking up. "He shot Cheyenne's boyfriend."

Christian was Brando's son. They lived in the same house, a little up the road from mine, but they had an odd living arrangement. The house, which was huge, was divided in two, with a wall separating Brando from his son and daughter, Cheyenne, who also lived on the other side of the wall and was eight months pregnant by Dag Drollet, her boyfriend and the guy Christian had just shot.

"What the fuck happened? Is he okay?" He had my full attention now.

Brando was now in full crying mode. "He's dead! Christian shot him!"

"You said that. Try to calm down. Why'd he shoot him?"

"A fight or something. Cheyenne told Christian that Dag hit her. And Christian had a gun over there and . . ." He trailed off.

"Did you call the cops?"

He had stopped weeping. "I'm gonna do that now, but you've gotta help me."

"Anything, Marlon. What do you need?"

"A lawyer, man, a really good lawyer." And the tears came again.

"Stand by. And don't talk to the police. Tell Christian the same thing. I'll have Robert Shapiro call you right away."

"Shapiro? He any good?"

I didn't have a good relationship with Shapiro; our last interaction had had me grabbing a phone out of his hand and hanging it up. He might've been an asshole, but he was a great lawyer.

"The best. I'm on it. Hold it together," I said, and hung up.

I had Shapiro's home number and called it. A man picked up on the second ring. He sounded like he was coming out of a deep sleep.

"Yeah? Who's this?"

"This Robert Shapiro?"

"Yeah, who's this?" he repeated.

"Gianni Russo. We met—"

"I know who you are." The fog was clearing up. "What the hell are you doing? It's almost two o'clock in the friggin' morning. What're you calling me for? You got some balls, you—"

"Shut the fuck up!" I bellowed into the phone. I wasn't going to get insulted a second time by this jerkoff. "You need to call Marlon Brando. His son just shot someone . . . killed him."

His attitude changed immediately. "Oh . . . okay. Sorry I—"

"Forget it; time's wasting." I gave him Brando's phone number.

"Thanks, Gianni. I owe you one," Shapiro said.

"Just take care of the kid. Call now; the cops are on their way to the house." I hung up.

After a restless night, I dragged myself out of bed and turned on the morning TV news. There was Shapiro, giving a press conference, with Brando at his side. I think they were in front of the courthouse. Shapiro talked eloquently about domestic abuse, said that Christian had been defending his sister, and answered questions posed by the army of press that was present.

I had to hand it to Shapiro: He looked and sounded sharp, all on very little sleep. Brando was composed, made a statement, and answered some questions. End of news conference.

Depending on which news source you wanted to believe, Christian Brando was either a hero or a cold-blooded killer. It was a hot story for weeks. As soon as the prosecutor filed murder charges, Brando spirited Cheyenne to Tahiti, where she would remain. No one thought she would flee, and her passport wasn't lifted. She was, after all, a witness, not a suspect. The DA felt he no longer had enough evidence to get a murder conviction without her, and so he allowed Christian to plead out to a manslaughter charge.

Marlon Brando took the stand during the sentencing phase, pleading for leniency for his son. "I think perhaps I have failed as a father," he said on the stand. My heart broke for him. He was a good man, and he was suffering. This period of time would begin a rapid decline for Brando, both in health and mental stability. I would be witness to his tragic end.

Christian got only five years in prison, thanks to top-notch lawyering by Robert Shapiro and his team.

Brando called me after the sentencing and told me that he was forever in my debt. I could never bring myself to call in that debt and have him relive what he'd just gone through with his son.

Le Bistro Restaurant was the place to be seen in Beverly Hills. Located on Canon Drive off Wilshire Boulevard, it was owned by Sidney Korshak, a very successful lawyer with strong connections to the Chicago Outfit. Sidney could've opened up a lunch wagon in Watts and the who's who of Hollywood would've eaten there, such was his power as a fixer and political powerhouse.

As it was, Le Bistro was an elegant eatery that was always packed with powerful people who liked to be fawned over. Regulars had "their" tables, which were always available, no matter when they arrived. I'd seen customers uprooted in the middle of a meal because some studio big shot or actor showed up without a reservation and asked for his usual table, which was occupied by unknowns.

Sidney and I were close friends, and every time I went to Le Bistro I was given his personal table, which was always left empty and made available to his friends. Sidney was a great guy—I miss him; he died in 1996—and his generosity was unparalleled. I never got a check in the place, no matter how big my party, but I would always leave a tip bigger than the check would've been anyway. I'd also pick up the checks at other tables occasionally, which Sidney comped, too.

I recall an episode in 1974 when Tony Curtis and I were having dinner at Sidney's table at Le Bistro one memorable night. Nancy Reagan—wife of the then second-term governor of California, Ronald Reagan—showed up with two friends and three plainclothes state police bodyguards. Tony and I had just finished making *Lepke*, the biopic of Louis "Lepke" Buchalter, a notorious gangster who met his end in the electric chair. Tony had played Lepke, and I'd played Albert "the Mad Hatter" Anastasia, who ran Murder, Inc., an infamous group of hit men for hire in the 1930s and 1940s. Tony and I had become good friends and would get together often.

The maître d' came over to us, leaned in, and said conspiratorially, "Gentlemen, this is Mrs. Reagan's regular table; would you mind moving?"

Tony started to say something, but I cut in. "Let me handle this," I said to him. I wasn't a fan of the governor's wife, and I wasn't alone. She was a snob and nasty. We little people were beneath her. She would later voice displeasure that I'd attended her husband's seventieth birthday party.

"We're not going anywhere," I told the maître d', and went back to enjoying my dinner.

The poor guy got flustered, and I can't say I blamed him. "Gianni, she's the First Lady of California."

I shrugged. "I don't really care. I'm a New Yorker." Tony thought this was hysterical, started to laugh, and didn't stop.

I knew the maître d' was envisioning a dressing-down by Sidney if he couldn't move us to another table, but I put his fears to rest.

"Don't worry," I told him, "Sidney doesn't like her, either."

He sighed, then went over and spoke to Mrs. Reagan in hushed tones. She gave me a withering look. I smiled and waved, at which point she whirled around and was gone.

Those who had witnessed her storming out began applauding, and a hotshot director at the table next to us sent over a bottle of champagne with a note attached, which read "Fuck her. She's a bitch."

I'll drink to that.

That wasn't my last Nancy Reagan experience.

Fast forward a few years and now her husband is president of the United States.

Every Sunday night, I'd have a standing reservation at Matteo's, another Hollywood hot spot. It was also Frank Sinatra's favorite L.A. restaurant. Matty Jordan, who owned the place, was delivered by Frank's mother, Dolly, who was a midwife back in Hoboken, New Jersey, before Frank was even contemplating becoming a singer. Matty and Frank were very tight, and Matty had a massive set of model trains in the place because Frank loved trains, and had a transformer at Frank's regular table so he could play with them while he dined.

Nancy was dining in Matteo's with an entourage one Sunday evening while I was there, and Matty stopped by her table and inquired if everything was satisfactory. Nancy, being the person she was, complained about the service and said that one of her dishes was cold.

Matty was a loud person normally, but when things weren't going well, he was known to be loud *and* swear like a sailor.

He summoned the waitstaff who had taken care of the table and began berating them.

"Do you know who this cunt is?" he hollered. "She's the fucking First Lady of the United States!" He continued yelling and screaming. Nancy and her party were mortified.

It's a night I'll never forget. Four Secret Service agents, who were at another table, leaped into action, but they didn't know quite what to do. Two went outside immediately—I assume to peruse the street—one stood there looking like a deer caught in headlights, and the last one spoke into his sleeve. I was sitting right next to him.

"Uh, there's a problem here," he said calmly into the radio. "A man just called Rainbow a cunt. He's screaming and making a scene."

Rainbow was Nancy's Secret Service code name.

The agent nodded while he got instructions, then whirled and said to Nancy and her party, "We're leaving. Now."

The First Lady of the United States and her friends hurried out of the restaurant like they were criminals doing a perp walk past the press.

I waved at her and smiled, hoping it would bring back memories of Le Bistro. She ignored me.

A group of us had a poker night a few times a month in a back room at Carmine's Restaurant on Little Santa Monica Boulevard and Beverly

Glen. One of those games turned into what resembled a scene from a Wild West movie.

The cardplayers were mostly regulars to the game—Frank Sinatra, Sammy Davis, Jr., Dean Martin, and myself—and were joined by a few others who sat in sporadically. Everyone at the table was armed, licensed to carry either because of celebrity or because they were involved in businesses where large sums of cash were carried or transported. And, of course, if you had a hook in the LAPD, you could be Public Enemy No. 1 and still get a pistol license.

On a warm night in October 1988, the game was progressing at its usual pace when Frank pulled his gun and placed it on the table. Whatever Frank did, everyone else was almost certain to follow, so we all did the same thing.

For no apparent reason, Frank picked up his gun and fired a shot into the ceiling. The rest of us thought this was a great idea, and we grabbed our guns and proceeded to shoot up the ceiling, emptying our guns. The noise was deafening, and my ears rang for hours.

Looking back on the incident, I would categorize this wildly irresponsible incident as an act of bravado. We did it because we could. No one was going to say anything about it, least of all Carmine, who owned the place and had joined in shooting up his restaurant with his own pistol.

Carmine's Restaurant is still around, and has been remodeled and painted many times . . . except for the back room we shot up. The bullet holes still remain and are considered part of Hollywood history.

Merv Griffin invited me on his show to be part of what he was going to call his "Tough Guys Show," featuring actors who had played tough guys on television and in the movies. In addition to me, Merv had as guests actors Robert Conrad and Jimmy Caan, and as a surprise guest real-life gangster Vincent "Fat Vinnie" Teresa. Teresa, a captain in the Patriarca crime family in New England, was the highest-ranking mobster at the time in any family to "flip" and become a federal informant.

I guess Vinnie was bored in the Witness Security Program (WITSEC) and decided he needed to get out more. He appeared onstage in silhouette from behind a curtain while two U.S. Marshals stood guard off-camera. The panel couldn't see him and he couldn't see us, only hear our voices.

We'd all been answering questions for a few minutes, when Vinnie paused and said, "Hey, Kid, is that you?"

He had recognized my voice from when I was known as "the Kid" during my early days in New York.

We began reliving old times, and I said, "You know, Vinnie, I could make five hundred grand right now by making one phone call to Providence and mentioning where you are."

Providence, Rhode Island, was a Patriarca stronghold, and there was a half-million-dollar bounty on Vinnie for ratting out the family.

I was joking, of course, but the marshals didn't have a sense of humor. They went into DEFCON 1 mode and wanted to get their charge out of there, for fear a busload of machine gun–toting gangsters could be on their way to the studio to take out Vinnie.

"Hey, relax!" I said. "It's a friggin' joke, and we're taping; it's not live." The show wasn't scheduled to air for five hours.

Everyone calmed down and taping resumed, and the mad-minute panic was edited out.

My acting career was moving along nicely. In 1999, while I was in Miami shooting *Any Given Sunday* with Al Pacino, Jamie Foxx, LL Cool J, Cameron Diaz, and Elizabeth Berkley, we thought it would be a good idea for all of us to go skinny-dipping on a Miami public beach. We did this early enough that the beach wasn't crowded. I'd come to realize a while ago that most actors have no filters, due to their celebrity; they do what they want to do, screw the general public. In another incident during the filming of the movie, LL Cool J decked Jamie Foxx after an argument.

After *Any Given Sunday*, I appeared in numerous pictures, including *The Family Man*, *Harvard Man*, *Red Dragon*, and *After the Sunset*. I also did the TV series *Prison Break*.

Pamela and I had two children, Deanna and Carmello. Frank Sinatra honored me by becoming my son's godfather.

I was loving the father role. In those days, my idea of a good time was spending it with my kids. I found great satisfaction in chartering a bus and hosting a bunch of my kids' school friends for a day at Disneyland, which became my new Las Vegas. I think I had more fun than the kids. Pamela and I were getting along great, and I envisioned myself growing old with her and having a platoon of grandchildren.

In early September 2001, I was invited to attend a fund-raiser for a children's hospital in Double Bay, Australia, hosted by Karl Suleman, an Australian businessman. Suleman also had another purpose in mind, in addition to raising money for sick kids.

He wanted to produce yet another sequel to *The Godfather*, which already had two sequels, one that won an Academy Award for Best Picture, and the other, which was a disaster. His idea was to make *The Godfather: Part IV* with former president of the United States Bill Clinton in a starring role and with me as a supporting actor and screenwriter. Clinton, unbelievably, liked the idea and flew to Australia, or maybe he just wanted to get as far away from Hillary as possible.

The former president was paid $500,000 basically to hang out and mingle with the other guests—some were potential investors in the picture, while others were there just for the fund-raiser. I got $125,000 to do the same. Serious business talks pertaining to the proposed movie weren't set to begin until we returned to the United States, so all we had to do was enjoy ourselves. I'm an expert at having a good time, and so was Bill Clinton. Eventually, the movie idea would die when the law finally caught up with Suleman and he went to prison for twenty-one months for defrauding investors and creative writing on bank loan applications, but for now he was planning on making the film.

We were given lavish rooms at the Double Bay Resort but spent the first three days mostly on Suleman's yacht, a massive floating version of Las Vegas on a wild weekend. Gambling casinos dotted the shoreline, and we'd use the boat to get to them, in addition to enjoying nonstop partying back on the boat.

I've met many influential people in my lifetime who would generate whispers when they walked into a crowded room. When Bill Clinton entered a room, it came to a standstill, and not because he was a former president of the United States; the man generated warmth and intelligence, and dripped charisma.

He insisted everyone call him by his first name, and he treated his Secret Service entourage as if they were family. And he liked to party. One of his Secret Service agents, whom I'll call "Bobby," was designated to approach women Clinton was hot for—which was most of them—and invite them to sit with him. He was surrounded with women wherever he went, and took at least one to his room with him every night. Clinton was always smiling, and I could understand why.

Suleman threw a party for the likely investors in the picture on his yacht on our third night in the country. The women I had seen the first two days in Australia were gorgeous, but the beauties in attendance that night made those we met initially look like witches. I made some of them to be hookers right away, but Clinton didn't, and I don't believe he ever figured out they were working girls. He had two of them on his lap and another hanging on his arm as the boat pulled into the dock after the raucous party was over. I decided to keep my distance from the bevy of beauties. I was invested in my marriage and didn't want to screw it up, particularly for a prostitute.

Clinton and I agreed to meet for breakfast at 9:00 A.M.; then he vanished into the hotel with the three girls, still smiling.

Later, in 2006, during one of my many guest appearances on *The Howard Stern Show,* I recounted my trip to Australia with Clinton, alluding to the great time we'd had, but leaving out the particulars.

An hour later, as I left the studio, I got a call from one of Hillary Clinton's female flunkies, requesting a full rundown of everything that had gone on in Australia with Bill Clinton. I hung up on her. She called back.

She started off by saying, "When Mrs. Clinton becomes president . . ."

I hung up on her again.

It was about 1:00 A.M. and I had just fallen into a booze-induced sleep from the party, when the unmistakable swoosh of helicopter blades woke me up. I saw two military helicopters hovering over the building where Clinton had his suite.

I got on the phone immediately and called Clinton's room. Bobby, the Secret Service agent, answered.

"What's going on?"

"Turn on your TV," he said, and hung up.

I flipped on the set and saw the horrendous reality of the September 11 attacks as they were occurring in real time. It was 10:30 A.M. the previous day in New York. I don't know how long I sat transfixed, watching the horror of the events unfolding in front of me, before the phone rang. It was Bobby.

"You've got your TV on?" he asked.

"Yeah, what the hell's going on?"

"Can't talk about it right now, but the president wanted me to call you to say he'll be unavailable for breakfast. He'll be leaving shortly."

I was confused. "Leaving for where?"

"A military base in Germany. All the former presidents are getting moved to different locations around the world."

I had to sit down. All this was overwhelming. The media was saying it was assumed to be a terrorist attack, but in the fog of the event, I didn't know what to believe. Bobby was talking, but I'd zoned him out, trying to comprehend the totality of what I'd been watching on TV.

". . . to your family, but all flights have been grounded over U.S. airspace."

"I'm sorry . . . what?"

"You should contact your family," Bobby said. "They know you can't fly home; all commercial fights are grounded."

My mind was racing. I was halfway around the world and I felt an urgent need to get home immediately, but that seemed like it wasn't going to happen. Then I had an idea.

"Can I hitch a ride to Germany with you guys?" I asked. I figured Germany was a lot closer to the United States than Australia, and when planes were permitted to fly again, there would be a lot more of them available heading to the States from Europe than there would be from Australia.

There was a moment of silence; then Bobby said, "Not with us, but stay in your room. I'll talk to who I have to talk to about that. Where do you want to go? Anywhere except the United States."

Between the urgency of the moment and a slight hangover, it took me a while to organize my thoughts. I blurted out, "Italy . . . Rome, to be specific." I had friends there, and if flights were at a premium to get back home, I knew I could depend on Vatican connections to get me there.

"Okay," Bobby said, "stand by." He hung up.

I heard the choppers leave in the next few minutes. I showered, packed, and sat glued to the television until the phone rang two hours later.

"This Gianni Russo?"

When I said that it was, the caller gave me his name, rank, and service branch and said, "Be in front of the hotel in twenty minutes. Can you do that?"

"Yeah, no problem," I replied. I tried calling home, but I couldn't get through. Lines must've been jammed.

I'm going to be a little vague as to my specific travel arrangements, assuming the people who were doing me this favor might still be in the military or connected to the government in some way.

I was helicoptered to a military base, where I transferred to a military fixed-wing aircraft. There were a handful of passengers on board dressed in civilian clothes, and looking as confused and anticipatory as I was. The body of the plane was bare-bones, with a row of uncomfortable seats facing one another on opposite sides of the fuselage. The engines were running as we buckled up. The noise was damn near deafening, which would make conversation almost impossible, but that was okay with me. All I wanted to do was get home whichever way possible, and talking up the guy next to me wasn't on my agenda.

A sergeant in fatigues and a helmet walked by us, checking fastened seat belts.

"Are we headed to Rome?" I asked above the din.

"Naples," he replied. "Rome's locked down."

Wonderful. The world was becoming unhinged.

Once in the air, the ambient temperature dropped to just bearable. The sergeant came by and handed out rough woolen blankets. After a few hours in the air, we were given military MREs (meals ready to eat). After eating what passed for food, I developed a new empathy for members of the military.

We stopped twice—I'm assuming to refuel. When I asked where we were, I was met by a smile and not much else.

When we arrived in Naples, the first thing I did was call home and speak to Pamela. Once assured that she and the kids were fine, I called the Vatican. A car was sent to pick me up and drive the three hours back to Rome, where I checked into a hotel and collapsed into a deep sleep.

I had to wait a little over a week to get a flight back to the States. During that time, I kept a low profile and ate most of my meals at a café in the nearby Excelsior Hotel. During my time in Rome, I had access to a chauffeur-driven Vatican car, replete with the papal flag waving from the front bumper.

There were advantages to being driven around in a papal automobile; traffic parted like the Red Sea, and in the chaos that is Rome traffic, that's saying something. The downside was that everyone thought the Pope was the passenger and the car was mobbed wherever we stopped. Once people realized I wasn't the Pope, they backed off.

The world calmed down considerably after a few days and commercial planes once again took to the air. While I awaited my departure day, I continued to eat all my meals at the Excelsior Hotel's café.

I had kept to myself and left the hotel primarily to eat, but I also shopped for some clothes, and gifts for Pamela and the kids, too. In the evenings, I'd sit in the outdoor café, have a few cocktails, and do a lot of thinking. Nothing like what occurred on September 11 for someone to take stock of his life.

I remember one night a few years back when I was in Rome. I'd just pulled up in a Vatican limo in front of Jackie O', a hot club at the time. Bob Newhart and his wife, along with Don Rickles and his wife, were at an outside restaurant table across the street and had spotted me getting out of the car, and observed the usual mob congregating around it. Rickles, ever the ballbuster, jumped up and shouted, "Look, Gianni Russo stole the Pope's car!" The next day, a headline in a local newspaper had a picture of the papal limousine outside the club with the headline POPE HAD A LATE NIGHT.

The Vatican pulled the limo for the remainder of my Rome stay.

I flew home on September 20, 2001. The passengers were dead quiet, each of us wondering if he or she was going to make it to the States. I had plenty of time to think. What thoughts didn't revolve around my family swirled around various business ideas I'd been toying with. I wanted to connect with investors who had enough cash to go into a major venture, exactly what was still evolving at the time.

I had met the Bakrie brothers in the Beverly Wilshire Hotel in early 2002. The two brothers were Indonesian billionaires and sole owners of Bakrie Telecom, a wireless telecommunications provider throughout Asia, and big *Godfather* fans. That picture opened a multitude of doors for me and continues to do so to this day.

In this case, the brothers wanted to produce a children's television show, coupled with DVDs, geared toward appreciation of the Koran, the Islamic sacred text, and looked to me for marketing ideas. While

I knew nothing about the Muslim religion or the Koran, I knew how to sell, so I did my research before committing myself to the project.

It didn't take a marketing genius to discover that there are 1.8 billion Muslims worldwide, which translates to about 24 percent of the world's population. That's a helluva potential market. I signed onto the project, envisioning making a killing.

I made several trips to Jakarta, Indonesia, to do research into a marketing plan.

What I found out is that Muslim communities are very cohesive, and their religious leaders, like other religious leaders, are always on the prowl to spread the word about their religion. These Muslim leaders hold great sway in their mosques, and what they "suggest" is to be taken seriously by their followers.

My idea was simple, as I portrayed it to Bakrie Telecom: Could the company see to it that every Muslim family bought a DVD for their family, one for their friends, and one for their non-Muslim friends? It didn't take much to do the math; we were sitting on an idea that could make Bakrie Telecom billions of dollars. The Bakrie brothers said sure, no problem.

And we were in business.

We agreed that the business would be headquartered in Los Angeles and that I would handle the production end. I was asked how much start-up money I would need. I figured thirteen million dollars was a nice number, and I was promised a wire transfer.

I was asking for a lot of money and I expected the usual approval delays until I got it. Apparently, they work quickly in Jakarta, because I had the money in four days. I couldn't believe my luck in meeting the brothers and the swiftness of the transaction. We were on our way to making a ton of money.

What could possibly go wrong? Just enough, it seems, to queer the deal.

Investors were frightened off by the terrorist attacks of September 11, 2001. We honestly thought that a kids' TV show wouldn't be impacted by what occurred on that terrible day, but anything involving the word *Muslim* was going nowhere fast. To say I was disappointed would be an understatement, but something good would eventually come of it.

I was getting increasingly concerned about Marlon Brando. He had dropped off the radar as far as the media was concerned, but I saw him occasionally because he was a neighbor and friend.

He had ballooned to 380 pounds. I believe bitterness at Hollywood and all it represented to him, combined with family problems and his confusion regarding his sexuality, had accelerated his rapid slide into depression and self-destruction. There had been rumors regarding Brando's sexual proclivities in fan media for years. Those of us who knew him were aware of his bisexuality because he freely admitted it and had had dalliances with many Hollywood types. Still, when he got a few drinks in him, which was often these days, he would become brooding, depressed, and would make veiled mention of his disgust with himself. He was a troubled man, but a good one, and a great friend.

The Godfather, his greatest triumph, was also his greatest disappointment. He believed that he had been taken advantage of—namely, getting lowballed when it came to his one-million-dollar salary. He reasoned that he'd deserved to have his contract renegotiated after the fact because the picture was arguably one of the best ever made, in large part due to his iconic portrayal of Don Corleone.

The studio had rebuffed him, and that began a feud with the producers that lasted for years. In *The Godfather: Part II,* there is a flashback scene at the end of the picture where Don Corleone's family is reunited at the dinner table and is waiting for him to join them. All the major actors from the original movie were brought back for that brief scene and paid well for their time. I made more money for that one scene than I did for the entire first movie, and the other players were similarly compensated.

Brando wanted one million dollars for that scene, and once again he got Hollywood's version of a fuck-you, and the scene was shot without him. The producers didn't even try to negotiate with Brando, not that he would have accepted a penny less, but the effort would've shown good faith.

I felt he deserved the money and the recognition a renegotiated salary would've provided him, plus the million dollars he wanted for the flashback scene. Marlon Brando was *The Godfather.* Almost half a century later, people who care about movies are still talking about his portrayal of Don Corleone, and I don't believe the movie would've done as well as it did without his being part of it.

His son Christian's incarceration, coupled with his daughter hanging herself at Brando's home in Tahiti—his only refuge from the inequity that was Hollywood—in 1995, propelled him to greater depths of despair. All this, combined with his bisexuality, left him with great feelings of guilt, which led to the perfect storm of despair and bitterness, which he assuaged with food and booze.

He was never one to commit his lines to memory—the scene with Don Corleone chastising Johnny Fontane in his office during his daughter's wedding had Brando reading his lines off actor Al Martino's chest, where they were written on his shirt—but in his later movies, most notably *The Island of Dr. Moreau,* he had to have his lines fed to him via an earpiece because his mind was beginning to deteriorate.

Brando was also a perfectionist. The iconic scene with Brando and Al Martino in the godfather's office, which culminated with Don Corleone slapping Johnny Fontane for not being a man, was actually the result of Brando's getting pissed off because Martino couldn't remember his lines.

The young Brando was a proud person whose good looks almost made him appear pretty. His earlier movies show a fit man, someone who obviously took care of himself. The Brando of the late 1990s was someone who had just given up on life. He ate anything he wanted and drank a bottle of Courvoisier cognac daily. In sum, he was one miserable person.

The Hollywood community is fickle and disingenuous; if you're not making money and your career is on the wane, everyone treats you as if you never existed. Elizabeth Taylor, Michael Jackson, and I—the only people who seemed to care about Brando—stuck with him and worried about what he was doing to himself.

Before the word *intervention* became part of the American lexicon, the three of us had one for Brando. He needed to go to a doctor immediately, only he didn't give a damn about his health, but we did, and finally convinced him to get a medical workup. The doctor took one look at him and the results of a myriad of tests and ordered his immediate hospitalization. Brando had pneumonia and didn't know it.

He entered UCLA Medical Center in June 2004, and his organs began to fail almost immediately. I got a frantic call from Michael Jackson at home on June 30, telling me Brando was dying. Jackson was crying uncontrollably. He blamed himself, Liz Taylor, and me for convincing Brando to go to a doctor, which he irrationally believed had led to his current deteriorating condition. I let it go; Michael Jackson loved Brando, and he was unable to come to grips with his impending death.

Marlon Brando died on July 1. I think about him often. He was a good friend, and without his tutelage I would never have made it as far as I did in pictures. He was eighty years old.

Family life was the best thing that ever happened to me. I was enjoying my kids, and Pamela was the perfect wife. My mob days appeared to be over, and I was constantly on the lookout for new business ventures.

The Bakrie Telecom TV show debacle kept playing in my mind. Of course, the downside was that I'd lost out on a thirteen-million-dollar deal; the upside was that I'd learned a lot about the production end of the TV business during the time I was putting the deal together.

An idea started to develop as I began to get sick of watching *Barney & Friends* on television with my kids. It didn't take long for that friggin' purple dinosaur to grate on my nerves. I knew I could do better than that show if I produced my own television series for kids.

And so I did.

I created, wrote, and produced *A.J.'s Time Travelers* for Gold Coast Entertainment. It had an ensemble cast, and I began by hiring comic Richard Lewis for the part of Edgar Allan Poe, and Sandra Bernhard for the part of Cleopatra—how's that for casting against type? The show was a success and went for forty-three episodes on the Fox Children's Network.

I hired quite a few people with experience in television to help in preproduction. One was a woman who approached me one day and asked if I would read a screenplay she had written that she intended to turn into a movie. It was a G-rated kids' story and I didn't think it was very well done, but I bounced it off some screenwriter friends of mine to make sure my critique was fair. It was; no one was enthused about the project. I let the woman down gently and forgot about the incident. She left my show shortly thereafter and I gave her no further thought.

A few weeks into production I was ambushed by a process server. While annoyed, I wasn't upset; the entertainment business is replete with pissed-off people who sue like other people brush their teeth.

When I read the summons I was shocked. The woman whose screenplay I had dismissed as poorly executed was suing me and most everyone connected with the show for stealing her idea and turning it into *A. J.'s Time Travelers*. After the initial shock wore off, I turned the paperwork over to my lawyer and let him earn his money.

About a week later, a longtime soldier in the Gambino family, Pasquale "Patty Rose" Florio, told me that the woman who was suing me was a "close friend," and he'd appreciate it if I'd come to a settlement with her. I had run into Florio over the years, but that's as far as our relationship went. I smelled a shakedown, and told him there was no way I was going to pay the broad off.

"You sure you want to blow this off, Gianni?" Florio said.

"You're goddamn right I'm sure." I hung up on him. Some of these guys knew no boundaries when it came to greed. I had called Florio's bluff, and I thought that would be the end of it.

My dreams of finally being free from that bloodsucker Patty Rose came to a crashing halt when I got home and received a call from Joe Watts, who was summoning me to New York for a sit-down—gangsterspeak for a meeting—to iron out differences with Patty Rose, with mob bosses acting as mediators. To my way of thinking there were no differences to iron out, but when you're summoned, you go. To disregard a sit-down is ill-advised; you go or you die.

I would be safe at the meeting; of that, I had no doubt. If I was going to get shaken down, killing me wouldn't get anyone paid. *After* the meeting was another story, however. If things didn't go as planned for the bosses, I'd never make it home. Of that, I had no doubt, either.

The meeting was to be held at Veniero's Pasticceria & Caffé at 342 East Eleventh Street in Manhattan's East Village in the spring of 1995. At least that's where I was told to go. Where we'd eventually sit down was another story. Whenever mob bosses get together, the gangster version of tactical awareness comes into play. Bosses could get arrested just for associating with one another, so I was expecting a move to another location at the last minute as a precaution in case word leaked out as to the initial location of the sit-down.

I took the red-eye to LaGuardia, then cabbed it to Veniero's after checking into a hotel room I hoped to get to sleep in later. Beats the hell out of the trunk of a stolen Caddy any day.

Veniero's has been a mob favorite since 1894, when it opened. Anyplace that makes good pastry is a mob favorite. I was greeted by a waiter who was old enough to have been at the grand-opening party. He was expecting me, and I was directed to walk through the kitchen, through an alley, and into the basement of the facing building. I did all that, albeit with my heart pounding like a kettledrum.

Seated around a beat-up table in a room the size of a walk-in closet were Vincent "the Chin" Gigante, boss of the Genovese family; my old nemesis John Gotti, boss of the Gambino family; and Patty Rose.

Gigante was famous for acting crazy to avoid prosecution; he'd often been seen wandering around Greenwich Village wearing pajamas and a ratty robe, supported by his sons, mumbling and drooling. Today he had dropped the bullshit nut act, but he appeared sullen. I was greeted by handshakes all around, which were about as sincere as the guy who had lured Paul Castellano to his death by saying, "Hey, boss, you should go to Sparks Steak House for a nice quiet dinner, get out of the house for a while."

Protocol stated that Patty Rose, as the accuser, would tell his side of the story, to wit, I stole his close friend's (the woman turned out to be his squeeze) "intellectual property," and then I would defend my position. Patty and I would be asked to leave the room so Chin and Gotti could make a decision as to who was right and a ruling—which mean who pays what to whom—would come down. Rulings were final; both parties had to comply.

Patty Rose gave his side of the story, conveniently omitting the fact that everything that he uttered were lies. When it was my turn, I related my version, which boiled down to that Patty's story was bullshit and that he was trying to shake me down. Gotti and Chin sat nodding like they were were Supreme Court justices.

I was certain things weren't about to go my way because when I was done I was the only one asked to leave the room. Patty Rose stayed. I was fucked, and knew that I was going to be shaken down big-time. I waited in Veniero's for the kangaroo court to reconvene.

When I was called back in, a smug John Gotti gave me the decision.

"Patty here"—Gotti pointed to Patty Rose—"will tell his friend to proceed with the lawsuit. And you gotta duck the summons to appear in court."

I couldn't believe what I was hearing. If I didn't appear in court I'd lose. A simple win for me would be ruled in favor of the plaintiff and

I'd have to pay up along with my investor. I realized now that Patty Rose's girlfriend wasn't a party to the scam; Gotti and Chin would never have trusted her. In the mob, women are good for only two things and one of them is cooking. They had nothing to do with mob business. I was livid, but if I wanted to survive for my trip home I had to keep my mouth shut. What I was thinking was, Fuck them. I'm going to get served, show up in court, and beat the lawsuit. If they wanted to come after me in L.A., let them. I'd be ready.

As if he read my mind, Gotti said, "I know what you're thinking, Gianni. Don't. Things will happen that you'll regret for the rest of your life if you go against us." Chin nodded. Patty Rose couldn't look me in the eye.

Gotti was telling me that if I showed up in court my family would be hurt . . . or worse.

Chin chimed in. "And when you get back to L.A., you gotta disappear."

Wonderful.

"What do you mean you have to leave? Leave to where? Why?" Pamela asked when I got home.

I told her the truth, knowing it would probably doom our marriage, but I had little choice. She was livid, and I couldn't blame her. Not only did I unwittingly fall back into the mob life, but I unintentionally put my family at risk. At least Pamela was an adult, albeit a pissed-off adult, but she knew what was going on. New York wanted me out of town so I wouldn't be served with a summons to appear in court. I didn't tell her that her life and those of my children had been threatened. I didn't want her angry *and* fearful.

How would I tell my kids I wasn't going to be around for a while, maybe a long while? I did what I had to do, and it broke my heart. I sat Deanna and Carmello down and put together a story they would believe. It took all my acting chops to get through the most gut-wrenching time of my life.

The kids accepted that I was going away on business with the wide-eyed innocence of youth. Whatever Daddy said had to be true, and they didn't question anything. It broke my heart that their love for me was unconditional and they would never doubt me.

I left town quickly; a just verdict would eventually be levied against me and the others in the lawsuit for fifty-five million dollars. The settlement would be for a lot less, but it was still seven figures. Chin, Gotti, and Patty Rose would be ecstatic.

I moved around a lot. My time was split between France, Monte Carlo, England, and other locales. I called home every day to talk to my family. Pamela was frosty; my kids were falling apart. They would eventually go to therapy to get through what I had inflicted upon them. I snuck back into the country once to attend Deanna's first communion and the word got back to John Gotti that I was back in town. He tracked me down and called me the next day.

"Gianni, don't be getting any fucking ideas. You know what the deal is. Wherever the fuck you were, go back. And don't show your face in this country until all this is over."

I felt terrible, but not as bad as I was about to feel.

Pamela filed for divorce, citing my mob ties, the three shootings that she knew about, and the "abandonment" of my family. She also sued to sever my parental rights. That cut me to the core. I had no reasonable defense. To refute the charges, I'd have to expose the sordid mess I'd gotten myself into, and by doing so, I'd piss off New York, and I knew what that meant.

The divorce was granted and I lost my parental rights. I was ordered to remove myself from my children's lives under penalty of a contempt charge. To this day, fourteen years later, I haven't seen them. My kids never found out that I had to leave when they were young to ensure their safety, but I hope they read my story and get a clearer understanding of the reasons I did what I did.

I never paid my end of the lawsuit, which was millions of dollars, but some of the other investors paid up an undisclosed sum. The rest is owed by me and Bakrie Brothers. No way were those bloodsuckers going to get a dime out of me. I'm using every legal means available to me to see that I'll never have to pay it, and over twenty years later, they're no closer to getting their scam money from me than they were when the judgment was first handed down.

I'm a realist. At seventy-five years old, I don't know what the immediate future will bring, but whatever it is, I want my children—and Pamela—to be part of it. It's time.

EPILOGUE

My life had come full circle. I had been abandoned at age seven, and survived for many years on my own. Now I find myself in the same position: abandoned and alone. I want desperately to reunite with my children, but I understand that I need to earn that right. I realize I wasn't a very good father because of the life I chose before my kids were born. To that end, I finally jettisoned the Mafia lifestyle once and for all, instead devoting myself to my show-business career and charitable work. I want them to know that whatever they may have heard about me, they did so without the benefit of hearing the story of my life from me. This book will change that, and it's my fondest prayer that once they realize who I am, I can resume being a father. This will be the biggest and best role of my life.

I'm fortunate to have a wonderful woman in my life. Maggie and I have been together ten years, and not a day goes by when I don't realize how lucky I am to be with her. She fully supports me in every aspect of my life, particularly in my efforts to reunite with my children. In many ways, Maggie reminds me of Marilyn Monroe; she's beautiful, giving, and kind, and I'm thankful she doesn't have any of Marilyn's bad habits.

I enjoy walking in Central Park, as I once did with Marilyn Monroe, and I feel the pain of missing her, but the good memories obscure my recollections of her last days. She was a remarkable person.

I don't get to Little Italy much anymore—mostly because I miss the cohesiveness of the old neighborhood, which has since been replaced by young invaders looking to score apartments in a historic area, without having any sense of what it used to be. They don't know what they missed.

Most of the old crowd, like Joe Watts, is serving lengthy prison sentences, and the old-school Mafia dons are gone. John Gotti and Vincent Gigante died in prison. The likes of Frank Costello, Tony Accardo, and Meyer Lansky will never be seen again. There is no reviving the old days, when the mob ran the city, if not the country. Too much damage has been done by crusading prosecutors and wiseguy turncoats to ever bring back the glory days. Gangsters were different when Frank Costello took me under his wing. They had a sense of style, knew how to keep their mouths shut, and when they gave their word, it meant something.

The Copa and most of the other mob haunts have disappeared, too. The Waldorf-Astoria Hotel is closed, but I can still envision Mr. C. in a custom-made suit, holding court in his booth in Peacock Alley, eyes twinkling, greeting me with a "How're you doing, kid?" as I slide onto the soft leather opposite him.

I'm doing fine, Mr. C., thanks to you.

The days of my youth are gone, and the men of this thing of ours are gone with it, and neither is coming back.

I'm still acting, have a few film and TV projects in the works, and I've also just launched a motivational-speaking career.

Since 2016, I have been traveling the world as the ambassador of the MJ Licensing Company, which owns Don Corleone Brands & Spirits, and Genco Olive Oil & Corleone Family Selections.

I am involved in many charitable undertakings, which include St. Francis Food Pantries, the American Cancer Society, the National

Kidney Foundation, American Catholic Charities, and the Wounded Warrior Project, and am always available for other causes. My work with these wonderful organizations goes beyond writing checks to them; I'm constantly on the road, making unpaid public appearances. Probably the easiest way to assassinate me would be to send a limo to my house, honk a few times, and I'd undoubtedly get in the car, such is my busy schedule for charitable events.

I've also put my cooking skills to good use. I prepare elaborate Italian meals for those groups well-heeled enough to afford me, and donate all the proceeds to charity. Almost everyone is a *Godfather* fan, so in addition to a great meal, they get to hear stories about the filming of that and other pictures.

I've led an interesting life, perhaps not all of it ethical. I've played to and profited from others' greed at times, but I've never physically hurt anyone unless it meant my survival.

My Catholic faith has always been important to me and I have never missed Sunday Mass since I was a kid on the streets of New York. Remember that little plastic Saint Anthony statuette I mentioned at the beginning of this book, the one I had as a child? I still have it and carry it with me daily, and have been collecting Saint Anthony statues all my life and keep them on a shrine I've erected in my bedroom.

I don't do charity work as penance; I do it because it gives me pleasure. The feeling of helping people in need is the most gratifying thing I've done in my life. I've been very successful in my endeavors, and I thank God for the blessings I've been given. Now it's time to give back.

I've bared my soul in this book, exposing portions of my life that I'd rather forget, but I've done so with good reason. This book is my chance to show young people, who perhaps don't have the benefit of money or education, that if you want something badly enough, and are willing to work *hard* for it, you can accomplish anything. If I'm not a perfect example of that, no one is. When I hear someone telling me that they are giving up on a dream, I tell them to pursue it no matter what the odds. I don't want to hear "I can't do it."

Yes, you can!

INDEX

ABOUT THE AUTHORS

GIANNI RUSSO has appeared in more than thirty movies, been involved in the production of several others, and appeared in numerous TV shows. His most well-known roles include parts in *The Godfather: Parts I* and *II; Goodnight, My Love; Lepke; Laserblast; Chances Are; The Freshman; Side Out; Another You; Super Mario Bros.; Any Given Sunday; The Family Man; Seabiscuit;* and *Rush Hour 2*. His lifelong association with organized crime has made him a witness to mob history. He is also a singer, whose shows are sold out across the country.

PATRICK PICCIARELLI is a retired NYPD lieutenant, Vietnam veteran, and private investigator. He is the author of *Street Warrior: The True Story of the NYPD's Most Decorated Detective and the Era That Created Him,* and other books. He resides in Pennsylvania.